Philosophy in the Time of Economic Crisis

T0270771

For over 2,000 years, economics was studied in the West as a branch of ethics, or moral philosophy. Presently, though, few economists and no textbook in economic orthodoxy claim any close connection between economic science and philosophy. However, might the current 'crises' in economics, and in the economics profession have their deep roots in the separation of economics from philosophy and ethics?

American pragmatism, among the various contemporary philosophic traditions, lends itself specially to dialogue with economics because of its view of philosophy as an instrument for solving the real, concrete problems of human life, both personal and social. The essays in this volume, drawing heavily on the tradition of pragmatism, suggest that the economic *crises* of our time (the 2008 collapse of real estate and finance markets) might not be merely technical in nature – that is, the result of faulty applications of economic tools by politicians and policy makers, based upon conventional economic models – but also due to the faulty philosophical assumptions underlying those models. These essays suggest that the overcoming of our current economic crises requires that economists once again become moral philosophers, or that philosophers once again engage themselves in economic matters. In either case, this volume aims to foster dialogue between the two disciplines and in that way, contribute to the improvement of contemporary economic life.

This book is suitable for those who study political economy, economic theory, and economic philosophy.

Kenneth W. Stikkers is Professor of Philosophy and Africana Studies at Southern Illinois University Carbondale, USA.

Krzysztof Piotr Skowroński teaches contemporary philosophy, aesthetics, cultural anthropology, Polish philosophy, and American philosophy at the Institute of Philosophy, Opole University, Poland.

Routledge Frontiers of Political Economy

Philosophy in the Time of Economic Crisis

Pragmatism and Economy

Edited by
Kenneth W. Stikkers and Krzysztof Piotr Skowroński

LONDON AND NEW YORK

First published 2018
by Routledge

2 Park Square, Milton Park, Abingdon, Oxfordshire OX14 4RN
52 Vanderbilt Avenue, New York, NY 10017

Routledge is an imprint of the Taylor & Francis Group, an informa business

First issued in paperback 2020

British Library Cataloguing in Publication Data
A catalogue record for this book is available from the British Library

Library of Congress Cataloging in Publication Data
Names: Stikkers, Kenneth W., editor. | Skowroânski, Krzysztof Piotr, editor.
Title: Philosophy in the time of economic crisis : pragmatism and economy /
edited by Kenneth W. Stikkers and Krzysztof Piotr Skowronski.
Description: Abingdon, Oxon; New York, NY : Routledge, 2017. | Includes
index.
Identifiers: LCCN 2017012355 | ISBN 9781138050303 (hardback) |
ISBN 9781315168869 (ebook)
Subjects: LCSH: Economics--Philosophy. | Economics--Moral and ethical
aspects. | Financial crises.
Classification: LCC HB72 .P465 2017 | DDC 330.01--dc23
LC record available at https://lccn.loc.gov/2017012355

ISBN: 978-1-138-05030-3 (hbk)
ISBN: 978-0-367-59467-1 (pbk)

Typeset in Times New Roman
by Taylor & Francis Books

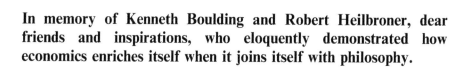

In memory of Kenneth Boulding and Robert Heilbroner, dear friends and inspirations, who eloquently demonstrated how economics enriches itself when it joins itself with philosophy.

Contents

Tables

Contributors

Guido Baggio, PhD, is postdoctoral fellow at Roma Tre University. He works on American philosophy, especially G. H. Mead, the classical pragmatists, and philosophy of economics in a pragmatist perspective. He published a monograph on Mead (*La mente bio-sociale: filosofia e psicologia in G. H. Mead* [The bio-social mind: philosophy and psychology in G. H. Mead], 2015) and many essays and articles on pragmatist thought and pragmatist philosophy of economics ("Sympathy and Empathy: G. H. Mead and the Pragmatist Basis of (Neuro)Economics," in *Pragmatism and Embodied Cognitive Science*, edited by Roman Madzia and Matthias Jung, 2016; "The Influence of Dewey's and Mead's Functional Psychology upon Veblen's Evolutionary Economics," *European Journal of Pragmatism and American Philosophy*, 2016; "The Concept of 'Behavior' in Psychology, Epistemology, and Economics, Starting from G. H. Mead," *Paradigmi*, 2016; and "Sen and Mead on Identity, Agency, and Economic Behavior," *EJPAP*, 2017).

Judith Green is Professor of Philosophy and Co-director of Women's Studies at Fordham University, in New York, having earned her PhD in philosophy at the University of Minnesota. She is the author of *Pragmatism and Social Hope: Deepening Democracy in Global Contexts* (2008) and *Deep Democracy: Community, Diversity, and Transformation* (1999), editor of *Richard J. Bernstein and the Pragmatic Turn in Contemporary Philosophy* (2013), and co-editor of *Pragmatism and Diversity: Dewey in the Context of Late Twentieth Century Debates* (2012).

Agnieszka Hensoldt received her MA in economics in 2000, her MA in philosophy in 2001, and her PhD in philosophy in 2005. She is an assistant professor of philosophy at Opole University (Poland). Her work is informed by pragmatic and analytic philosophy of language. Her publications include a book, *Concepts of C. S. Peirce's Pragmatism and Their Revival in Twentieth-Century Philosophy of Language* (in Polish), and a number of articles on pragmatism and analytic philosophy. Her forthcoming book will be devoted to the issue of the theory-practice relation in

American pragmatism, with special account of the social responsibility of philosophy.

Henry Kelly studied economics at Trinity College, Dublin, and Edinburgh University. He is currently completing his doctoral thesis on "Ethical and Economic Perspectives to Value." His interests include rhetoric and linguistics, in addition to heterodox approaches to economic theory.

Marcin Kilanowski, PhD, LLM, is an Assistant Professor at the Department of Law at Nicolaus Copernicus University, in Toruń, Poland. After completing his studies at Nicolaus Copernicus, Utrecht, and Harvard universities, he was a visiting researcher and scholar at the Freie Universität in Berlin, The Institute for Social Research at Johann Wolfgang Goethe-Universität, the Department of Philosophy at Harvard University, and the Science-Po École de droit in Paris. His research focuses on the development of democracy, civil society, and strengthening human rights through overcoming private-public dichotomies in philosophy and law, and was supported by grants from the Kościuszko Foundation, the State Committee for Scientific Research, European Commission, and French government. He is the author of two books, dozens of scientific papers and articles published in Poland and abroad, and an opinion contributor for various media. He teaches classes in the fields of philosophy, jurisprudence, and global governance.

Liu Mu is an associate professor in the School of Economics and Management at Beijing University of Chemical Technology, in China. He was born in Heilongjiang Province, China, on June 29, 1973. He received his doctoral degree in political economy from Peking University in 2004 and after graduation began teaching at Beijing University of Chemical Technology. His main research interests are the methodology of economics and the philosophy of economy. Based on Max Scheler's phenomenological value theory, he finds mainstream economics has ignored the objective order of values in favor of the lower grade of welfare values. He has written a series of papers from this perspective, including "Phenomenological Analysis of the Hypothesis of Economic Man: *Ressentiment* in New Institutional Economics."

Maja Niestrój, Chair, Berlin Practical Philosophy International Forum e.V.; lectures at Viadrina University, Frankfurt (Oder), Germany. Fields of specialization: philosophy of language (especially metaphors); practical philosophy in education and coaching. Recent publications: "Zur Rolle metaphorischer Ausdrücke in Lernprozessen: Metaphern der Demokratie," in *Philosophie und Bildung: Philosophie als Lehrerin kritischen Denkens*, edited by Iwona Alechnowicz-Skrzypek, Dorota Barcik, and Hans Friesen (2017); and "The Solomonic Strategy: The Brain as Hardware, Culture as Software – Re-reading Rorty's Criticism of Cognitive Science," in *Rorty and Beyond*, edited by Randall Auxier and Krzysztof Piotr Skowroński (forthcoming).

Matteo Santarelli (University of Molise) is a scholar in philosophy and social sciences. His main research interests are American pragmatism, social theory, and contemporary psychology. His first PhD dissertation focused on the relation between the individual and the social dimensions of experience. Presently he is working on the concept of interest in sociology and social theory, focusing particularly on authors such as John Dewey, Karl Marx, and Pierre Bourdieu. He has written articles, published in Italian, French, and English, speaking books, and scientific journals. He recently co-edited, with Maura Striano and Stefano Oliverio, *Nuovi usi di vecchi concetti: il metodo pragmatista oggi* (New uses for old concepts: the pragmatist method today).

Michael Schleeter began teaching as an assistant professor at Pacific Lutheran University in 2011, having received a BA in philosophy, comparative literature, and biology from the University of Minnesota and a PhD in philosophy from Penn State University. He regularly teaches courses in ethics, social and political philosophy, and business ethics, as well as in early modern philosophy, nineteenth- and twentieth-century continental philosophy, and the philosophy of race. His areas of scholarly interest include political philosophy, political economy, German Idealism, and phenomenology. In his free time, he enjoys cooking, watching films, playing music, reading literature and poetry, studying history and politics, and sampling beers from around the world.

Krzysztof (Chris) Piotr Skowroński, PhD, teaches contemporary philosophy, aesthetics, cultural anthropology, and Polish and American philosophy at the Institute of Philosophy, Opole University, Poland. He co-founded the Berlin Practical Philosophy International Forum e.V. He co-organized thirteen editions of the American and European Values international conference series. He authored *Values, Valuations, and Axiological Norms in Richard Rorty's Neopragmatism* (2015); *Beyond Aesthetics and Politics: Philosophical and Axiological Studies on the Avant-garde, Pragmatism, and Postmodernism* (2013); *Values and Powers: Re-reading the Philosophical Tradition of American Pragmatism* (2009); and *Santayana and America: Values, Liberties, Responsibility* (2007). He edited *Practicing Philosophy as Experiencing Life* (2015), and co-edited, with Matthew Flamm, *Under Any Sky: Contemporary Readings of George Santayana* (2007); with Matthew Flamm and John Lachs, *American and European Values: Contemporary Philosophical Perspectives* (2008); with Larry Hickman, Matthew Flamm, and Jennifer Rea, *The Continuing Relevance of John Dewey: Reflections on Aesthetics, Morality, Science, and Society* (2011); with Cornelis de Waal, *The Normative Thought of Charles S. Peirce* (2012); with Kelly Parker, *Josiah Royce for the Twenty-First Century: Historical, Ethical, and Religious Interpretations* (2012); with Tom Burke, *George Herbert Mead in the Twenty-First Century* (2013); and with Jacquelyn Kegley, *Persuasion and Compulsion in Democracy* (2013). He blogs about Santayana's philosophy.

Kenneth W. Stikkers is Professor of Philosophy and Africana Studies at Southern Illinois University Carbondale, where he has been since 1997. He earned his PhD in philosophy from DePaul University, in Chicago, in 1981, and previously was Professor of Philosophy at Seattle University. He has been a visiting professor at the Autonomous University of Sinaloa, in Mexico, the University of Warsaw, in Poland, the National University of Ireland, Maynooth, and Ca' Foscari University of Venice, and he is former President of the Society for the Advancement of American Philosophy. His main areas of scholarly interest and research are philosophy of the social sciences (especially economics), contemporary continental philosophy (especially Max Scheler and Michel Foucault), American philosophy (especially Puritanism, William James, and African American philosophy), and thematic and historical connections between American and continental European philosophy, on which he has authored and edited over sixty publications.

David W. Woods is the Deputy Director of Planning for the City of Stamford, Connecticut. He has twenty-five years of experience as a planning consultant and public servant in New York, New Jersey, Connecticut, Washington, Florida, and Minnesota, and he teaches at New York University. Previously, he was the Commissioner of Planning, Environment and Land Management for the Town of Brookhaven, New York, and Vice-president/ Chief Planner for Urbitran Associates, a major New York metropolitan area consulting firm, and he served on the American Planning Association's Board of Directors as the Director for the Northeast United States and Canada. He earned his PhD in urban sociology from Fordham University, as well as a BA in political science from California State University at Hayward, an MA in government from the University of Maryland, and an MS in urban and regional planning from Florida State University. His recent book, *Democracy Deferred: Civic Leadership after 9/11*, focuses on developing an experience-based planning framework for building better communities, while discussing the lessons learned in trying to influence decision-makers in rebuilding the World Trade Center and Lower Manhattan after 9/11.

Part I

The crisis in philosophical and historical perspective

1 Philosophy and the crisis of economic science

Kenneth W. Stikkers

John Dewey warned in 1917 that philosophy, as an academic discipline, faced a crisis: it could continue down a path toward irrelevancy by increasingly becoming merely an aristocratic pastime of solving mental puzzles posed by professional philosophers, or it could recover itself by re-engaging with personal and public experience. "Philosophy recovers itself," he famously proclaimed, "when it ceases to be a device for dealing with the problems of philosophers and becomes a method, cultivated by philosophers, for dealing with the problems of men" (Dewey 1917, 46). Following Dewey's suggestion here, we might say something similar about the contemporary state of economics as a discipline: economics recovers itself when it ceases to be a device for dealing with the problems of professional economists, in the guise of *homo economicus*, and becomes a method, cultivated by professional economists, for dealing with the economic problems of democratic citizens and publics.

What I wish to demonstrate in this chapter is how the central crisis of economics, of which the recent, global financial crisis was but one manifestation, is the growing gap between pronouncements by professional economists, on the one hand, and the concrete, material conditions of life as they are actually experienced by ordinary citizens, on the other. Nobel laureates Joseph Stiglitz and Amartya Sen point to this crisis in their report "on the Measurement of Economic Performance and Social Progress," commissioned by former French president Nicolas Sarkozy, *Mismeasuring Our Lives: Why GDP Doesn't Add Up*:

> Metrics that seem out of synch with individuals' perceptions are particularly problematic. If GDP is increasing, but most people feel they are worse off, they may worry that governments are manipulating the statistics, in the hope that by telling them that they are better off, they will feel better off. In these cases, confidence in government is eroded, and with the erosion of this confidence, the ability of government to address issues of vital public importance is weakened.
>
> (Stiglitz et al. 2010, xxi)

One specific incidence of their point is seen in the growing global inequality in wealth whereby per capita incomes rise but median incomes fall: aggregate wealth is increasing, but the experienced living conditions of many are diminishing. There is an old joke about the physician who proclaims, "The operation was a success, but the patient died." It is no joke, however, when economists and policy makers following them proclaim that policies are working, economies are growing, and recessions are ending, but the material conditions of people's lives, as they actually experience them, decline.

Professional economists are increasingly recognizing that the traditional measure of economic well-being, namely, per capita gross domestic product, is a very poor indicator of how people actually experience the quality of their material existences, and increasingly governments, such as France and now Great Britain, are moving away from GDP metrics, following the Prince of Bhutan, who famously declared that he did not care at all about gross domestic product but only about "gross domestic happiness." What exactly is the relationship between economic well-being and human well-being, or happiness? The current crisis in economics, which Stiglitz and Sen describe, is presently forcing economists to become once again moral philosophers, as they were until the twentieth century, and to address such elementary philosophical questions if they are to regain credibility. It has also spawned the rise of 'happiness studies,' as economists ponder the true meaning of human flourishing and recognize that there is no empirically demonstrable, consistent correlation between economic wealth and human happiness or well-being, and many, like Sen, have turned back to Aristotle for help, for Aristotle reminds us that wealth does not consist in ever-greater quantities of material goods but in the appropriate kind and amount of material goods necessary for human flourishing (*eudaimonia*). It is as foolish to believe that having more and more consumable goods will make one happier as it is to think that having more and more pots and pans in one's kitchen will make one a better cook.

I wish to show here, first, how this crisis in economics is part of a much larger crisis in Western philosophy and science, which can be traced at least to the beginnings of modernity itself; second, how both the philosophical movements of pragmatism and phenomenology began as responses to this crisis in Western science; and third, how pragmatism and phenomenology offer complementary antidotes to that crisis.

The crisis of Western science, of which the current crisis of economic science is a part, was centuries in the making. Throughout the Middle Ages and well into the eighteenth century notions of '*philosophia*' and '*scientia*' were intimately connected: indeed, those terms were virtually interchangeable. With the Renaissance, however, a new notion of science emerged – often termed 'new philosophy' – that set itself sharply apart from philosophy as traditionally understood. Ancient and medieval philosophy/science had tended to explain nature in terms of final causality – natural purposes and ultimate ends. The beginning of modern science, by contrast, can be dated to those early efforts, by Hasdai Crescas, Nicholas of Cusa, Giovanni Francesco Pico della Mirandola, and Giordano Bruno, among others, to reject teleological explanations in favor of simpler principles of efficient causality, which Galileo, Copernicus, Kepler, Descartes, and Newton, among others, described mathematically. Frances Bacon and others saw talk of ultimate ends and purposes as mere speculation and imagination and a carry-over from an older, unenlightened age of superstition, idols, and myth. True science, such thinkers suggested, confines itself to the 'real,' directly observable, and mathematically describable efficient causes of events, and hence began a separation of such science from philosophy, which increasingly became identified with speculative metaphysics, that is, thinking seeking to explain nature by reference to imagined final causes.

The moral sciences, constituting the other great branch of the tree of *scientia/philosophia*, stood in awe and envy of the seeming progress that the natural sciences were making, as the great historian of economics Albert O. Hirschman has well described: Newtonian mechanics marked unquestionable advancement over Aristotle's physics and metaphysics, but who would dare argue that the ethical theories of the eighteenth century offered comparable improvement over the ethical systems of the ancients and scholastics? What might moral philosophy, which included economics, learn from the enormous successes of the natural sciences?

Ancient and scholastic natural law ethics rested upon the speculative, teleological metaphysics that 'new science' had rejected, whereby morally proper human behavior conformed to our presumably true and proper ends as humans. Thus, just as natural science was able to progress by jettisoning notions of final causality, so moral philosophy, including economics, needed to break free from unscientific, metaphysically speculative, teleological foundations. Hence, Machiavelli, followed by Hobbes, Mandeville, and others, would urge fellow moral philosophers to concern themselves no longer with 'man as he ought to be' (in accord with true and proper metaphysical ends) but with 'man as he really is,' whom, without the aid of cultural anthropology, they imagined to be not a very nice person (Hirschman 1997, 12–14).

Furthermore, just as natural philosophers, most notably Newton, had come to view the universe as a complex machine governed by interacting forces, moral philosophers came to see human societies as complex machines, rather than as living organisms. They described such social machines as governed by intricate relations between desires and power, seen as analogous to the natural forces, such as gravity and inertia, described by Newton – what Gilles Deleuze aptly termed "desiring machines" (Deleuze and Guattari 1983), that is, machines driven by desires – giving rise to modern social sciences as positive sciences of human power and interests: just as natural bodies stay in motion, with a mathematically describable inertia until acted upon by opposing forces, so too humans pursue their self-interests, their desires, with varying degrees of power, or intensity, until acted upon by contrary self-interested forces. The new sciences of society – political science, economics, and sociology – would set as their principle task, describing such interacting forces, the machinery of society, with the same sort of mathematical precision found in Newtonian mechanics. Indeed, August Comte called the discipline that he founded "social physics" before coining the term "sociology."

Adam Smith offered the earliest thoroughgoing and most brilliant effort to apply principles of Newtonian mechanics to moral life and moral philosophy. Newton had described the harmonious relationships between planets and their moons in terms of counterbalancing forces: the centrifugal force of Jupiter's moons perfectly counterbalances Jupiter's gravitational pull, which Smith described as an "invisible hand" in his treatises on astronomy, well before his more famous writings on economics, where that infamous phrase again appears. Analogously, Smith described the ideal 'market mechanism' in terms of counterbalancing interests of buyers and sellers, operating under conditions of "perfect liberty," as an "invisible hand" leading markets to equilibrium – the most fair, just, efficient, and happy of all possible (economic) worlds.

Smith did not yet know how to quantify and thereby describe mathematically the economic forces of human self-interest as Newton had done with natural forces. Jeremy Bentham took up that challenge with his proposed 'hedonic calculus,' which would be refined by the marginalist economists, such as Léon Walras, William Stanley Jevons, and Alfred Marshall, culminating in F. Y. Edgeworth, who boldly proclaimed in his *Mathematical Psychics* (i.e., the mathematics of the soul) that he had achieved the dream of modern economic science, namely, the establishment of ethics as an exact, mathematical science, as indicated by the subtitle of that famous and influential work, *An Essay on the Application of Mathematics to the Moral Sciences*. Human beings, he tells us, are "pleasure optimizing machines," and their souls are their utility calculators. As Newton had developed a *"Mécanique Celeste,"* based upon the quantification of cosmic energies, Edgeworth claimed to have developed a *"Mécanique Sociale,"* based upon the quantification of "pleasure energy," thereby completing the task of liberating ethics from speculative metaphysics and making it entirely a matter of positive science, on par with physics (Edgeworth 1881, 12). Similarly, German economist Hermann Heinrich Gossen would claim that the meaning of life could be reduced to a simple mathematical formula: it is "the magnitude ... measured exactly by the magnitude of the pleasure that it [life] gives us" (Gossen 1854, 4), and that pleasure in turn is measured by the monetary value of the pleasurable goods that persons consume – an assumption that remains at the foundation of mainstream GDP measurements of economy. As John Maynard Keynes noted, these late nineteenth-century economists, having now answered definitively, in their judgment, all the major perennial questions of moral philosophy, allowed moral philosophers to take early retirement (Keynes 1926, 275): moral philosophers were no longer needed to speculate about our true and proper human ends when now economic scientists – the new moral positivists – could describe with mathematical precision the exact conditions under which human happiness, understood as the satisfaction of desires, or 'consumer demand,' is optimized. (Keynes praised G. E. Moore's *Principia Ethica* for calling moral philosophers back out of retirement.)

From its very beginning this mechanistic world-view, whereby both nature and human societies are broken down into atomic units – particles and autonomous, self-interested selves – governed by forces and interests, respectively, all mathematically describable, met with complaints that, in questioning traditional understandings of nature and society, it was undermining life's everyday sense of meaning – what some, including Richard Rorty, have termed "the disenchantment of the world." One finds such protests, for example, in Elizabethan authors such as William Shakespeare (e.g., *The Tempest*), Edmund Spenser (*The Faerie Queene*), and John Donne ("Anatomy of the World"). The latter, for instance, complained that "new Philosophy cals all in doubt, ... [and] freely men confesse, that this world's spent ... . [All] is crumbled out againe to his Atomis. 'Tis all in pieces, all coherence gone." Donne accused "new Philosophy" of having murdered the world's beauty: "Shee, shee [the world's beauty] is dead," Donne loudly and chillingly complained: "she's dead; [and] when thou knowest this, Thou knowest how ugly a monster this world is."

Donne's complaints about "new philosophy" came at exactly the same time that the enclosure of land in England into parcels of 'private property' was reaching its peak and reducing English society to atoms, that is, into an aggregate of self-interested individuals. Karl Polanyi, the founder of economic anthropology, described this process in his classic work, *The Great Transformation*, as a "catastrophic dislocation of the lives of the common people" (Polanyi 1944, 33).

> Enclosures have appropriately been called a revolution of the rich against the poor. The lords and nobles were upsetting the social order, *breaking down ancient law and custom*, sometimes by means of violence, often by pressure and intimidation. They were literally robbing the poor of their share in the common, tearing down the houses which, by *the hitherto unbreakable force of custom*, the poor had regarded as theirs and their heirs'. The fabric of society was being disrupted: desolate villages and the ruins of human dwellings testified to the fierceness with which the revolution raged, endangering the defenses of the country, wasting its towns, decimating its population, turning the overburdened soil into dust, harassing its people and turning them from decent husbandmen into a mob of beggars and thieves.
>
> (Polanyi, 35; emphases added for the sake of later analysis)

Robert Heilbroner commented: "The market system ... was ... born in agony. Never was a revolution less well understood, less welcomed, less planned. But the great market-making forces would not be denied. Insidiously they ripped apart the mold of custom, insolently they tore away the usage of tradition"; that is, these economic forces defied traditional morality (Heilbroner 1986, 33).

R. H. Tawney perhaps most succinctly and pointedly described enclosure as "an acid dissolving all customary relationships" (Tawney 1926, 137). Indeed, Queen Elizabeth I, upon completing a tour of her kingdom, complained that within a relatively few decades England's prosperous, happy peasantry – the envy of Europe – had been transformed into roving mobs of "beggars and thieves" (Heilbroner, 31). In short, the theoretical atomizing of nature by New Philosophy paralleled the atomizing of society by economic forces that was taking place at precisely the same time, and both were turning the world ugly.

The first to speak extensively of a 'crisis' in European reason and science was perhaps Friedrich Schelling: according to him the assumption of an absolute separation (*Scheidung*) of Nature from Spirit (*Geist*), upon which Europe had built its boasted edifices of reason and science, had led to a crisis with respect to human freedom and self-understanding. How could the presumably utterly irrational impulse of life (*Seele*) give birth to mind and reason? How could spirit then become alienated from soul and take command over life as its lord and master? And, once it does, once life is thoroughly subjected to mind's logic and laws of causal determinacy, what becomes of human freedom? This 'crisis,' created by reason's triumph over life, of Spirit over Nature, "first appeared [in] that conflict between mind and heart" and culminated in "Spinozism," to be condemned not only for its fatalism but mainly for its utter lifelessness and absence of feeling (Schelling 1809, 19–20).

Some of the manifestations of such a crisis in economics should be evident. First, at the same time it would shout so loudly slogans of human freedom – 'free markets,' 'free enterprise,' 'free labor,' 'freedom to choose' – the literature of classical and neo-classical economics would be developing iron laws of causal determinacy to explain the market mechanism, which would seem to preclude any such human freedom. Second, as Max Weber described the matter, the spirit of capitalism is a strange blend of reason and anti-reason: agents in the market pursue, produce, market, and distribute in hyper-rational ways, economic goods that satisfy utterly irrational wants, a condition that Sen aptly captured in the title of one of his books, *Rational Fools*. Third is the absolute dichotomy between facts and values, enshrined as economic dogma by Lionel Robbins (1932), as Hilary Putnam recently identified and criticized: facts express the objective state of the world in itself, and hence are matters of rational science, while values express merely subjective preferences, and hence have no place in scientific reasoning. Indeed, as Putnam noted, economics, among all the sciences, natural and social, continues to cling most tightly to this absolute fact-value dichotomy (Putnam 2004).

Concerns over this 'crisis' in Western reason and science are found throughout the nineteenth century, for example, in the writings of Kierkegaard and Nietzsche, and it was the principle motive behind the phenomenological movement, as the title of Edmund Husserl's last and most impassioned and provocative book, *The Crisis of European Sciences and*

Transcendental Phenomenology, expresses. This 'crisis' entailed for Husserl, as it did for Schelling, a growing tension between metaphysical principles of Nature and Spirit, Life and Reason (Husserl 1965, 152), but it was most profoundly manifest in a growing chasm between scientific, theoretical accounts of the world and the experienced, everyday sense of the world, or what Husserl termed the '*Lebenswelt,*' the realm of existential meaning. Husserl identified Galileo's mathematical schematization of nature as a key event in the history of this crisis. The experienced world, wherein the sun rises and sets, was displaced by a view in which such life-world experiences were rendered as mere illusions: the sun only appears, to the primitive, pre-scientific eye, to rise and set. Later, seemingly solid matter was said to be but minuscule particles whizzing about in largely empty space and giving only the appearance of solidity. We imagine ourselves to experience a world of objects, such as books and chairs, but what we 'really' experience are mere atomic sense data, which we then synthesize into objects of understanding. Seemingly 'free' persons are merely causally determined mechanisms. The 'real world' that 'new science' describes is ultimately no longer the one experienced first-hand, through the senses, but an array of circles, vortices, and forces – a world of Platonic forms – described best mathematically.

The issue behind the displacement of the life-world by such theoretical, mathematized formalisms, according to Husserl, was not one of truth: it was not a question of whether or not such scientific accounts provide accurate, 'correct,' or 'true' depictions of the world as it is in itself. Rather, the question for Husserl – someone trained primarily as a mathematician – was, "*What is the meaning of this mathematization of nature?*" (Husserl 1970, 23). As he wrote in perhaps the most pointed description of the crisis of European science:

> Merely fact-minded sciences make merely fact-minded people … . In our vital need – so we are told – this science has nothing to say to us. It excludes in principle precisely the questions which humanity, given over in our unhappy times to the most portentous upheavals, finds the most burning: questions about the meaning or meaninglessness of the whole of this human existence … . What does science have to say about … us humans as subjects of … freedom? The mere science of bodies has nothing to say; it abstracts from everything subjective … . Scientific, objective truth is exclusively a matter of establishing what the world, the physical as well as the spiritual world, is in fact. But can the world, and human existence in it, truthfully have meaning if the sciences recognize as true only what is objectively established in this fashion, and if history has nothing more to teach us than all the shapes of the spiritual world, all the conditions of life, ideals, norms upon which life relies, form and dissolve themselves like fleeting waves, that it always was and ever will be so, that again and again reason must turn into nonsense, and well-being into misery? Can we console ourselves with that? Can we live in this world,

where historical occurrence is nothing but an unending concatenation of illusory progress and bitter disappointment?

(1970, 6–7)

Husserl thought not. As European science had become increasingly sophisticated in explaining the mechanisms by which we exist and the universe operates, it became less and less able to address the question of the meaning of human existence. The issue was not one of the 'truthfulness' of science but whether or not human life, with all its suffering and despair, could find such a world-view bearable, that is, sufficiently meaningful to be worth living in. Europe, Husserl proclaimed, was spiritually "sick": "Europe," he claimed, "is in critical [spiritual] condition" (1965, 150).

The manifestation of this 'crisis' in economic science should be clear: as economists have become increasingly adept at explaining and controlling the mechanism of the market, they have become decreasingly able to address the question of the relationship between economic wealth, well-being, and growth, on the one hand, and human well-being, growth, and happiness, on the other. What is the *meaning* of ever-bigger GDP numbers in terms of the quality of human life as it is concretely lived?

Husserl's remedy for the crisis of European science was transcendental phenomenology, which did not romantically reject positive science, as some like Schelling did, but whose genetic and generative methods trace the growth and development of science's abstractions out of their life-world origins, thereby retrieving the everyday meanings of those abstractions from their obscurity and revealing the organic, experiential connections between them and scientific theorizings. Among the social scientists most influenced by Husserlian phenomenology, Georg Simmel saw its implications for economics and in his monumental *Philosophy of Money* (Simmel 1978) applied phenomenological method to provide a genetic account of how monetary abstractions grew out of concrete, face-to-face, life-world exchanges. (Unfortunately Simmel accepted uncritically an assumption long held by social scientists, namely, that money developed to facilitate barter exchanges. Anthropologists, such as Daniel Graeber, have now shown this notion to be a myth and that barter was never a dominant form of economic exchange [Graeber 2011], thus illustrating the need for phenomenology – and philosophy generally – to be properly informed by the most recent findings from cultural anthropology.) Simmel's pioneer efforts to apply phenomenology to economics unfortunately had few followers.

Max Scheler, the other major founder of the phenomenological movement, described the crisis of European science as a perversion of the relationship between life and the machine, between vital and useful values: "With the development of modern civilization," he proclaimed in his *Ressentiment*, "*the machine* has grown to dominate life. 'Objects' have progressively grown in vigor and intelligence, in size and beauty – while humans, who created them, have more and more become cogs in their own machines ... . The mere means are developed and the goals are forgotten. And that precisely is decadence" (Scheler 1961, 172, 174). Western science had succeeded, with cruel irony, in keeping alive human life that was experiencing itself as less and less worth living. As with Husserl, for Scheler, too, Western man was dying, not from any shortage of food but from spiritual malnutrition, a lack of meaning. "Everything living and vital is eliminated from this strange picture. This world is an accumulation of logicians standing in a huge engine-room – bloodless, emotionless, without love or hate" (Scheler, 164). To what extent does Scheler describe the modern economist, financier, or captain of industry? Scheler traced the Great War to this crisis: fueling the war hysteria was the belief deeply held by many in Germany and elsewhere, including many leading intellectuals, that Europe needed a good war to shake it out of the decadence of its own abstractions and back to life.

The body of literature in nineteenth- and twentieth-century continental philosophy and literature that speaks of such a crisis in Western scientific reason is vast, but classical American philosophers, starting with the Transcendentalists, although seldom invoking the language of 'crisis,' expressed concerns strikingly similar to those of their European counterparts, and those concerns formed much of the impetus behind the rise of pragmatism. Indeed, it is perhaps William James who, among both European and American philosophers, best personified and embodied the crisis of European science. Once an aspiring painter, he was educated in the biological sciences of the day and became a physician, only to discover that those sciences had nothing to say to him about the meaning of the life that they classified and whose mechanisms they described. Indeed, note the stunning similarities between the following biting commentary from James's "The Will to Believe" and the lengthy passage from Husserl quoted above:

> When one turns to the magnificent edifice of the physical sciences, and sees how it was reared; what thousands of disinterested moral lives of men lie buried in its mere foundations; what patience and postponement, what choking down of preference, what submission to the icy laws of outer fact are wrought into its very stones and mortar; how absolutely impersonal it stands in its vast augustness … . Can we wonder if those bred in the rugged and manly school of science [like James was] should feel like spewing [all] subjectivism out of their mouths? The whole system of loyalties which grew up in the schools of the science go dead against its toleration; so that it is only natural that those who have caught the scientific fever should pass over to the opposite extreme, and write sometimes as if the incorruptibly truthful intellect ought positively to prefer bitterness and unacceptableness to the heart in its cup.
> It fortifies my soul to know
> That, though I perish, Truth is so –
>
> (James 1968, 720)

As with Husserl, the issue for James was not one of science's truthfulness but one of meaning: can scientific 'truth' adequately console us in the face of inevitable death? James, like Husserl and Scheler, did not think so. Elsewhere James wrote:

> This systematic denial on science's part of the personality as a condition of events, this rigorous belief that in its own essential and innermost nature our world is a strictly impersonal world, may conceivably, as the whirligig of time goes round, prove to be the very defect that our descendants will be most surprised at in our boasted science, the omission that to their eyes will most tend to make it look perspectiveless and short.
>
> (James 1896, 136–37)

Similarly, will future economists laughingly look upon twentieth-century efforts to separate facts from values and economic science from ethics as embarrassingly "perspectiveless and short"?

Whatever James's own organic disposition, much of his personal depression stemmed from a sense of hopelessness that was fueled by modern science's account of the world as a causally determined mechanism, which, to James, made a joke of human longings for freedom and meaning. James felt paralysed and crushed, as he recorded in his journal: "Hitherto, when I felt like taking a free initiative, like daring to act originally, without carefully waiting for contemplation of the external world to determine all for me, suicide seemed the most manly form to put my daring into" (Diary, April 30, 1870, in James 1968, 8). Why struggle, why bother to assert oneself boldly, when, according to modern scientific accounts, all is causally determined, freedom is but illusion, and human quests for meaning are greeted by a cold, indifferent universe, which, frankly, doesn't give a damn?

James, like Husserl, proposed, already in his *Psychology*, a genetic method, whereby abstract scientific concepts are traced back to concrete, everyday experience. He also proposed renewal of the power of belief and radical empiricism as antidotes to the debilitating effects of the objective science that he described. Active belief, for James, powerfully broke through the cold indifference of a purely objective world of facts by asserting the role of human subjectivity in the creation of facts. "My first act of free will will be to believe in free will," he boldly asserted in working his way out of his depression (Diary, in James 1968, 7–8). Radical empiricism, much like Husserl's phenomenology, was a return to the primacy of concrete experience, against the tyranny of abstract generalization.

Dewey, like Schelling, Husserl, and James, criticized, with a strong sense of urgency, in his call for the reconstruction of philosophy, noted at the beginning of this chapter, how the sciences of his day – natural and social sciences alike – anchored in an array of false metaphysical dichotomies, had grown increasingly disconnected from everyday, practical experience. Like the others, Dewey attacked a notion of 'reason' as detached from life, as extra-experiential. This detachment of reason from life manifests itself in philosophy's increasing preoccupation with solving logical puzzles created by professional philosophers and decreasingly with the actual, concrete problems of life – social as well as personal.

Dewey's remedy for the increasing disconnection of science and philosophy from life was nothing less than the radical reconstruction of philosophy, aided by his postulate of immediate empiricism, Dewey's term for what James had called "radical empiricism." According to this postulate, "things – anything, everything, in the ordinary or non-technical use of the term 'thing' – are what they are experienced as" (Dewey 1905, 241). Philosophy, following this postulate, thus recovers and reconstructs itself in a double-barreled manner. In the name of philosophical rigor, Dewey insisted, first, that every intellectual inquiry begin with clear articulation of the concrete problem that motivates it: why is this an existential, human problem, rather than merely an intellectual puzzle for the professional scholar? Second, once we arrive at our theoretical conclusions, we return to the existential problems that motivated the inquiry at the beginning, to be certain that our conclusions do not provide merely intellectual satisfaction but contain practical value in solving the problems of life that motivated the inquiry in the first place.

Among economists most influenced by pragmatism Thorstein Veblen, founder of the institutionalist school of economics, criticized capitalist and socialist theories alike for their apriorism, and he aimed to reconstruct economics radically by starting not with some theoretical model but with careful observations of actual economic behaviors. Thus he developed his theory of the leisure class, and with it his famous notion of "conspicuous consumption," not from some intensive analysis of capital and the logic of capitalism, as did Marx, whom Veblen severely criticized, but from detailed descriptions of the actual practices of business leaders of his day, using their own language, often in sarcastic and satirical ways.

Contemporary institutionalist economist, and perhaps the leading economic pragmatist, Daniel Bromley, observes that mainstream economists aim mainly at satisfying the conceptual concerns of other professional economists and not the lived concerns of ordinary citizens. As he wonderfully writes, "citizens demand justifications [for economic policies] based on grounds that matter to them – and few citizens are waiting to be told that particular policies are Pareto optimal, or that they can be proven socially preferred by the application of potential compensation tests" (Bromley 2006, 148). What Bromley proposes, in the spirit of John Dewey, is that the test of any economic policy is how well it experimentally satisfies actual citizens and publics, and not the theoretical *homo economicus*.

So what I have suggested here is that the crisis in economics is not merely the recent crisis of financial markets that brought about the recent global recession, but a manifestation of a much deeper crisis in Western science, centuries in the making, that has been described and diagnosed by phenomenologists and pragmatists alike. It is a crisis in meaning, wherein theoretical, mathematized accounts of the world seem increasingly out of touch with the concrete experiences of actual persons. Economics today is the primary manifestation of this crisis, and pragmatism, along with phenomenology, offers powerful resources, largely untapped, for diagnosing the current crisis in economics and reconstructing that discipline and remedying its crisis.

References

Bromley, Daniel W. 2006. *Sufficient Reason: Volitional Pragmatism and the Meaning of Economic Institutions.* Princeton, NJ: Princeton University Press.

Deleuze, Gilles, and Félix Guattari. 1983. *Anti-Oedipus: Capitalism and Schizophrenia*, trans. Robert Hurley. Minneapolis: University of Minnesota Press.

Dewey, John. 1905. "The Postulate of Immediate Empiricism." In *The Middle Works of John Dewey, 1899–1924*, vol. 3: *1903–1906, Essays*, ed. Jo Ann Boydston. Carbondale: Southern Illinois University Press, 1977.

Dewey, John. 1917. "The Need for a Recovery of Philosophy." In *The Middle Works of John Dewey, 1899–1924*, vol. 10: *1916–1917, Essays*, ed. Jo Ann Boydston. Carbondale: Southern Illinois University Press, 1980.

Edgeworth, F. Y. 1881. "Mathematical Psychics: An Essay on the Application of Mathematics to the Moral Sciences." In *Mathematical Psychics and Further Papers on Political Economy*, ed. Peter Newman. Oxford: Oxford University Press, 2003.

Gossen, Hermann Heinrich. 1854. *The Laws of Human Relations.* Cambridge: MIT Press, 1983.

Graeber, David. 2011. *Debt: The First 5000 Years.* Brooklyn, NY: Melville House.

Heilbroner, Robert. 1986. *The Worldly Philosophers: The Lives, Times, and Ideas of the Great Economic Thinkers*, 6th ed. New York: Simon & Schuster.

Hirschman, Albert O. 1997. *The Passions and the Interests: Political Arguments for Capitalism before Its Triumph.* New Haven, CT: Yale University Press.

Husserl, Edmund. 1965. "Philosophy and the Crisis of European Man." In *Phenomenology and the Crisis of Philosophy*, trans. Quentin Lauer. New York: Harper & Row.

Husserl, Edmund. 1970. *The Crisis of European Sciences and Transcendental Phenomenology: An Introduction to Phenomenological Philosophy*, trans. David Carr. Evanston, IL: Northwestern University Press.

James, William. 1896. "Address of the President before the Society for Psychical Research." In *Essays in Psychical Research*. Vol. 16 of *The Works of William James.* Cambridge, MA: Harvard University Press, 1986.

James, William. 1968. *The Writings of William James: A Comprehensive Edition*, ed. John J. McDermott. New York: Modern Library.

Keynes, John Maynard. 1926. "The End of Laissez Faire." In *Essays in Persuasion.* New York: Palgrave Macmillan, 2012.

Polanyi, Karl. 1944. *The Great Transformation: The Political and Economic Origins of Our Time.* Boston: Beacon Press.

Putnam, Hilary. 2004. *The Collapse of the Fact/Value Dichotomy and Other Essays.* Cambridge, MA: Harvard University Press.

Robbins, Lionel. 1932. *An Essay on the Nature and Significance of Economic Science*, 2nd ed. New York: Macmillan, 1962.

Scheler, Max. 1961. *Ressentiment*, trans. William W. Holdheim, ed. Lewis Coser. New York: Free Press of Glencoe.

Schelling, Friedrich. 1809. *Of Human Freedom*, trans. James Guttman. Chicago: Open Court, 1936.

Simmel, Georg. 1978. *The Philosophy of Money*, trans. Tom Bottomore. London: Routledge.

Stiglitz, Joseph E., Amartya Sen, and Jean-Paul Fitoussi. 2010. *Mismeasuring Our Lives: Why GDP Doesn't Add Up*. The Report by the Commission on the Measurement of Economic Performance and Social Progress. New York: The New Press.

Tawney, R. H. 1926. *Religion and the Rise of Capitalism: A Historical Study*. Gloucester, MA: Peter Smith, 1962.

2 On the shadow and the substance

Adam Smith, John Dewey, and the Great Recession

Michael Schleeter

In 1917, John Dewey argued in his essay "The Need for a Recovery of Philosophy" that philosophy should "develop ideas relevant to the actual crises of life, ideas influential in dealing with them and tested by the assistance they afford" and, further, that its recovery would be accomplished only "when it ceases to be a device for dealing with the problems of philosophers and becomes a method, cultivated by philosophers, for dealing with the problems of men" (Dewey 1917, 43, 46). From a Deweyan perspective, then, it would seem that philosophers in our time should be spending at least some of their energies developing ideas relevant to what is perhaps the most significant of the "actual crises of life" the world has experienced since the turn of our new century: the recent economic crisis that has come to be called the 'Great Recession.'

The ideas that will be most influential in dealing with this crisis would seem to be those that will assist the general public, first, in understanding the causes and consequences of the crisis and, second, in evaluating the practices that gave rise to it along ethical lines, with an eye in both cases to preventing similar crises from happening in the future. The ideas that will assist the general public in the first way are ideas drawn from the sort of careful empirical work that is perhaps best performed by economists and political scientists. Such ideas will find their bases in careful empirical analyses of the activities that caused the crisis (including those of homebuyers, mortgage brokers, home appraisers, commercial bankers, investment bankers, ratings agents, insurance agents, and investors), of the various public policies that enabled those engaged in these activities to act as they did, and of the consequences of these activities for all who were affected by them. The ideas that will assist the general public in the second way, however, are ideas drawn from the sort of careful theoretical work that is perhaps best performed by philosophers and political theorists. Such ideas will find their bases in careful interpretations of principles drawn from ethical theory and careful applications of these principles to the above activities.

Many schools of ethical theory have developed principles that may be usefully applied to the various practices that caused the Great Recession, but given that this crisis was economic in nature, it may be the case that the principles that are most appropriate in this context are those developed in the body of theory that is known as 'political economy.' This body of theory is concerned, among other things, with the ethical dimensions of different economic systems – with the values they are supposed to promote, the principal ways in which they may be promoted, and the principal ways in which they may be undermined. The history of political economy has produced a body of theory that ranges from the radical socialism of Karl Marx to the laissez-faire capitalism of Friedrich Hayek and Milton Friedman. However, given that the economic crisis happened within the context of a nominally capitalist economic system, it may be the case that the principles that are most appropriate here are those drawn from the political economy of the so-called 'Father of Capitalism,' namely, the political economy of Adam Smith.

Smith's principles explained

For Smith, a central figure in the classical liberal tradition, the ideal society was one that promoted above all else the value of liberty for all of its citizens. Such a society, he argued, would be characterized by what he called a "system of perfect liberty," a system of basic rights and freedoms that would enable each of its citizens to "pursue his own interest his own way" (Smith 1776, 719). Such a system, he argued, would include not only basic political and civil rights and freedoms, but also basic economic rights and freedoms, such as the right to own and the freedom to exchange private property. In order to secure these basic economic rights and freedoms, the ideal society would have to erect and maintain institutions that would work not only to establish private property itself, but also to ensure that, when it was exchanged, it would be exchanged freely. Indeed, Smith argued that one of the three essential duties of the ideal society was to establish what he called "an exact administration of justice," the duty "of protecting, as far as possible, every member of society from the injustice or oppression of every other member of it" (766). This duty, with respect to the freedom to exchange private property, meant that the ideal society would have to erect and maintain institutions that would ensure that, as a rule, its citizens would not be 1) blocked from exchanges they wanted, 2) forced into exchanges they did not, or 3) duped into exchanges they would not have wanted had they not been denied relevant information.

The phrase 'as a rule' here is significant because Smith allowed for two exceptions to the first and second of these conditions for the free exchange of private property. He argued that the ideal society could block its citizens from exchanges that they wanted or force them into exchanges that they did not want if doing so was either 1) in the service of liberty itself or 2) in the service of some other important public good that could not otherwise be promoted. With respect to the first of these exceptions, Smith argued that the ideal society could, for example, block its citizens from exchanges that they wanted if those exchanges would "endanger the security of the whole society" (353). Along similar lines, it could force its citizens into exchanges they did not want (e.g., by taxing them) if doing so was necessary to erect and maintain the institutions required for protecting them from violations of their liberty, both those committed by other citizens and those committed by other societies. Indeed, Smith argued that the ideal society had not only the duty to establish an exact administration of justice, but also the duty to establish "a military force," the duty "of protecting the society from the violence and invasion of other independent societies" (745).

With respect to the second of these exceptions, Smith argued that the ideal society could, for example, block its citizens from exchanges that they wanted by granting some of them temporary monopolies on the production and/or distribution of their writings and inventions in order to promote innovation and creative work. Along similar lines, it could force its citizens into exchanges they did not want (e.g., by taxing them) if doing so was necessary to erect and maintain such things as roads and bridges for the facilitation of commerce, post offices for the facilitation of communication, and schools for the promotion of scientific and religious instruction. Indeed, Smith argued that another of the three essential duties of the ideal society was the duty of "erecting and maintaining certain public works and certain public institutions, which it can never be for the interest of any individual, or small number of individuals, to erect and maintain; because the profit could never repay the expense to any individual or small number of individuals, though it may frequently do much more than repay it to a great society" (745). For Smith, these two exceptions were entirely compatible with a system of perfect liberty.

Importantly, Smith argued that the ideal society, in promoting above all else the value of liberty, would also promote the value of prosperity for all of its citizens, for Smith assumed that most individuals were driven in general by the desire of bettering their condition, "a desire which, though generally calm and dispassionate, comes with us from the womb, and never leaves us till we go into the grave," to augment their fortunes (372). He further assumed that, within a system of perfect liberty, most individuals would be driven by this desire 1) to increase their productivity and 2) to enter only into advantageous exchanges, and that this would ultimately occasion "that universal opulence which extends itself to the lowest ranks of the people" (12). In fact, Smith went even further and argued that the ideal society, in promoting above all else the value of liberty, would also promote not only the value of prosperity, but also the value of equality for all of its citizens. He assumed that "[i]f, in the same neighborhood, there was any employment evidently either more or less advantageous than the rest, so many people would crowd into it in the one case, and so many would desert it in the other, that its advantages and disadvantages would soon return to the level of other employments" (114). Thus, he argued, "the whole of the advantages and disadvantages of the different employments of labour and stock" would "in the same neighborhood, be either perfectly equal or continually tending to equality" (114). Indeed, Smith thought that the ideal society need not choose between liberty, on the one hand, and prosperity and equality, on the other, for he thought that the one would lead naturally to the other.

Smith thus argued that the free exchange of private property would be, by and large, a very good thing for the citizens of the ideal society. However, he also recognized that citizens, being driven in their exchanges by the desire of bettering their condition to augment their fortunes, could end up posing a significant threat to their liberty, prosperity, and equality, for he recognized that this desire could lead some of them to violate the basic economic rights and freedoms of others – to block them from or force or dupe them into exchanges – and thereby lead them to turn against the system of perfect liberty itself. This in two ways. First, he argued, it could lead them simply to disregard those public policies designed to protect others from such violations. That is, the desire to better their condition could lead citizens to acts of overt criminality. Second, he argued, such a desire could lead them to influence the legislative process so as to weaken, repeal, or prevent the passage of public policies designed to protect others from such violations. In both of these ways, Smith recognized, citizens could be driven by the desire of bettering their condition to violate the basic economic rights and liberties of others, and insofar as they were so driven, he noted that not only liberty, but also prosperity and equality would be diminished.

Smith himself was particularly concerned about the second of these ways, whereby citizens could be driven to violate the basic economic rights and freedoms of others. In fact, he coined a special term for the desire that would lead them to influence the legislative process in the above ways. He called it the "corporation spirit," and he found it to be so prevalent among the order of merchants and manufacturers in his own time that he was led to observe, "People of the same trade seldom meet together, even for merriment or diversion, but the conversation ends in a conspiracy against the public, or in some contrivance to raise prices" (148). Indeed, he even went so far as to issue a warning to the members of the other orders of society, to the landlords and laborers:

> The proposal of any new law or regulation of commerce which comes from this order, ought always to be listened to with great precaution, and ought never to be adopted till after having been long and carefully examined, not only with the most scrupulous, but with the most suspicious attention. It comes from an order of men, whose interest is never exactly the same with that of the public, who have generally an interest to deceive and even to oppress the public, and who accordingly have, upon many occasions, both deceived and oppressed it.
>
> (228)

For Smith, this warning to the landlords and laborers was made all the more necessary by the fact that, even though their interests tended not to be advanced by the proposals of the traders and artisans of his day, "the clamour and sophistry of merchants and manufacturers easily persuade them that the private interest of a part, and of a subordinate part of the society, is the general interest of the whole" (147).

Smith's principles applied

The above ideas could be quite influential in dealing with the Great Recession inasmuch as they outline a set of principles that could assist the general public in evaluating the practices that gave rise to it along ethical lines, and they could do so in a rather powerful way. Indeed, since this set of principles is developed not in the standard schools of normative ethical theory, but in the political economy of Adam Smith, it could enable the general public to ask not whether the practices that gave rise to the Great Recession were in line with, for example, Aristotelian, utilitarian, Kantian, or even pragmatist principles, but instead whether they were in line with the basic principles of capitalism itself (at least as Smith understood them). In fact, many of these practices were not, but in order to see this, a very brief overview of the story of the Great Recession is necessary.

The story of the Great Recession is now well understood. In the early 2000s, American investment banks and bank holding companies began to purchase large amounts of debt from commercial lenders in order to create debt securities (as well as related derivative products), which they then sold to investors all around the world. The debt was quite diversified, but much of it was home-mortgage debt, which was turned into mortgage-backed securities. Later, in the mid-2000s, they began to purchase larger and larger amounts of comparatively risky subprime home-mortgage debt in order to entice investors with higher interest payments. At the same time, they began to purchase large amounts of credit default insurance on these securities in case home-buyers defaulted on their mortgages before the securities were sold. In response to the increased demand from the investment banks and bank holding companies, commercial lenders began to issue more and more of these comparatively risky home-mortgage loans. Indeed, from 2000 to 2006, subprime lending in the United States rose from 10.1% to 23.5% of all mortgage originations (FCIC 2011, 70). Eventually, in 2007, homebuyers began to default on their mortgages in large numbers. Many of the companies that had issued credit default insurance, and American International Group (AIG) in particular, did not have sufficient reserves to pay the claims and, without them, many of the banks did not have sufficient reserves to remain solvent. As a result, Bear Stearns and Lehman Brothers went bankrupt, while AIG and the other large investment banks and bank holding companies, all on the brink of bankruptcy, received the largest government bailout in American history.

The story of the Great Recession offers numerous instances of violations of the basic principles of capitalism (at least as Adam Smith understood them). That is, it offers numerous instances of violations relating to individuals being blocked from or forced or duped into exchanges of their private property. Perhaps the most obvious violations were those relating to individuals being duped into exchanges they would not have wanted had they not been denied relevant information. Such violations happened on an industrial scale in the exchanges between homebuyers and commercial lenders as well as mortgage brokers, on the one hand, and in the exchanges between investment banks as well as bank holding companies and investors, on the other. With regard to the former, in many cases the banks and brokers that originated the comparatively risky subprime home-mortgage loans placed homebuyers into excessively large mortgages by pressuring home appraisers to inflate home values. According to the Financial Crisis Inquiry Commission (FCIC) Report, "One 2003 survey found that 55% of the appraisers had felt pressed to inflate the value of homes; by 2006, this had climbed to 90%" (91). Moreover, in many cases the banks and brokers placed homebuyers into excessively high-interest mortgages, even though they qualified for lower-interest ones, or into adjustable-rate mortgages whose terms they did not understand. According to Charles Ferguson, an MIT-trained political scientist, former Brookings Institution senior fellow, and Academy Award-winning director of *Inside Job*, "Several studies have concluded that at least one-third of people receiving subprime loans during the bubble *actually would have qualified for a prime loan*" (Ferguson 2012, 57–58). And, according to the FCIC Report, "A study by two Federal Reserve economists estimated at least 38% of borrowers with adjustable-rate mortgages did not understand how much their interest rates could reset at one time, and more than half underestimated how high their rates could reach over the years. The same lack of awareness extended to other terms of the loan" (90).

With regard to the latter, in many cases the investment banks and bank holding companies that sold debt securities to investors all over the world convinced them to purchase these securities by pressuring nationally recognized statistical rating organizations such as Moody's and Standard and Poor's to give them inflated ratings. According to the FCIC Report, "because issuers could choose which rating agencies to do business with, and because the agencies depended on the issuers for their revenues, rating agencies felt pressured to give favorable ratings so that they might remain competitive" (150). As a result, the rating agencies gave many of the debt securities backed by comparatively risky subprime home-mortgage loans their highest rating of 'AAA.' As Kyle Bass of Hayman Capital Advisors testified before Congress, "They convinced investors that 80% of a collection of toxic subprime tranches were the ratings equivalent of U.S. government bonds" (FCIC, 148). In both of the sites where these violations happened, then, individuals were duped into exchanges they would not have wanted had they not been denied relevant information, and in many cases these violations were of the first type: they were acts of overt criminality. Indeed, Ferguson argues convincingly that the commercial lenders, mortgage brokers, investment banks, bank holding companies, and ratings agencies in question were all guilty of securities fraud under Rule 10b-5 of the 1934 Securities Exchange Act (Ferguson, 190–93).

But the story of the Great Recession offers up instances of violations of the second type as well. That is, it offers instances of the 'corporation spirit' at work, particularly relating to individuals being blocked from or forced into exchanges. Indeed, Ferguson asserts that, in general, the United States has become a "political duopoly," wherein the financial services industry and others (such as the energy, defense, telecommunications, health-care, and food/agribusiness industries) have effectively established control over both political parties in order to influence the legislative process so as to weaken, repeal, or prevent the passage of public policies designed to protect others from violations of their basic economic rights and freedoms. As he explains,

> Over the past quarter century, the leaders of both political parties have perfected a remarkable system for remaining in power while serving America's new oligarchy. Both parties take in huge amounts of money, in many forms – campaign contributions, lobbying, revolving-door hiring, favors, and special access of various kinds. Politicians in both parties enrich themselves and betray the interests of the nation, including most of the people who vote for them.
>
> (Ferguson, 11)

Indeed, Ferguson continues, representatives from these industries desire "to translate their wealth and cohesion into political power in order to shelter themselves, their families, their personal assets, and their industries from competition, prosecution, effective regulation, proper corporate governance, and taxes" (283).

Interestingly, Dewey advanced a remarkably similar critique of the American political scene over eighty years ago. In 1931, in the early years of the Great Depression, he wrote a series of articles for *New Republic*, which he entitled "The Need for a New Party." In this series, he observed that "the malefactors of great wealth" had established control over both political parties, and he hoped that the "realization that both are alike because both are servants of big business" would be "a step toward the creation of a new alignment of political forces" (159, 167). Indeed, he even went so far as to echo Smith's warning about the "clamour and sophistry of merchants and manufacturers" when he remarked that "men of large business and wealth" were given to "rationalize their behavior by making themselves believe that it is in the interest of general welfare" (158).

In Dewey's time, the malefactors of great wealth had influenced the legislative process in order to further policies that served "production purposes at the cost of consumption" (Dewey 1931, 160). In our time, and within the context of the Great Recession, they did so in order to violate the basic principles of capitalism in other ways. Perhaps the most important violations relating to blocked exchanges were those having to do with deregulation. As

Ferguson notes, "The evidence is now overwhelming that over the last thirty years, the U.S. financial sector has become a rogue industry. As its wealth and power grew, it subverted America's political system (including *both* political parties), government, and academic institutions in order to free itself from regulation" (Ferguson, 2). And it has done so in multiple ways.

In 2002, the financial services industry used its political power to prevent the passage of legislation recommended by Sheila Bair, the assistant secretary for financial institutions at the Department of the Treasury at the time, and proposed by Senator Paul Sarbanes, which would have placed constraints on predatory lenders. According to the FCIC Report, "Sarbanes introduced legislation to remedy the problem, but it faced significant resistance from the mortgage industry and within Congress" (79). In 1999, the industry used its political power to secure passage of the Gramm-Leach-Bliley Act, which overturned what remained of the Glass-Steagall Act, the Depression-era legislation that prohibited bank holding companies from selling securities and insurance products and services. After its passage, Sandy Weill, the CEO of Citigroup, reportedly hung in his office "a hunk of wood – at least 4 feet wide – etched with his portrait and the words 'The Shatterer of Glass-Steagall'" (FCIC, 55). In 2000, the industry used its political power to secure passage of the Commodity Futures Modernization Act, which "in essence deregulated the [over-the-counter] derivatives market and eliminated oversight by both the CFTC [US Commodity Futures Trading Commission] and the SEC [US Securities and Exchange Commission]" and thus eliminated oversight over the sale of credit default insurance as well as exotic derivative products such as synthetic collateral debt obligations. According to the FCIC Report, Robert Rubin, who served as the Secretary of the Treasury at the time, was "'not opposed to the regulation of derivatives' … but that 'very strongly held views in the financial services industry in opposition to regulation' were insurmountable" (49). Finally, in 2004, the financial services industry used its political power to convince the SEC to allow investment banks and bank holding companies to increase their leverage limits with respect to the securities they held by employing "a new methodology to calculate the regulatory capital that they were holding against their securities portfolios" (FCIC, 151). In some cases, this allowed them to increase their leverage ratios to 30:1 or higher, which is why, in 2007, when homebuyers began to default on their mortgages in large numbers, many of them did not have sufficient reserves to remain solvent.

Why do these cases of financial deregulation represent violations of the basic principles of capitalism? Recall that, for Smith, the ideal society would ensure that its citizens would not be blocked from exchanges they wanted *unless* doing so was either in the service of liberty itself or in the service of some other important public good that could not otherwise be promoted. In these cases, by unblocking certain exchanges between homebuyers and commercial lenders, as well as between investment banks, bank holding companies, their investors, and their creditors, the world financial system was placed at systemic risk, and it would seem that if avoiding systemic risk is not in the service of freedom itself, it is certainly in the service of an important public good that could not otherwise be promoted.

Now, if the most important violations relating to blocked exchanges are those having to do with deregulation, perhaps the most important violations relating to forced exchanges are those having to do with the bailout. Indeed, American taxpayers were overwhelmingly opposed to being forced to spend $150 billion bailing out AIG and an additional $700 billion bailing out the remaining investment banks and bank holding companies through the Troubled Asset Relief Program (TARP). In fact, TARP failed to pass the first time around because representatives' offices were being flooded with calls from concerned citizens. However, it passed a few days later after what Dean Baker, one of the few prominent economists who had been warning the public about the impending crisis for years, called "a full-court press to members of Congress," whereby "some members got special pork barrel projects added to the bill in exchange for their votes" and others "were told that they would face serious consequences if the bill went down to defeat, and they had voted against it" (Baker 2010, 74–76). And this is only part of the story of the bailout. For, beyond TARP, the Federal Reserve lent hundreds of billions of dollars to the banks through ten special lending facilities, which, at one point, had more than $1.6 trillion in outstanding loans, and the Federal Deposit Insurance Corporation (FDIC) guaranteed hundreds of billions of dollars in private loans to the banks through the Temporary Liquidity Guarantee Program (Baker, 79–80). Importantly, the banks received TARP money with virtually no strings attached, Fed loans at virtually no interest, and FDIC guarantees for nominal fees. For this reason, the fact that much of the money was repaid is quite beside the point. For the lost revenue in interest and fees alone represents a substantial subsidy – and a substantial forced exchange – from American taxpayers (Baker, 80–81).

For Smith, insofar as citizens are driven by the desire to better their condition to violate the basic economic rights and freedoms of others, not only liberty, but also prosperity and equality, would be diminished. The fact that many players in the financial services industry have been so driven may help to explain why they have done so well in terms of both income and wealth relative to the general population. As Ferguson suggests, "America's new elite has obtained much of its extreme wealth not through superior productivity, but mainly via forced transfers from the rest of the American, and world, population. These transfers were frequently unethical or even criminal, and were enormously aided by government policies … . Those government policies were, with varying degrees of subtlety, bought and paid for by their beneficiaries … . Much of the new wealth of the U.S. financial sector was acquired the old-fashioned way – by stealing it" (16).

Conclusion

The preceding analysis represents an attempt to demonstrate that a great many of the practices that gave rise to the Great Recession were not in line with the basic principles of capitalism itself (at least as Smith understood them) and were thus antipathetic to the values of liberty, prosperity, and equality. Some of these practices involved individuals in the financial services industry disregarding public policies designed to protect others from violations of their basic economic rights and freedoms. Others involved individuals in the financial services industry influencing the legislative process so as to weaken, repeal, or prevent the passage of such policies. But all of them point to profound failures on the part of the American government, whether in enforcing such policies or in legislating them. These failures would seem to invite at least two possible responses, one that is necessarily counterproductive and one that is at least possibly productive.

The necessarily counterproductive response, which is exemplified in the views of many members of the Tea Party movement, is to advocate for a radical reduction in the size and power of government as such. In his series of articles for *New Republic*, Dewey anticipated the problem with this response when he wrote, "As long as politics is the shadow cast on society by big business, the attenuation of the shadow will not change the substance. The only remedy is new political action based on social interests and realities" (Dewey 1931, 163). Indeed, to advocate for a radical reduction in the size and power of government as such is not only to aim at the wrong target – at the shadow rather than the substance – but also to aid and abet the right one. For it is to advocate for a reduction in the size and power of the only thing that could potentially provide an effective counterforce against the right target, namely, big business and concentrated capital. It is perhaps for this reason that the Tea Party movement has (and always has had) corporate sponsorship.

The possibly productive response, which is exemplified in the views of many members of the Occupy Wall Street movement, is to advocate for a no-less-radical reform of government as it presently exists in America. In his series of articles, Dewey himself advocated for a "return to representative government," which had been rendered necessary by the fact that "economic privilege [had] taken possession of government," and he even went so far as to say that "[the] issuance of securities needs regulation. It would be a good deal to expect that those who profit by manipulation will undertake this regulation. In default of such action, the millions who are now the victims of this lack of regulation cry out for governmental control" (1931, 174, 178). Such a return to representative government and such a reform of the financial services industry are no less necessary today than they were in Dewey's time, and philosophy has a role to play in this reform project. In "The Need for a Recovery of Philosophy," Dewey wrote that "philosophy in America will be lost ... unless it can somehow bring to consciousness America's own needs

and its own implicit principle of successful action. This need and principle ...
is the necessity of a deliberate control of policies by the method of intelligence," which will "forecast what is desirable and undesirable in future possibilities" and will "contrive ingeniously in behalf of imagined good" (1917,
47–48). Perhaps the set of principles outlined above, the principles of classical
political economy, could be of some service toward this end.

References

Baker, Dean. 2010. *False Profits: Recovering from the Bubble Economy.* Sausalito, CA:
PoliPoint Press.

Dewey, John. 1917. "The Need for a Recovery of Philosophy." In *The Middle Works
of John Dewey, 1899–1924,* vol. 10: *1916–1917, Essays,* ed. Jo Ann Boydston, 3–48.
Carbondale: Southern Illinois University Press, 1980.

Dewey, John. 1931. "The Need for a New Party." In *The Later Works of John Dewey,
1925–1953,* vol. 6: *1931–1932, Essays,* ed. Jo Ann Boydston, 156–181. Carbondale:
Southern Illinois University Press, 1985.

FCIC (Financial Crisis Inquiry Commission) 2011. *The Financial Crisis Inquiry
Report.* New York: Public Affairs.

Ferguson, Charles. 2012. *Predator Nation: Corporate Criminals, Political Corruption,
and the Hijacking of America.* New York: Random House.

Smith, Adam. 1776. *The Wealth of Nations.* New York: Random House, 2000.

3 John Dewey

A philosophy for times of crisis

Matteo Santarelli

The complexity and immensity of the current crisis makes it difficult to reflect upon it from a purely philosophical standpoint. The very nature of the object of discussion and reflection seems to call for a multidisciplinary effort, involving economics, sociology, psychology, and environmental sciences. This call does not mean that philosophy should be silent about the crisis. A recollection of what has been written and said in the past about this type of problem could be useful. The present chapter will not sketch a history of past 'philosophies of crisis.' Rather, attention will be focused on the way in which the American philosopher John Dewey reflected upon the crisis of his times, trying to single out its causes and to point explicitly to a positive solution.

Dewey proposed a complex approach, involving philosophy, history, economics, science, and technology. Specifically, his attempt aims at integrating two dimensions that are rarely discussed together: a long-term historical and philosophical perspective on the background factors of the crisis and a concrete account of its social and economic aspects. The first part of this chapter aims at reconstructing Dewey's complex theory of the crisis by focusing on its historical, economical, and political aspects. This reconstruction will include a discussion of Dewey's writings concerning the theme of the crisis, from the early 30s (e.g., *Individualism, Old and New* and "The Need for a New Party") to the early 40s ("The Crisis in the Human History"). I will also briefly compare Dewey's position with that of Edmund Husserl, based on his writings on *Krisis*.

I will draw particular attention to the multifaceted nature evident both in Dewey's approach to understanding the crisis, and in his proposed solutions. Specifically, Dewey takes into account both the need to reconstruct collective and public intelligence by following the model of scientific communities, as well as the more immediate need of a political answer to the crisis by means of the construction of consensus. In the final part of the chapter, I will discuss the possibility of reinterpreting Dewey's complex thesis in order to deal with the contemporary crisis.

The nature of the crisis

At the beginning of the 1930s, a large part of the Western world was still struggling to emerge from the disastrous economic breakdown that history calls the Great Depression. The USA was the epicenter of this earthquake. Given Dewey's ongoing participation in American public political discussion, it comes as no surprise that his considerations about the crisis deal straightforwardly with the economic depression and its effects.

In 1932 Dewey was fully aware of the historical relevance of the events prompted by the Black Tuesday stock market crash (October 29, 1929): "we are in a crisis the greatest anyone living in this generation has seen, a crisis of the world and this nation" (Dewey 1932, 239). Dewey easily expresses the size of this breakdown by simply listing its effects on American economy and society:

> Banks failed, building and loan societies gone down in ruin, savings that were invested in bonds, domestic and foreign, wiped out; factories shut down, millions of men and women wholly out of work, millions more working for reduced wages and salaries and on part time; mortgages foreclosed; homes lost; farms taken for taxes or for security on money loaned; mutual confidence gone; everywhere insecurity, fear, black depression.
>
> (242)

This is his discouraging portrayal of the Great Depression, whose destructive power cannot be overstated. However, Dewey does not restrict his focus to the economic dimension. A crucial role is indeed played, or rather it is tragically abdicated, by politics. The Economic crisis cannot be separated from the Political crisis. Dewey engages this issue in the 1931 article "The Need for a New Party."

According to Dewey, the Great Depression showed how the two big American parties – the Republican Party and the Democratic Party – were equally powerless against the uncontrolled private interests that provoked the financial and industrial breakdown. Both the presumably progressive and conservative parties appeared as 'property-minded.' This meant that their subjugation to private profit was not reducible to an explicit alliance with big economic powers. Rather, it was mainly a matter of acquired habits. Even when they acknowledged the need to limit the range and power of private interests, their habits forced their actions in the opposite direction:

> In the clash between property interests and human interests, all their habits of thought and action fatally impel them to side with the former. They make concessions, but do not change the direction of their belief or behavior … the parties are too committed and too habituated to purposes and policies diametrically at war with their intentions.
>
> (Dewey 1931, 161)

The deeply ingrained habit of submission distanced both parties from the concrete reality of the crisis. The shared view that the "only remaining reality is the next election" (162) made the Democrats and the Republicans substantially equivalent in their common helplessness when faced with the aggressiveness and short-sightedness of property interests. The exclusive focus on short-term consensus makes any serious program of political reform impossible, and the result is perpetual domination by degenerated capitalism.

The connection between the economic breakdown and the political crisis thus produces a paradoxical and tragic situation. The huge effects of the economic crisis call for political decision, that is, for a planned change in society, but given their subjugation to private interests, political parties are impotent and devoid of any autonomy of action. Far from being the simple effect of brute and uncontrolled economic power, this subjugation was ideologically grounded in a specific philosophical justification, which Dewey summarizes in the following way:

> In the face of all law, natural and moral, we have supposed that social harmony could be secured by the competitive efforts of individuals, each to promote his own personal advantage; that men could become the keepers of their brothers' welfare by pursuing them with weapons of destruction on battlefields of war and of industry; that the planning of privileged individuals for their own private gain was an effective substitute for social planning; that society could deliberately cripple its only agent of self-control, popular government, and yet maintain its order and health.
>
> (1932, 241)

Individualism – or rather, a precise kind of individualism – is then the ideological background of the primacy of the economic dimension over the political one. According to Dewey, during the years preceding the crisis the individualist dream had come true, as most of the old institutions had crumbled away. If the assumption of economic individualism were true, the dissolution of social bonds would have corresponded with the triumph of the individual and her vitality. Unfortunately, things went differently. Since "stability of individuality is dependent upon stable objects to which allegiance firmly attaches itself" (Dewey 1930, 66), social dissolution and disorganization produced the "lost individual," instead of complete freedom of individuality. Therefore, Dewey seems to identify a third aspect of the crisis, alongside the economic and the political dimensions. This aspect involves its moral and socio-psychological repercussions.

Dewey analyzes the relation between the crisis and the individual in *Individualism, Old and New*, a volume published in 1930 which collects articles written between April 1929 and April 1930. Curiously, the word 'crisis' hardly ever appears in the book.[1] The connection between individualism and the crisis is explicitly pointed out in the 1943 essay, "The Crisis in the Human History," whose eloquent subtitle is "The Danger of the Retreat to Individualism." However, this connection is already set out in this 1929–30 series of articles, whose starting point is the analysis of the condition of the "lost individual." According to Dewey, this condition is marked by insecurity, confusion, bewilderment, precariousness, impatience, irritation, and above all, loss of meaning. None of these features develop in a vacuum, nor do they stem from an endogenous pathology of the individual. Rather, they can be traced back to the underlying social conditions: "Fear of loss of work, dread of the oncoming of old age, create anxiety and eat into self-respect in a way that impairs personal dignity. Where fears abound, courageous and robust individuality is undermined" (Dewey 1930, 68). Individual insecurity is then grounded in social insecurity: "the loyalties which once held individuals, which gave them support, direction and unity of outlook on life, have well-nigh disappeared. In consequence, individuals are confused and bewildered" (65).

There is one specific aspect which is worth noting. The condition of the lost individual, as Dewey describes it, shows that the psychological and moral insecurity characterizing the crisis is deeply related to the economic and political dimensions, and yet it is not reducible to them. The insecurity that reigns in times of crisis is not simply the immediate effect of poverty or the spontaneous consequences of the loss of faith in the political system. Rather, it seems to point to a deeper disorganization produced by a fundamental and non-harmonic change that has occurred in society. Even if this change is inconceivable in the absence of its material, economic, and political conditions, its nature and consequences appear complex and multifaceted. Most probably it is this complexity that explains Dewey's adoption of a pluralist and anti-reductionist approach to the problem of the crisis.

Understanding the crisis: an historical point of view

More than ten years after writing his articles concerning the political and economic crisis and his reflections on the "lost individual," Dewey tackled these issues together in the above-mentioned essay, "The Crisis in Human History." This paper draws explicit connections between individualism, social conditions in the life of individuals, economic breakdown, and political confusion. The key to a full understanding of the crisis is an historical perspective. Dewey maintains that "we can understand the crisis only as we take it out of its narrow geographical and temporal setting and view it in long historical perspective" (1943, 212). In order to pursue this complex task, the 1943 essay starts by expanding three points from *Individualism, Old and New*. First, there is a crisis of human beings in their status as individuals. Second, there is also a crisis of human beings "in their status as caught up in a complicated meshwork of associations, and ... one crisis cannot be viewed in separation from the other" (212). Third, the social crisis of the individual has been reinforced by a widespread – Marx may have preferred 'ideological' – conception of the relations between the individual and the social. According to Dewey, the opposition between the individual and the social has been a crucial factor in producing and intensifying the crisis. Particularly, this presumed dichotomy is shared by "the movement that goes by the name of Individualism" and which is "very responsible for the chaos now found in human associations – the chaos which is at the root of the present debasement of human beings" (212). Since the history of this movement covers a long period of time, a full understanding of the relation between individualism and the crisis requires a long-term, historical perspective.

In a first historical phase, which Dewey does not specifically date, individualism was a movement of liberation, fighting against oppressive institutions, such as the Church and the State. However, this emancipatory movement was not conceived as a social movement opposing *specific* social institutions. Rather, these institutions were identified as being themselves uniquely 'social,' in contrast to the individuals they repressed. Consequently, emancipation and freedom were "regarded largely as the cutting loose of 'the individual' from the 'social'" (212). This transformation of a social conflict into an ontological, moral, and political dualism between 'the Social' and 'the Individual' is not to be understood in terms of a purely cultural and intellectual procedure. A complex entanglement of economic, political, and cultural factors sustains the individual/social dichotomy, which is responsible for the troublesome situation called 'the crisis.'

This tendency was most marked at first in the development of the new physical sciences and in the efforts made by agencies of belief-attitudes embodied in old institutions to suppress it by force. Subsequent events in politics and in the industrial and commercial aspects of life continued and intensified the belief that social organization was the enemy of human enlightenment and progress (213).

So far, Dewey's analysis in "The Crisis in Human History" delves deeper into the points already advanced in *Individualism, Old and New*. However, the events which occurred between the production of the two essays (the rise of totalitarianism and the outbreak of World War II) make possible a wider acknowledgment of the political effects of the social realization of individualism. Evoking Karl Polanyi's *The Great Transformation* (Polanyi 1944), Dewey underlines how individualist policies went far beyond the attack on oppressive, traditional institutions. As already stated, they had been directed against 'the Social' itself, in this way menacing a wide range of affective and existential bonds and human interests. Individualism thus gave rise to uncertainties and fears, creating a need for specific political and social measures. Unfortunately, this need for special measures has been largely ignored by all but the totalitarian regimes. These governments stood alone in the defense of 'the Social,' and people preferred the 'road to serfdom' and its relative stability to the recurrent pains and sufferings produced by the dominance of 'the Individual.' In this way, the political answer to the crisis produced even more unstable and dramatic conditions, as witnessed by the tragedy of World War II.

The outbreak of the crisis is then related to the established dichotomy between 'the social' and 'the individual,' conceived as two separated entities.

In addition, the historical perspective proposed by Dewey makes clear how this opposition is itself closely connected with an even older dichotomy, which opposes ends and means. In order to understand fully this key connection, it is necessary to focus first on Dewey's painstaking discussion of the nature and history of the ends/means dichotomy, whose historical range extends to ancient history.

In *Experience and Nature* Dewey asserts that Greek metaphysics was built upon a strict dichotomy opposing means, as "menial, subservient, slavish," and ends, as "liberal and final" (Dewey 1925, 102). The sanctity of ends was heavily questioned beginning with the Renaissance. Thanks to the scientific revolution of the seventeenth century, science was finally freed from the classicist cage of pure contemplation and disinterest. Those ends, which Greek philosophy conceived as self-sufficient and unchanging, had been later brought back to immanence: "Liberation from a fixed scheme of ends made modern science possible" (120), as long as objects were reduced "from their status of complete objects as to be treated as signs or indications of other objects" (106). Modern and early modern philosophers threw ends out of transcendence, banishing them into individual consciousness: "The doctrine of natural ends was displaced by a doctrine of designs, ends-in-view, conscious aims constructed and entertained in individual minds independent of nature" (81).

The logical result of this process was to cut off consciousness and ends from nature and reality. The overturning of the ancient dualism then produced an inverted dichotomy. This sharp separation between ends and means should not be understood as a mere philosophical opposition. Particularly, the identification of means (i.e., the only existing things) with the economic and the material dimensions of life became entangled with the affirmation of the primacy of the individual. This connection gave rise to the "most successful" and "most harmful myth" of modern life: the idea that "economic activities in production, commerce and finance are carried on by 'individuals' in their individual capacity" (Dewey 1943, 218). As long as only means count in producing consequences, "the economic aspect of human association decides the conditions under which human beings actually live":

> Separation of 'ends-in-themselves' from the conditions that are the only active means of ends actually accomplished, renders the former utopian and impotent, and the actual conditions brought about by the means in use, inequitable and inhuman.
>
> (219)

Since moral values are separated from the economic dimensions, the individual must rely on her conscience in order to organize her social and interpersonal relations ethically. According to Dewey, this solution must be considered as "moral poultice." It is impossible to appeal to a moral dimension that has been previously devoid of any concreteness and causal power. At the same time, the individualist alliance between the primacy of the economic dimension and moralism cannot be solved by means of "a sheer swing of the pendulum," that is, by adopting a socialist approach. This swing "is but an effective perpetuation of the old separation with a change in the kind of suppressions it inevitably entails" (219).

It should now be clear how Dewey's approach to the crisis is a paradigmatic instance of his anti-dichotomist perspective. Instead of taking a side with one of the two contending positions in old, long-standing conceptual oppositions, such as mind versus body, reason versus practice, individual versus social, science versus humanities, he tried to show how these oppositions are both theoretically misleading and morally harmful. Furthermore, their apparent internal conflict conceals the deep complicity between the two opposite terms.[2] If only economic means should be considered as real and concrete, then moral ends will be confined necessarily to a transcendent dimension. If the individual and her economic means-relations are the only existing entities, then ends and morality must be somehow 'imported' from an external source. Any viable solution to the crisis must look beyond the conceptual and social dyadic system produced by the connection between these two oppositions.

By distancing himself from the modern tyranny of means, Dewey asks for the recognition of the inescapable importance of ends. The "lost individual" portrayed in *Individualism, Old and New* is an individual either devoid of ends or provided with obsolete and ineffective ends. But where should these ends be found? How should they be constructed?

Dewey was not the only philosopher of the time who connected the issue of crisis with the problem of ends. A similar connection was drawn by Edmund Husserl. Husserl posed the key question: how could human beings be reconnected to ends? How could they be reconnected to the meaning of their lives? Before proceeding with the analysis of Dewey's proposal, it will be interesting to consider how Husserl tackled this very same issue.

Husserl and Dewey: a viable comparison?

Edmund Husserl wrote his unfinished masterpiece, *The Crisis of European Sciences and Transcendental Phenomenology*, during the years 1935–37. This far-reaching work was both a general survey of the theoretical outcomes of phenomenology and a passionate answer to the dramatic problems gripping Europe. Particularly, Husserl's philosophy of history and history of philosophy trace European decadence back to the crisis of science.

According to Husserl, European spiritual form, which he identified with the essence of all humanity, consisted of an imminent teleology, revealing itself through the rise of a new humanity, in which men decided to live according to the sole authority of reason. Spiritual Europe had a precise place and time of birth: ancient Greece, sixth and seventh centuries BC. During that period, Greeks developed a new attitude towards reality, which contested the evidence of the immediately perceived world and of shared opinions. Truth became the object of endless research, guided by reason and inspired by the infinite ideal of truth and knowledge. This new philosophical attitude shaped a brand new humanity, which was permeated with the spirit of free critique and of free normativity and the infinite ideas of truth and knowledge.

After the medieval decadence, the Renaissance revolution looked at the ancient world as a model to follow. This return to Greek origins implied the affirmation of the primacy of philosophical life and of theoretical philosophy. Philosophy became a source of emancipation and freedom and a privileged discipline, embracing all sciences and all meaningful questions into a unitary theoretical system. Unfortunately, this ideal of a universal philosophy failed. In fact, it turned out that the alleged universal method was partial, since it worked successfully only in the domain of positive sciences. As a reaction to this disappointment, the whole world had been restricted to the natural and quantitative world, which is the object of the natural sciences. But this mathematization and naturalization of reality entailed losing touch with sense perceptions and the related rejection of secondary qualities, considered to be devoid of any scientific value. After this sharp distinction, science circumscribed its domain of action and validity, becoming fragmented into the different, and often unrelated, single disciplines. Reason became an instrument of science, conceived as the only source of legitimate knowledge.

According to Husserl, this beheading of reason, which in his time was well represented by logical positivism, was the main cause of crisis for two main reasons. First, any objectivist reduction of reality excludes the subjective dimension from the field of legitimate experiences. Nevertheless, the subjective and intersubjective ground of any experience, which Husserl called *Lebenswelt* (life-world), is the reservoir of any possible sense and meaning to be found in human activities, including scientific and theoretical ones. Therefore, by repressing the life-world, naturalistic reason forgoes any contact with the sense of its own activity. Second, the mechanistic world depicted by naturalist reason is nothing but facts and means. However, "merely fact-minded science makes merely fact-minded people" unable to deal with ends and with "questions which are decisive for a genuine humanity" (Husserl 1970, 6).

Then, this European crisis showed how reason is unable to tackle problems concerning sense and meaning. However, this failure was not due to an inherent weakness in reason: rather, it was the inescapable outcome of its unhappy reduction to naturalist and objectivist naïveté. The rise of irrationalism, dramatically perceived by Husserl, was based on this misunderstanding. The faculty of reason was charged for a crime perpetrated by a degenerated rationality. This is why Husserl invoked a new "heroism of reason" (Husserl 1970, 299), overcoming naturalism and leading reason back to itself by means of a "radical and universal self-understanding" (17) of *Geist*. The discipline in charge of this task was a radically new form of philosophy, named phenomenology. Into this innovative phenomenological inquiry, every problem concerning Being, norms, and existence was supposed to find its place. Thanks to this new self-reconstruction of reason, humanity could grasp once again its *telos* – i.e., its authentic philosophical attitude – and a deeply renewed scientific thought could be reconciled with that life-world in which the sense of every human activity lies.

Husserl's profound and insightful analyses seem to lean, however, on a conception of nature and science that is problematic under many aspects. Specifically, his criticism of naturalism is viable as long as naturalism is identified with naïve realism and with a mechanistic conception of nature. It is undeniable that such a philosophical naturalism would cut reality in two: on the one hand, objective reality, which is the object of natural sciences and is governed by stiff, causal relations; on the other, subjective and psychological reality, which is 'less real' and wherein secondary qualities, values, and ends are confined, having been "banned from the realm of science" (Husserl 1970, 7). Given this irreconcilable dichotomy, scientific reason is in principle forbidden to deal with meaningful, profound, and finally illusory questions.

Dewey would surely agree with Husserl's criticism of the dualistic structure of modern thought, which witnesses the incompleteness of modern revolution as described in *Experience and Nature*. Also, he would agree in identifying the crisis with a profound lack of meaning due to the banishment of ends from the realm of reality. Nevertheless, this agreement ends when it comes to their definitions of 'nature' and 'science.' Husserl grounded his skepticism towards science on a modern conception of nature. Now, what if this background conception changes? What if nature appears not only as a set of static causal relations, but rather as a dynamic evolutionary process (Wetz 2003, 110)? What if nature encompasses ends and values, and what if the mind is conceived as a natural phenomenon, emerging from the natural continuum?

This alternative conception of nature is exactly that envisaged by the Darwinian revolution. Given his commitment to naturalist evolutionism, we should not be surprised that Dewey's conception of science and its philosophical diagnoses and prognoses of the crisis are radically different from Husserl's arguments. While according to the latter the naturalistic reduction was the source of the discontinuity between reason and meaning, which characterizes crisis, the former conceived 'naturalism' as the inescapable framework of any possible philosophical reflection upon contemporaneity. Again, this disagreement implies two different conceptions of nature and scientific activity. In contrast to Husserl, Dewey espoused a rich conception of nature, encompassing human-specific traits which old mechanists had banished from the objective world:

> 'Naturalism' is a word with all kinds of meanings. But a naturalism which perceives that man with his habits, institutions, desires, thoughts, aspirations, ideals and struggles, is within nature, an integral part of it, has the philosophical foundation and the practical inspiration for effort to employ nature as an ally of human ideals and goods such as no dualism can possibly provide.
>
> (Dewey 1930, 114)

The skeptical and pessimistic attitude towards science is then completely reversed. Recovery from the crisis will be achieved through the application of science and the scientific method. This method being intrinsically democratic, its extension also means expanded participation in public discussion. The broadening of social applications of science is of a piece with the growing democratization of society, and thus with the overcoming of the crisis. These contrasting viewpoints on democracy and the role played by the social dimension are the final points of discontinuity between the two perspectives discussed in this section.

According to Dewey, the causes of individual disorientation are not to be found in an allegedly pure spiritual dimension. Rather, they are deeply embedded in the social context. If the individual is lost and frightened, it is because the bonds that once kept individuals together and gave them support have almost completely disappeared. Like Husserl, Dewey interpreted this dismay as a perceived lack of meaning and ends. But how can this meaning and these ends be reconstructed? And who is the agent responsible for this reconstruction?

Husserl's phenomenological revolution has to be fulfilled by the community of philosophers. This community is responsible for the true being of mankind and then for the critical and "radical self-understanding" of what "was originally and always sought in philosophy," of "what, in respect to the goals and methods (of philosophy), is ultimate, original, and genuine" (Husserl 1970, 17–18). Thanks to this recovery of the original philosophical attitude, human beings will then be engaged again with their authentic *telos*. Therefore, the effects of the redeeming action of an elitist community will spread to all humanity.

Unfortunately, Husserl did not say anything about *how* this philosophical revolution should influence the broad audience of non-philosophers. Philosophy and philosophers seem to be equipped with the magical power of changing the world by simply turning their phenomenological gaze in the right direction.[3]

On the contrary, Dewey dealt straightforwardly with this problem, which is not simply a political and sociological issue, but rather a key philosophical matter. Ends cannot be drastically separated from means, as long as pure ideal ends are nothing but a metaphysical invention. Thus, every discussion about ends and values must necessarily be a discussion about means and about the consequences involved by the realization of elected purposes and intermediate means. Therefore, "evaluating" (Dewey 1939b) the relation between means and ends does not involve, as Husserl seems to maintain, dismissing the role which ends play in our life. Dewey's instrumentalism is not a perpetuation of the banishment of ends from human life. Rather, it is the logical consequence of the acknowledgment of the constitutive entanglement between ends and means. Given this entanglement, achieving a solution to the crisis must involve a reconstruction of the relation between means and ends. According to Dewey, the collective agent responsible for this reconstruction is intelligent democracy, in this case, a certain kind of democracy which is able to reconstruct a new order starting from the existing conditions. 'Intelligence' and 'democracy' are the very key words of Dewey's proposals for the recovery from the crisis.

Beyond the crisis: intelligence and democracy

While Dewey shares Husserl's view about the necessity of reconnecting human beings and ends, he disagrees with the father of phenomenology about the way in which this reconnection should be realized. Generally speaking, Dewey's solutions are as multifaceted as his definition and understanding of the crisis. These proposed solutions lean on three methodological conditions, which allow for a proper understanding of the nature of the crisis and thus open the path to its possible solution.

The first methodological condition is the adoption of a pluralistic view-point. Instead of endorsing an epistemologically untenable individualism and a morally debatable egoism, attention should be focused on the plural conditions of association under which individuality can positively develop. At the same time, a monist employment of terms such as 'the society' and 'the social' should be equally rejected: "The gangster is as highly 'social' in one connection as he is anti-social in other connections" (Dewey 1943, 221). Both individual and social monisms should then be abandoned, as long as their mutual opposition plays a key role in obscuring the nature and causes of the crisis. Instead of calling into question the alleged entities of 'the social' and 'the individual,' Dewey's purpose is to say that the events that constitute the present crisis can be dealt with in a way that produces a desirable outcome only to the extent that they are viewed in their own concrete context, with due consideration for economic, political, social, and historical factors.

The second methodological recommendation concerns the correct posture (Bourdieu 1990b, 2000) to assume in order to deal properly with the crisis. This posture is difficult to assume because it requires a reflexive attitude, which is at odds with the general attitude of "impatience and haste" (Dewey 1943, 223) characterizing Dewey's times. Thus, a further dichotomy appears. Emotional reactions are necessarily part of the moral and political evaluation of the nature and effects of the crisis. However, emotions cannot be allowed to restrict intelligent vision by blocking observation and planning. By rejecting any opposition of emotions and intelligence, Dewey believes that the former can and should be integrated with intelligent and rational understanding of phenomena.[4] These emotions are themselves as legitimate as they are inevitable in every rightly constituted human being, but they should be used to promote – not to impede – wide observation and large-scale planning, that is, large enough in scale to integrate the economic with the moral and humane (Dewey 1943, 223).

The third methodological point involves an attempt to overcome the deep imbalance between technological and human knowledge – i.e., sciences whose object is constituted by human activities. While the latter field is "speaking in an infantile state" and is "left under the control of a complex of institutions and traditions that took shape in a static period when changes in life were the work of chance, often of catastrophe," the former holds a monopoly on the "entire impact of systematic observation and report" (Dewey 1943, 222–23). As could be easily seen in Husserl's *Krisis*, many influential authors tried to challenge this monopoly by calling for a renewed spirituality, but in Dewey's view, this ultra-humanistic perspective entails a perpetuation of that tragic division in humanity which is at the core of the crisis.

This broad, anti-dichotomist approach involves some important consequences for understanding and resolving the crisis. As already stated, Dewey traces the condition of the lost individual back to the destruction of old social habits and bonds, but this loss cannot be reduced to mere manifestations of insecurity and disorganization. The discomfort characterizing the crisis arises because inherited beliefs and values have lost their meaning in a society that has dramatically changed. In the absence of reliable social supports, individuals continue to believe in values that have become devoid of any sense. Similarly, the two old parties "perpetuate and cling to ideas and ideals of a past that has forever departed," becoming "so out of vital contact with the times, that the people are out of touch with them" (Dewey 1931, 160). The crisis is then strongly related to that kind of social phenomena which Pierre Bourdieu labeled as "hysteresis": the habits that have been formed by specific social conditions survive the disappearance of these conditions, remaining active in a new social context in which their meaning is lost (Bourdieu 1990a).

Consequently, overcoming the crisis implies a creative work of adaptation. But is not adaptation an instance of conformism?[5] Not necessarily. In fact, Dewey is far from proposing a simple submission to the power of the existing conditions. On the contrary, he maintains that the crisis is born from a lack of meaning. That is why the individual condition can be improved only by creating new social perspectives and organizations starting from the status quo. This creation is not an *ex nihilo* production,[6] as it requires the intervention of socially directed intelligence. Since "stability of individuality is dependent upon stable objects to which allegiance firmly attaches itself" (Dewey 1930, 66), renewing individuality implies working on social conditions:

> The inner man is the jungle which can be subdued to order only as the forces of organization at work in externals are reflected in corresponding patterns of thought, imagination and emotion. The sick cannot heal themselves by means of their disease, and disintegrated individuals can achieve unity only as the dominant energies of community life are incorporated to form their minds.
>
> (73)

In contrast to Husserl, Dewey does not believe that the re-connection between human beings and ends should be provided by means of purely philosophical and phenomenological activity. In order to create new ends and values, intelligence must select those aspects of society that make possible a reconstruction of the individual and create new ends, starting from the possibilities opened by actual social conditions. Looking at his own society, Dewey believed that the practical ends of a socially renewed individual were anticipated by the existence of small scientific communities:

> there is a movement in science which foreshadows, if its inherent promises be carried out, a more human age. For it looks forward to a time when all individuals may share in the discoveries and thoughts of others, to the liberation and enrichment of their own experience.
>
> (Dewey 1930, 115)

Now, this promise was not mere idealism, nor just wishful thinking. On the contrary, it was a possible development of the democratic tendency already present in scientific research:

> No scientific inquirer can keep what he finds to himself or turn it to merely private account without losing his scientific standing. Everything discovered belongs to the community of workers. Every new idea and theory has to be submitted to this community for confirmation and test.
>
> (115)

By generalizing the attitude of small scientific communities, political, ethical, and existential problems could be dealt with in a revolutionary way. The solution to the crisis must then be democratic and scientific at the same time. In other words, Dewey's solution to the crisis updates Thomas Jefferson's conception of democracy as an ongoing experiment (Calcaterra 2011, 88). The democratic solution can resolve all the features characterizing the complexity of the crisis: the lost individual, who could be recovered, thanks to the new social reconstruction; and the submission of politics to economic interests, which would be overcome by reasserting the primacy of intelligent democratic power.[7]

This proposal might appear overly optimistic. Why should economic and political powers obey this deep democratic and intelligent change? How could this melioristic revolution be accomplished in practice? Dewey deals with these problems in his 1931 article, where he calls for the establishment of a new party. The new party sketched by Dewey is a middle-class party whose main aim is "the use of government to effect the subordination of economic forces to the maintenance of human justice and happiness" (Dewey 1931, 177). The supremacy of people's needs over private interest has to be restored by asserting the social control of credit (Dewey 1932, 243). For this purpose, economic policy will revolve around three core issues: planning, distribution of wealth, and industry and finance directed toward the interest of consumption.

However, Dewey acknowledges that people are generally unfavorably disposed towards changes. Therefore, the following question has to be raised: how could this new party become appealing and attractive to American citizens? Dewey introduces then three conditions that could guarantee the needed amount of consensus. First, the party's political program has to be focused on a single "great issue on which all others converge" (Dewey 1931, 175). This unity is necessary because a successful reformist party must be able to grasp that particular opportunity which emerges only once in a while in history: "there are times when a large number of social tendencies previously more or less separated draw together, and masses of people feel, even if they do not clearly see, their unity. Such a time is here" (175). Second, the new movement has to be built not only on a rational ground but also on an emotional background: "no movement gets far on a purely intellectual basis. It has to be emotionalized; it must appeal to the social imagination" (175). In order to fulfill these two conditions, a third one has to be introduced. An important way of achieving unity and of gaining emotional involvement is steering conflict towards a clear target: "a sense of conflict and battle is a necessary part of any movement which enlists the imagination and the emotions" (176).

To summarize, in his works devoted to the issue of the crisis Dewey stresses respectively two sides of his democratic solution to the crisis. The first focuses on the intelligent reconstruction of society; the second concentrates on the populist problem of consensus. The use of the term 'populism' might appear as misleading in this context. Dewey's approach promotes the development of common intelligence and common inquiry. On the contrary, populist movements seem to indulge every attitude and desire of people by means of an oversimplification of reality and by discrediting pluralism.[8] At first sight, Dewey's attention to the issue of consensus has nothing in common with "populism."

This potential confusion disappears once it is made clear that the terms 'populist' and 'populism' are employed here in the technical sense introduced by Ernesto Laclau. Laclau (2005) defines populism as the "the very essence of the political" (222), as long as the construction of a 'people' is "the political operation par excellence" (153). This construction is made possible by a floating signifier, that is, a name – e.g., 'freedom,' 'race,' 'nation,' 'democracy' – which is able to unify the different conflicts and demands emerging from society. The Dewey-Laclau connection should now be clearer. As Dewey wishes for the birth of a party that is able to draw together "a large number of social tendencies previously more or less separated," by creating a unity that "masses of people feel, even if they do not clearly see," he is asking for a populist political operation in Laclau's terms.[9] As Brendan Hogan points out, referring to Dewey's article "The Need for a New Party," "Dewey's theory of new political action as presented five years earlier in *The Public and Its Problems* takes up the challenge of mobilizing the people through an alternative arrangement of collective action via the establishment of a public sphere that is essentially a more populist and pluralist version of Gramsci's party organ in *The Modern Prince*" (Hogan 2015, 111).

Dewey's reflections then seem to swing between these two different approaches to democracy – democracy as intelligent collective inquiry; democracy as the populist construction of 'the people.' However, this swinging should not be conceived in terms of ambiguity or contradiction. Instead of focusing solely on the question, 'What is democracy?,' Dewey is also engaged in explaining *how* democracy should be applied and how it should work. This 'how' is the necessary boundary between idealism and realism.

In the *Individualism, Old and New* essays Dewey points at then-current social conditions that might anticipate a future democratic and intelligent organization of society. To this purpose he proposes to model this renewed society after small scientific communities, in which individual expression is both guaranteed and limited by public discussion and mutual agreement. However, it is not clear how to involve the so-called ordinary people in this sophisticated change. Small scientific communities are made up of scientists endowed with certain features – a certain educational level, a certain acquaintance with rational discussion, a certain interest in scientific issues – which are not necessarily shared by all the participants in the democratic community. Here Dewey seems to project his social posture onto all the social actors, in this way falling into the scholastic fallacy described by Pierre Bourdieu (2000). People do not deal with ordinary and extraordinary problems in a scientific way. Of course, a scientific organization of society might be imposed from above. Technocracies and Stalinism are classical examples in this sense. However, these attempts are at odds with Dewey's concern about democracy. Therefore, the questions arises: could a real democratic society be modeled after scientific communities?

First, a Deweyan answer to this question should of course mention education. It is not by a matter of chance that education plays a key role in Dewey's thought (Spadafora and Hickman 2009). Education is able to build up a steady connection between participation and knowledge, scientific organization and democracy. However, the dramatic nature of the crisis also requires more immediate answers. How could a new democratic movement actively involve people in its conflict against the runaway predominance of private interests? Here comes Dewey's call for a new party, whose consensus has to be built by means of a flexible agenda focused on a big, unifying issue and by means of the 'emotionalization' of the movement.

To sum up, the populist and scientific approaches to democracy do not necessarily contradict each other. Rather, each one seems to answer questions raised by the other approach. The populist construction of a new party without intelligent direction is blind and empty; the intelligent construction of society without the populist construction of a movement is ineffective. Unfortunately, Dewey never explicitly defined the relationship between these two core problems of democracy. This is why his political solutions might appear at times as either idealistic or superficial.[10] However, the reconstruction of these different positions reveals the richness and complexity of his reflections on the crisis. This complexity is necessary, since the object of investigation is an extremely complex and multifaceted one.

A Deweyan reading of the contemporary European crisis

Dewey's analyses clearly refer to a particular historical context: the Great Depression, its background, its nature, its consequences. However, his considerations seem pertinent to some general features of the concept of 'crisis.' As Federico Zappino points out, both the etymology and the employment of the Greek word '*krisis*' refer to judgment and decision (Zappino 2014). Dewey's reflections seem to be very sympathetic with this forgotten but still valid meaning. In his perspective, understanding the crisis implies a judgment about the social context in all its complexity. Moreover, overcoming the crisis requires a decision regarding which traits in the existing social conditions have to be taken as starting points for a positive reconstruction. In particular, Dewey's judgments and decisions call for a new democratic organization of society, which is made possible by eliminating damaging dichotomies, such as individual/social, political/economic, rationality/emotions. Surprisingly, some of these same dichotomies and ambivalences continue to play a key role at the present time in the current European crisis.

In the first place, the connection between the economic and the socio-political dimension is still at the core of the crisis. Once again this relation appears in terms of subjugation, and financial domination is still paired with unequal distribution of wealth. This correlation between economic crisis and growing inequality is probably not accidental. According to Thomas Piketty, in general terms wealth grows faster than economic output. Therefore, in order to support social and economic equality, suitable means (e.g., taxation) must be used to maintain an appropriate relationship between economic growth and wealth accumulation by the financial sector (Piketty 2014). Consequently, in this period, which combines economic crisis with uncontrolled financial power, the owners of capital and financial goods are gaining an even more privileged position, and workers devoid of wealth are sinking deeper into poverty.

Additionally, in recent years financial concerns have been dictating the rules in the political economy of many European countries. Austerity has been the core value inspiring national budget plans, conceiving them essentially as budgetary constraints. Without taking political sides, it is worth noting a curious historical trend: immediately following the 2008 Western crisis, public opinion, journalists, and right-wing and left-wing politicians blamed 'the financial system' for what happened in the USA and, successively, throughout almost all of the Western world. Some years later, a substantially unchanged version of the same 'financial system,' supporting the austerity system of values, is exerting its even-more-uncontrolled influence over European political economies. In this regard, what Dewey wrote in 1931 seems to fit adequately with the current situation:

It would be ludicrous, were it not tragic, to believe that an appeal to the unregulated activities of those who have got us into the present crisis will get us out of it, provided they are relieved from the incubus of political action. The magic of eating a hair of the dog which bit you in order to cure hydrophobia is as nothing to the magic involved in the belief that those who have privilege and power will remedy the breakdown they have created. As long as politics is the shadow cast on society by big business, the attenuation of the shadow will not change the substance. The only remedy is new political action based on social interests and realities.

(Dewey 1931, 163)

Democratic political control over financial power and private interests appears again as the most promising way to overcome this vicious cycle, but democracy is struggling with worrisome questions in Europe today. Curiously, some of these problems seem to be tied to the ends/means dichotomy. As Dewey pointed out in his 1939 essay *Theory of Valuation*, ends are often considered as ideals that must be fulfilled in themselves, apart from the outcomes involved by their achievement, but the realization of these ends by any specific means results in different consequences for everyday life. Taking the ends/means entanglement seriously entails caring about the real import of any practical realization of ends.[11]

This looks like a banal remark, but it might be useful in times of reigning technocracy and rising, demagogic movements. From a political point of view, southern Europe is swaying between the inexorability of technocracy and the obsessive and incessant mistrust towards political institutions. In both cases, ends are drastically divided from means. In the former case, the technocratic goal of austerity is separated from democratic discussion and considered as a sort of indisputable principle,[12] despite important challenges to its validity by many influential economists. In the latter case, insistence on immediacy leaves out any realistic consideration about which means are needed in order to fulfill certain ends. In both cases, democracy might be undermined, either by the holy dogmas of financial power or by ignorance and fear. A Deweyan conception of democracy can overcome this political dichotomy, whose influence seems to grow in current political debate. As Dewey would suggest, a democratic solution to the crisis requires citizens – and organizations of citizens, of course – to be able to discuss existing ends critically and to cooperate on the establishment of new ones if the former are deemed unfair. The capacity of taking part in such a discussion exemplifies the shift from "the method of discussion" to the "method of inquiry." That is, from superficial conversation to the reflexive and critical acknowledgment, settlement, and resolution of problems (Dewey 1935).[13] This discussion also involves the consideration of all viable means that will bring about the desired ends: "The fundamental principle of democracy is that the ends of freedom and individuality for all can be attained only by means that accord with those ends" (Dewey 1937, 334).

Of course, this change can be achieved only by acting on social conditions, that is, education, social policies, and incentives promoting new forms of social organization. At the same time, any effective solution to the crisis requires an intelligent selection that is far from being an uncritical acceptance of the status quo. This balance between past and present, realism and idealism, habit and change, is often hard to reach. The current debate about job-related issues illustrates this difficulty.

The European welfare system, whose structure has been defined by a social context characterized by a growing economy, sometimes proves to be ineffective when facing the new conditions produced by the crisis. Specifically, in some countries – Italy among others – any welfare assistance, e.g., unemployment benefits, is strictly related to a job previously held. Consequently, labor unions often focus exclusively on job issues, such as wages, battles against short-term work contracts, and improvements in working conditions. Despite the importance of these concerns, which represent a legitimate defense of rights acquired during the past decades, they ignore a large part of the population which is drastically separated from work – for instance, unemployment among Italy's youth is actually 39.2% (as of August 2016).[14] This begs the question: is an exclusively job-centered welfare-state still viable today? This question lies at the very core of the current discussions about the adoption of basic income, a form of income supplied by public institutions in order to guarantee dignified living conditions regardless of job market trends.[15]

Surprisingly, Dewey cleverly foreshadowed this issue some decades ago. An interesting passage in his criticism of the policies of the Democratic and the Republican parties concerns the relation between production and consumption. According to him, both the old parties tried to answer to the economic breakdown by means of policies that were focused on production. This policy proved to be unsatisfactory. Not only was it unable to guarantee a decent standard of living for the populace, but it also proved ineffective at stabilizing employment. Unemployment and precarious work then show how the "problems and needs of life for the masses have to do with consumption" (Dewey 1931, 160) and not with production. The former should be considered as a means to incentivize the latter, and not vice versa. Despite the use of the ambiguous word 'consumption,' Dewey found the key point of current discussions about basic income and welfare state: should the ultimate goal of democracy be the safeguard of production rates in themselves, or the warranty of decent living conditions for all the citizens? Of course, the two issues are deeply connected. However, the crisis seems to require a judgment and a decision in this respect. If the safeguard of the material conditions for individual dignity is conceived as the main purpose of the welfare state, then the necessary means have to be either selected or created in order to fulfill this end.

To sum up, Dewey's theory of the crisis seems to provide useful insights and plausible strategies for dealing with some crucial contemporary issues contributing to the complexity of the European crisis. I would like to conclude by sketching a proposal concerning one of these specific issues, something we could provisionally call the crisis of evaluation.

Democracy as a way of life requires the broadest possible participation in public discussion. At the present time this participation is fostered by the widespread diffusion of new means of communication. Thanks to Facebook, Twitter, and all the other social networks, people can post comments on online journals; they can like or dislike posts on Facebook; they can participate in opinion polls. However, these evaluations generally consist in mere one-sided expressions of pleasure or displeasure. Being the object of immediate experience, these hedonistic ends are immune to discussion and debate: who would ever question something as private and subjective as expressions of pleasure? As Dewey made clear in his 1939 essay *Theory of Valuation*, if the only valuations available are of this kind, some serious problems arise.

In general terms the crisis of democracy is then entangled with the crisis of evaluation. As Dewey clearly understood, participation is the core of real democracy (Westbrook 1993; Talisse 2005). However, popular participation in public discussions is impaired by the one-sidedness of the available evaluations in the market of opinions. As Dewey pointed out, democracy is neither made exclusively of interactions between fully rational agents, nor can it be grounded on purely emotional reactions and behaviors. The radical split between emotions and rationality establishes one of the dichotomies that was at the core of the crisis in Dewey's time, and still plays a crucial role in the current situation. In more general terms, the two crises appear to be related to a specific set of dichotomies whose enduring existence impairs any possible solution. Dewey's conception of democracy involves a serious anti-dichotomist approach and thus appears as a source of viable solutions to the painful divisions characterizing the current crisis:

> Democracy as compared with other ways of life is the sole way of living which believes wholeheartedly in the process of experience as ends and means; as that which is capable of generating the science which is the sole dependable authority for the direction of further experience and which releases emotions, needs and desires so as to call into being the things that have not existed in the past.
>
> (Dewey 1939a, 229).

Is democracy compatible with the hegemony of one-sided and allegedly immediate evaluations? Does the current crisis call for new ways of evaluating? Can the current issue of post-truth be understood in terms of the ontological and moral fight between reason and emotions? Or, is the growing appeal of this dichotomy a symptom of the crisis itself? Although I do not have an answer to these difficult questions, I believe Dewey could help us in formulating these issues in a clearer and more effective way.

Notes

1 More precisely, it appears once in the title of chapter 7, "The Crisis in Culture," and in the text of the chapter, as Dewey writes: "The solution of the crisis in culture is identical with the recovery of composed, effective and creative individuality" (1930, 109).
2 This point has been brilliantly made by Pierre Bourdieu (2000) and Gregory Bateson (1972).
3 Of course, this criticism does not apply to the phenomenological method in itself but to Husserl's conception of the relation between phenomenology and the crisis.
4 On Dewey's conception of emotions, see Garrison 2003.
5 This exact point is precisely made by Max Weber (1949).
6 A brilliant pragmatist account of creativity can be found in Joas 1996. A more recent pragmatist account of creativity, can be found in Maddalena 2015.
7 On Dewey's theory of democracy, and on its relations with other influent contemporary theories, see Frega n.d..
8 On a contemporary interpretation of populism as anti-pluralism, see Müller 2016.
9 The connection between pragmatism and Laclau's theory of populism has been discussed by Koczanowicz (2015). The relation between Dewey, Gramsci, and Gramscian tradition, to which Laclau somehow belongs, has been discussed by Brendan Hogan (2015).
10 Moreover, Dewey has been often accused of not taking into consideration the issue of Power. However, the importance of Dewey's insights in this regard have been discussed by, among others, Midtgarden (2012).
11 A clear account of Dewey's overall refusal of the means/ends dichotomy can be found in Joas 1996.
12 In 2012, the balanced budget principle was introduced into the Italian Constitution. This means that in a certain sense economic policies which challenge this principle must be considered unconstitutional.
13 I came across this insight in Oliviero, forthcoming.
14 Istat 2016.
15 For an overall understanding of the debate about basic income, see Van Parijs 2004, Friedman 1962, and van Donselaar 2008.

References

Bateson, G. 1972. "Morale and National Character." In *Steps to an Ecology of Mind: Collected Essays in Anthropology, Psychiatry, Evolution, and Epistemology.* Northvale, NJ: Jason Aronson.
Bourdieu, P. 1990a. *In Other Words.* Stanford, CA: Stanford University Press.
Bourdieu, P. 1990b. *The Logic of Practice.* Stanford, CA: Stanford University Press.
Bourdieu, P. 2000. *Pascalian Meditations.* Stanford, CA: Polity Press.
Calcaterra, R. 2011. *Idee concrete: percorsi nella filosofia di John Dewey.* Genova-Milano: Marietti.
Calcaterra, R. 2014. "John Dewey and Democracy as Regulative Ideal." *Cognitio: Revista de Filosofia* (São Paulo) 15(2): 275–288.
Dewey, J. 1925. *Experience and Nature.* Vol. 1 of *The Later Works of John Dewey, 1925–1953,* ed. Jo Ann Boydston. Carbondale: Southern Illinois University Press, 1981.
Dewey, J. 1930. *Individualism, Old and New.* In *The Later Works of John Dewey, 1925–1953,* vol. 5: *1929–1930, Essays, The Sources of a Science Education, Individualism, Old and New, and Construction and Criticism,* ed. Jo Ann Boydston, 41–144. Carbondale: Southern Illinois University Press, 1984.

Dewey, J. 1931. "The Need for a New Party." In *The Later Works of John Dewey, 1925–1953*, vol. 6: *1931–1932, Essays*, ed. Jo Ann Boydston, 156–182. Carbondale: Southern Illinois University Press, 1985.

Dewey, J. 1932. "Democracy Joins the Unemployed." In *The Later Works of John Dewey, 1925–1953*, vol. 6: *1931–1932, Essays*, ed. Jo Ann Boydston, 239–246. Carbondale: Southern Illinois University Press, 1985.

Dewey, J. 1935. *Liberalism and Social Action*. In *The Later Works of John Dewey, 1925–1953*, vol. 11: *1935–1937, Essays, Liberalism and Social Action*, ed. Jo Ann Boydston, 1–65. Carbondale: Southern Illinois University Press, 1985.

Dewey, J. 1937. "Democracy is Radical." In *The Later Works of John Dewey, 1925–1953*, vol. 11: *1935–1937, Essays, Liberalism and Social Action*, ed. Jo Ann Boydston, 296–301. Carbondale: Southern Illinois University Press, 1987.

Dewey, J. 1939a. "Creative Democracy – The Task before Us." In *The Later Works of John Dewey, 1925–1953*, vol. 11: *1935–1937, Essays, Liberalism and Social Action*, ed. Jo Ann Boydston, 224–230. Carbondale: Southern Illinois University Press, 1987.

Dewey, J. 1939b. *Theory of Valuation*. In *The Later Works of John Dewey, 1925–1953*, vol. 13: *1938–1939, Essays, Experience and Education, Freedom and Culture, and Theory of Valuation*, ed. Jo Ann Boydston, 189–258. Carbondale: Southern Illinois University Press, 1988.

Dewey, J. 1943. "The Crisis in Human History." In *The Later Works of John Dewey, 1925–1953*, vol. 15: *1942–1948, Essays*, ed. Jo Ann Boydston. Carbondale: Southern Illinois University Press, 1989, 210–223.

Frega, R. n.d. "The Democratic Project." Unpublished manuscript.

Friedman, M. 1962. *Capitalism and Freedom*. Chicago: Chicago University Press.

Garrison, J. 2003. "Dewey's Theory of Emotions: The Unity of Thought and Emotion in Naturalistic Functional 'Co-ordination' of Behavior." *Transactions of the Charles S. Peirce Society* 39(3): 405–443.

Hogan, B. 2015. "Pragmatic Hegemony: Questions and Convergences." *Journal of Speculative Philosophy* 29(1): 107–117.

Husserl, E. 1970. *The Crisis of European Sciences and Transcendental Phenomenology*, trans. David Carr. Evanston, IL: Northwestern University Press.

Istat (Istituto Nazionale di Statistica). 2016. "Work and Incomes in Italy" [in Italian]. Istat, Rome. <www.istat.it/it/lavoro-e-retribuzioni>.

Joas, H. 1996. *The Creativity of Action*. Chicago: University of Chicago Press.

Koczanowicz, L. 2015. *Politics of Dialogue: Non-consensual Democracy and Critical Community*. Edinburgh: Edinburgh University Press.

Laclau, E. 2005. *On Populist Reason*. London: Verso.

Maddalena, G. 2015. *The Philosophy of Gesture: Completing Pragmatists' Incomplete Revolution*. Montreal: McGill-Queen's University Press.

Midtgarden, T. 2012. "Critical Pragmatism: Dewey's Social Philosophy Revised." *European Journal of Social Theory* 4: 505–521.

Müller, J. W. 2016. *What Is Populism?* Philadelphia: University of Pennsylvania.

Oliverio, S. Forthcoming. "La democrazia come educazione e l'epoca della post-verità: civitas educationis." *Education, Politics, and Culture* 5(2).

Piketty, T. 2014. *Capital in the Twenty-First Century*, trans. Arthur Goldhammer. Cambridge, MA: Harvard University Press.

Polanyi, K. 1944. *The Great Transformation*. New York: Farrar & Rinehart.

Spadafora, G., and L. Hickman, eds. 2009. *John Dewey's Educational Philosophy in International Perspective: A New Democracy for the Twenty-First Century.* Carbondale: Southern Illinois University Press.

Talisse, R. 2005. *Democracy after Liberalism: Pragmatism and Deliberative Politics.* London: Routledge.

van Donselaar, G. 2008. *The Right to Exploit: Parasitism, Scarcity, Basic Income.* Oxford: Oxford University Press.

Van Parijs, P. 2004. "Basic Income: A Simple and Powerful Idea for the Twenty-first Century." *Policy & Politics* 39(1): 7–39.

Weber, M. 1949. "The Meaning of 'Ethical Neutrality' in Sociology and Economics." In *The Methodology of the Social Sciences.* Glencoe: The Free Press.

Westbrook, R. 1993. *John Dewey and American Philosophy.* Ithaca: Cornell University Press.

Wetz, P. 2003. *Husserl.* Bologna: Il Mulino.

Zappino, F. 2014. "Crisi." In *Genealogie del presente*, ed. F. Zappino, L. Coccoli, and M. Tabacchini. Milan-Udine: Mimesis.

Part II

The narrative and rhetoric of 'crisis'

4 Neopragmatist ethnocentric rhetoric on economic crisis

Richard Rorty and social amelioration by redescription

Krzysztof Piotr Skowroński

There are some doubts regarding the need for philosophy in the present world. Its impracticality is raised especially by those who despair of getting some definite conclusions from philosophical debates and applying those conclusions to social life quickly and effectively. The present chapter intends to show that philosophy can contribute to social amelioration in various ways, and one of these ways is by paying special attention to the preconditions and assumptions of using narratives and descriptions to tell stories about social (also economic and financial) progress and crisis. Philosophers, who are sensitive to the normative dimension of such terms as 'duty,' 'obligation,' 'loyalty,' 'necessary,' 'worthy of doing,' 'progress,' 'growth,' 'success,' and many others, can detect the hierarchy of values upon which such a normative system is constructed or from which such a system stems.

They can ask whether such a hierarchy of values manifests the power structure of a given society as described by some of its representatives rather than an unbiased presentation of the real goods to be aimed at by members of the public. If so, I mean, if the discourses about 'success' and 'duties' do not present the world to us as it factually is, one can ask, to what facts, or, perhaps, to whose goods and interests, do these narratives mostly refer, and whose do they ignore? If there are as many possible descriptions of the world as it seems, then what about the alternative narratives? And what is the mechanism, or what are the mechanisms that make some narratives dominate others? Is it because some are useless? untrue? unrealizable? unwanted? Can a 'free market of narratives' be a part of the free market of goods? And, if so, can it be regulated or controlled by similar mechanisms?

These issues also concern the discussion about the economic crisis. The story about the economic (and/or financial) crisis usually stems from one about economic growth and success, and the preconditions of both are, at many points, similar. If we agree that some definite group of people are especially predisposed to monopolize the truth about economic success, most probably we will accept the news about the crisis from the same group of people; if we accept the narrative about the factors that make for progress, for example, more consumption from our (the consumers) part, we most likely admit that the lack of these factors (e.g., diminishing consumption) will make for crisis; and if we admit that some given social mechanisms are responsible for the generation of the narratives on what should be done and what should be avoided, most likely similar types of mechanisms will be used to overcome stagnation and regression.

A special status of philosophers is not an issue here: I do not claim that philosophers as such are more detached or autonomous so as to see the social reality better than anyone else, as if from a bird's-eye view, nor that they are able to provide us with more reliable solutions. Philosophers themselves get frequently involved in the assumptions that are typical of the cultures and traditions in which they have been living and which are hardly acceptable for other cultures and traditions. For example, philosophers from democratic countries may easily get morally puzzled, if not trapped, when, while promoting worldwide freedom and tolerance, as understood by Western standards, they are seen as 'oppressive,' 'intolerant,' and 'colonizing' by representatives of other cultures, for whom the introduction of Western values equals the undermining of long-standing and commonly accepted social orders there. Hence, a special status of philosophers is not at stake here but rather the special status of the tools that they can provide, in the first instance critical thinking about the assumptions of the discourses that deal with progress and crisis.

Rorty's neopragmatist philosophy of redescription

In *American Philosophy: An Encyclopedia* (2008), under the entry "Economics," we can read that the theory of choice is one of the main things that American philosophy, especially in its pragmatic version (John Dewey), can teach economists; 'choice' is understood as the experience of agents dealing with the selection of goods and the achievement of goals. The main assumption is that agents make more or less free choices in their activities and they do not act according to some fixed features of human nature that dictate to them their courses of action. Rather, agents act freely and according to their experience within the social conditions that make it possible for them to thrive and develop in one way or another. Little is said about the choice that deals with alternative descriptions and redescriptions that change vocabulary and redirect the agent's attention regarding goals and ways of talking about these goals. I say "little" because it is admitted that pragmatism, "with its emphasis on the relevance of context and meaning, can provide a needed conceptual backbone" (Khalil 2008, 204) to institutional economics, according to which institutions provide paradigms and theories, not just customs and laws, and to behavioral economics, according to which agents "have been found to reverse their choices once the incentive is worded differently – as if a half-empty glass differs substantially from a half-full one" (ibid.). Here, I propose to develop these suggestions and to think whether the choice of narratives about the economic dimension of living can also be a part of the pragmatist project, this time in its neopragmatist version, and I think of Richard Rorty (1931–2007) in the first instance.

Rorty, one of the most influential American philosophers today, developed a philosophy that pays special attention to the role of new narratives in the process of ameliorating social life in general; at the same time, he put these attempts into the framework of the democratic society and free market economy. Rorty's anti-foundationalism claims that the discourses do not refer to the world as it really is. Sciences, and this must include economics, have their own discourses and vocabularies that serve certain aims, yet their aims are neither 'telling us the ontologically true story' nor 'cognitively showing us how things objectively, mind-independently, factually work.' Rorty is quite definite on the socio-political dimension of descriptions made by some people for certain reasons: "there are lots of descriptions of the world, some more useful and some less, but none that match the way the world independently is" (Rorty 2001, 131). His prioritizing democracy over philosophy, or, as he put it, "that our responsibility for other people comes first" (in Auxier and Hahn 2010, 20), promotes using narratives and descriptions for the betterment of the communal life. This betterment should serve both 'us' and 'them' (that is, those who frequently (and unjustifiably) are left outside of 'our' descriptions of 'our' hopes for a fair and just world). So should his idea of *cultural politics* (also, *cultural policy*), or "the attempt to create a change in the intellectual world" (ibid., 23), by means of redescription or changing vocabularies. Redescription is "a slow process, stretching over decades and centuries" (ibid., 104), and its aim is to make the world more adaptable for all of us, rather than maintaining the status quo as suitable for some.

In Rorty's "Love and Money" (*Philosophy and Social Hope*), we can see his exemplary approach towards people suffering from poverty. Rorty regrets the impotence of philosophers at doing something particularly efficient and quick so as to help the poor in their hopelessness. He identifies those who are marginalized and in plight as 'unthinkable,' 'unconversable,' 'unconnectable,' and merely subjects of studies for statisticians and ethnologists, without being recognized as genuine agents and heard as persons having dignity. Those people who are 'unthinkable,' 'unconversable,' and 'unconnectable' suffer not only from their economic plight and social degradation but also, which is even more crucial in the long-term perspective, from social and political unrecognition within the discourses and narratives of those who have the power to make a difference. Hence, in this very text, Rorty suggests the way philosophy (he prefers the term 'literature' for this kind of redescriptive activity) can help in the long-term perspective: it can demand the redescription of the lot of those others and make this function in the narratives of the public, the mass media, and the institutions, especially powerful ones, effectively involved in the practice of both cultural policy and real politics. It should be noted that redescription as such, as a merely 'oral' or 'written' project, is not enough: it must be assisted by the practical action of factually implementing this new description into the system of social and political life.

A similar redescriptive strategy is proposed by Rorty in other places. For example, while discussing the unfortunate plight of Black Americans and the possible ways of helping them, Rorty says the following: "Do we say that these people must be helped because they are our fellow human beings? We may, but it is much more persuasive, morally as well as politically, to describe them as our fellow *Americans* – to insist that it is outrageous that an *American* should live without hope" (Rorty 1989, 191). Here the redescription of the status of those in trouble is not seen as the only and ultimate way to ameliorate their condition and to make them recognizable as worthy human beings; however, it is an important thing to do, and philosophers are those who can and should at least try to contribute to this project, in order to implement it into the current language of public opinion and influential institutions. If we want to talk about the responsibility of philosophers for anything, building bridges between 'us' (happy, successful, powerful, and included in narratives) and 'them' (marginalized and not included) is the priority for Rorty.

Rorty does not say that everything should be redescribed, nor that all new descriptions bring good results. How redescriptions can at times make a difference for the worse we can see through the example of the postcolonial world. The change in description of present Black Africa from 'colonial' to 'postcolonial' can actually bring worse effects, although morally and politically, the ex-colonial nations are 'independent' and can decide about their own 'development.' However, in the era of globalization, these nations are not heard by those living in the richer part of our planet, and have been left alone in their self-expression and their self-invention: "The postmodern fear of being ill-conceived in the representation that the other could make of us made it so important for us to have the self-representation that circulates in the image market, that ensures our existence, no more after death, but in real life and in the here and now. And so nowadays, the failure to have one's self-image in circulation signifies non-existence" (Jewsiewicki 2000, 216).

What Rorty calls 'redescription' has also been used by many others and in other contexts, e.g., postmodernism, post-structuralism, feminism, ecologism, neo-Marxism, gender studies, neopragmatism, and, perhaps most conspicuously, commercial narratives. The modern era witnesses an enormous scale of redescriptions whose messages are amplified by commercials in the omnipresent mass media, so that millions of people are ready to rearrange their ways of looking at their own needs, pleasures, and expectations according to what they hear from those commercials. The power of the richest corporations, which is much bigger than the financial power of many independent states, makes it possible for these corporations to spread convincing narratives about what is needed and not needed to the extent that it reaches the level of a factually monopolized coercion, instead of pluralistic information to be had by those who want to hear it.

Such a set of limitations on free choice can and often does result in a serious reordering of people's basic and biggest needs, something described by Bill Gates in the following way: "The malaria vaccine in humanist terms is the biggest need. But it gets virtually no funding. But if you are working on male baldness or other things you get an order of magnitude more research funding because of the voice in the marketplace than something like malaria" (quoted in Solon 2013). Likewise, the narrative of the pharmaceutical and cosmetics companies reads that cosmetics are basic needs for everyone and the choice of the customers should be directed towards the selection of the most suitable cosmetics rather than towards reflection upon whether they are needed at all. A similar strategy had been assumed by the banking system in the richest countries before the recent crisis. They produced a narrative to the effect that, say, an independent house for every family should be standard rather than a luxury. The alternative discourses, that houses are not basic goods for each and every family and there are needs more basic for millions of people, seemed to have been weak, and not reliable.

While discussing such examples we can hardly escape, I claim, discussion about power structures, for example, the institutional support that certain discourses receive (and other discourses do not receive), along with their reliability and the vision, if not the utopian illusion, of the progress they encompass.

Ethnocentric rhetoric on growth and development

Rorty's neopragmatist philosophy provides us with tools to explore the question of social importance, communal recognition, and public acceptance of the discourses claiming to depict the realizable arena of action. The notions of 'the great books,' 'ethnocentrism,' 'cultural policy/politics,' 'the priority of democracy to philosophy,' 'science as a useful vocabulary for a given human purpose,' and others, show the mechanism for prioritizing some descriptions over others. In one of his most notable ideas – ethnocentrism – Rorty claims that it is hardly possible for us to transcend the boundaries of an ethnocentric set of discourses, which means, among many other things, that we are doomed to narrate the most fundamental affairs and basic criteria by means of the vocabulary, descriptions, and language that are at our culture's disposal. Ethnocentrism can be applicable to the cultures of different nations and civilizations as well as to lifestyles, statuses, and traditions, sometimes functioning side by side: the rich and the poor, the white and the black, the majority and the marginalized, and many others, depending upon the given context. Moreover, probably each ethnocentric framework is able to give us many incompatible yet solid narratives for the justification of preferable discourses to which many articulators of purposes, aims, and interests will implicitly or explicitly refer. This observation leads us to the question as to what makes some discourses dominate the other discourses, as well as the question as to what makes some discourses more reliable than others.

Rorty reiterates, there are no better or worse languages as such; there are, as he says, languages that are more useful for some purposes and less useful for other purposes: "There are as many descriptions as there are uses to which the pragmatist can be put, by his or her self or by others. This is the stage in which all descriptions (including one's self-description as a pragmatist) are evaluated according to their efficacy as instruments for purposes, rather than by their fidelity to the object described" (Rorty 1999, 134). This is a controversial point, because, one can argue, the efficacy of instruments as well as their purposes are socially arranged, and this means that some groups of people impose their purposes and visions of a better future (as they see it) or a more attractive utopian illusion upon other groups of people. The purposes, the ways of their realization, and the criteria by which they are assessed as either excellent or deplorable, as noble or ignoble, do not always result from dialogue and conversation. More often than not, they result from people's struggles, somewhat in the same way as the English language has become an international tool for communication, thanks to British colonization of many nations around the globe and, later (in the twentieth century), because of American economic, political, and cultural dominance in the world, and not thanks to having had any dialogue whatsoever or settling things at a negotiating table.

In my opinion (which can be very different from Rorty's and other pragmatists on this point) we can hardly avoid thinking about the possible relationship between the rhetoric of growth and the rhetoric of crisis, on the one hand, and, on the other, the ethnocentric matrix of power, along with the cognitive justification it employs. By 'ethnocentric matrix of power' I understand a set of discourses and narratives so well established in the socially influential institutions of a given culture that it assumes and enjoys the status of reliably telling most members of that culture what the factual arrangement of discourses is and how it is possible to criticize other discourses. The reliability of discourses comes partially from reliable socio-political institutions rather than exclusively from the discourses and vocabularies themselves, and it is dependent, to a great extent, upon the condition of these institutions. This is the main reason why I strongly recommend recognizing the practical mechanisms for implementing discourses and why I focus on the role of publicly *important* discourses, discourses that are articulated by 'great books' and 'great texts' that function within socially and politically strong institutions.

Emphasis upon the 'socially important discourses' is compatible with Rorty's understanding of 'inspirational' discourses, or, as he sometimes calls them, 'the great books.' In his "The Inspirational Values of Great Works of Literature," he confesses that such 'great books' should be able to "recontextualize much of what you previously thought you knew" (Rorty 1998, 133), to be able to self-transform, give hope, and inspire many people: "We should see great works of literature as great because they have inspired many readers, not as having inspired many readers because they are great" (Rorty 1998, 136). To put it differently, great or inspirational or influential descriptions have social significance and should not be limited to just their literary, artistic, and philosophical meaning. In order to be such, they must exercise some influence upon the users of these discourses, and a part of my discussion with Rorty is, to what degree the social power of these discourses has an institutional character and to what degree it is textual, literal, philosophical, and theoretical – all this for pro-social aims: "The only way in which the rich can think of themselves as part of the same moral community with the poor is by reference to some scenario which gives hope to the children of the poor without depriving their own children of hope" (Rorty 1996, 15).

Any skilful group of writers and humanists (he calls such people 'great poets') is able to undertake the projects of redescription of different aspects of the world and to indicate new categories, fresh hierarchies of values, and updated norms that seem better applicable than others. Whether these attempts will have any intersubjective significance is my bone of contention with Rorty. These descriptions have to become a part of the mechanisms by which they are recognized and function more effectively than others no less suited to perform comparable functions. In a similar way, many pragmatists and neopragmatists put forward the claim, and justify it abundantly, that the pragmatist description better suits the needs and expectations of contemporary society than, for example, metaphysical and religious descriptions, though the latter have functioned for millennia in some cultures and traditions. In a similar vein, the followers of Enlightenment-type discourses elevate the role of natural sciences as the main, if not the only, genuine articulator of what is real and factual, and disfavor other, alternative ways of narrating as mythical and prejudicial. The very suggestion that discourses are more significant the more they rely on influential socio-political institutions is pronounced by Rorty himself, and in "The Priority of Democracy to Philosophy" he makes clear that liberal democracy is the ultimate framework to which all other concepts should refer: "the philosopher of liberal democracy may wish to develop a theory of the human self that comports with the institutions he or she admires. But such a philosopher is not thereby justifying these institutions by reference to more fundamental premises, but the reverse: He or she is putting politics first and tailoring a philosophy to suit" (Rorty 1991, 178).

The philosophical tradition of American pragmatism is for Rorty one of such ethnocentric matrixes as I have just mentioned. The American transcendentalists as well as the American pragmatists themselves have been engaged in the 'production' of discourses about America and her mission within the framework of democracy and democratic values. Ralph Waldo Emerson, in *The American Scholar*, pronounced something we can call the 'cultural and discursive independence of America from Europe,' and in this way he himself was a strong articulator of the idea, to use Rortyan language, of redescribing American culture as mature and strong enough to free itself from European types of narratives.

Two decades later, Emerson was proud enough of his land to write, in "Success," about the Americans' multiple achievements, and justified America's moral superiority in terms of the country's economic growth, territorial expansion, technological achievements, and rapid increase in population. Emerson wrote the following: "Our American people cannot be taxed with slowness in performance or in praising their performance. The earth is shaken by our engineries [instruments of war]. We are feeling our youth and nerve and bone. We have the power of territory and of sea-coast, and know the use of these. We count our census, we read our growing valuations, we survey our map, which becomes old in a year or two. Our eyes run approvingly along the lengthened lines of railroad and telegraph. We have gone nearest to the Pole" (Emerson 1837, 179).

Also for the main figures of American pragmatism, that is, for William James and John Dewey, ethnocentric rhetoric was a significant factor. Patrick K. Dooley and Sergio Franzese pay attention to the warlike and heroic vocabulary that James uses in his ethics, and suggest that it manifests "the motifs of the American age of energy" (Franzese 2008, 160). Dooley writes about "the extent to which a cultural endowment of concepts, issues and problems provided a matrix for intellectuals and public figures," and he goes on to show that James "extolled the value of the strenuous mood" at the same time when "Theodore Roosevelt celebrated the benefits of the strenuous life" (Dooley 2001, 162) and when other heroic activities were highlighted from 1890 to 1900 in the US. Indeed, James, in his well-known and influential texts, used the type of rhetoric that well suited the spirit of activity, progress, and success. In "The Energies of Men" James linked his ethics of energy and progress with the political aims of the nation and the educational character of its schools: "a man who energizes below his normal maximum fails by just so much to profit by his chance at life; and that a nation filled with such men is inferior to a nation run at higher pressure. The problem is, then, how can men be trained up to their most useful pitch of energy? And how can nations make such training most accessible to all their sons and daughters. This, after all, is only the general problem of education, formulated in slightly different terms" (James 1906, 673).

At the same time, democracy and the practical implementation of democratic ideals into the practice of socio-political life had been among the fundamental projects and most noticeable narratives for other American pragmatists, for Dewey in the first instance. A leading American neopragmatist these days, Hilary Putnam, for whom Dewey is a philosophical hero, interprets Dewey's philosophical and epistemological writings as having been closely connected with Dewey's views on the role that democratic institutions should play in contemporary society. Putnam claims that Dewey's "purely epistemological writings cannot be understood apart from that concern. That concern is with the meaning and future of democracy" (Putnam 1990, 330), and it includes the role of description and vocabulary, along with the practical attitude that is articulated by this vocabulary. Putnam defines himself by taking on the vocabulary of Deweyan democracy, and in this he sees the best available way to deal with problems of political liberty and, we may suspect, of economic issues as well. In one of his books, Putnam writes that "Democracy is not just a form of social life among other workable forms of social life; it is the precondition for the full application of intelligence to the solution of social problems. The notions from Dewey's vocabulary that I have employed are, of course, *intelligence* [...] and *problem solving*" (Putnam 1990, 331).

Yet such types of indications may cause different sorts of reactions in other commentators, especially those having other ethnocentric backgrounds. Seeing Dewey from his non-Western cultural perspective, Paulo Margutti, in "Pragmatism and Decolonial Thinking: An Analysis of Dewey's Ethnocentrism," claims that Dewey (like Immanuel Kant) uses in his democratic philosophy his own ethnocentric background: "under the guise of universality," Margutti says, Dewey articulates "the particularism of Western modern imperial view of the world" and sees "modern Western culture as the goal towards which all other cultures should direct their respective historical evolutions" (Margutti 2013, 80). Interestingly, a similar aspect was taken up by Rorty himself, and I'm thinking of a paper devoted to George Santayana ("Genteel Synthesis, Professional Analyses, Transcendentalist Culture"), in which Rorty writes that Santayana "was able to laugh at us [Americans] without despising us," and "he saw us as one more great empire in the long parade. His genial hope was that we might enjoy the imperium while we held it" (Rorty 1980, 228). We can use Margutti's (and Santayana's) remarks to put forward a more general question: do we have any idea how to deal better with the discourses than trying to tell others a story about ourselves, our traditions, and our vision of progress, regress, and crisis? Do the American pragmatists have such a proposal in their philosophical deliberations?

Political, economic, and discursive democracy

The processes of democratizing the modern world tend to favor differentiation and pluralization of people's decisions about their needs, pleasures, and pains. Free market discourses seem to strengthen this 'democratic' message by saying that it is up to the people (customers) themselves and their free choices as to what they factually want to do and want to consume. On the other hand, however, free choice in the selection of goods and the sense of personal liberty in setting the limits of one's own consumption make it easier for corporations and other mercantile institutions to stimulate potential clients into expected directions, I mean, expected by those mighty institutions. The discourses that deal with democratization and liberty, when used by a tiny, yet influential minority, can lead to dangerously divergent and undemocratic consequences, and the monopolization of the axiological character of the mainstream discourses may become the most problematic: innumerable narratives telling us more or less the same mercantile messages and referring to more or less the same (consumptive) values. In my view, the process of generating the discourses and narratives should be more pluralistic, with more alternative discourses accessible (I mean alternative in character; I do not mean various discourses saying more or less the same thing). The origin and use of the discourses should be more transparently investigated so as to avoid, or limit at least, double standards while using discourses – freedom for everyone but more freedom for some. This is not incompatible with the view of most pragmatists on the way in which the amelioration of the social life should go.

With engagement and belief in the sense of their message, nearly all the American pragmatists averred that the fair and transparent arrangement of political institutions and the institutional protection of individual rights should go hand in hand with the perspicuous settlement of economic institutions that would facilitate fair access to goods for everyone. Also, all of them claimed that the socio-political order must not stimulate economic disorder. For example, Sidney Hook does not discuss the economy and economic crisis by means of just economic terms. In "The Democratic Way of Life" he directly links political democracy with what he calls "economic democracy" and avers that the former is inefficient in the situation where "differences in economic power are so great that one group can determine the weal or woe of another by non-political means" (Hook 1938, 157). Being able to imagine the consequences of the monopolization of discourses and its consequences in a non-democratic economic world, he takes on far-reaching remedies in the democratization of such socially important institutions as education and the mass media. He claims that political and economic relations are not free, not only if deprived of information, but also if – and this is significant for the present discussion – they are reliable on "*only* the official information, if [one] can hear only one voice in the classroom, pulpit, and radio" (158). This view can stimulate an answer to the question of what can be done to cope with the situation of economic crisis in a longer term perspective and what philosophy has to say on this. I wonder whether Hook's suggestion about 'political democracy' and 'economic democracy' can be extended into something that we could call 'discursive democracy' and whether Rorty's neopragmatism is close or even sympathetic to this idea.

Rorty, a liberal democrat, was sensitive to the role of descriptions and narratives in the hands of a small group of people who are on a higher rung of the social ladder and enjoy more institutional possibilities for promoting their discourses and narratives among much larger groups of people, who are nonetheless more impotent and defenseless regarding the possibility of describing and redescribing the world and narrating their roles in it. He realized that such a struggle among groups of people having alternative descriptions at hand takes place both in positive and negative contexts, and he presented an example taken from both American and international history: "Fifty-one years ago, a set of rich and lucky people imagined themselves to be 'we, the people of the United Nations.' One reason they chose those words was that, a hundred and fifty six years earlier, some equally rich and lucky people had imagined themselves to be 'We, the people of the United States'" (Rorty 1996, 10–11).

However, he continues, those who wrote the US constitution should not be credited with referring to the people of the US, nor should they have called themselves the representatives of the nation. More appropriately, they should be seen as "the representatives of the property-owning white males of the

United States," showing no reference to "[t]heir black slaves, their white servants, and even their wives and daughters" (11). We can see that it is not
merely rhetoric, vocabularies, narratives, and telling stories that are at stake
here, but the groups that articulate their aims by means of given discourses.
This insight can stimulate us to ask the following question: can the pluralization of such groups and the democratization of the economic institutions
which they represent result in the democratization of discourses about progress and crisis? In my opinion, the answer to this question can be positive.
Rorty's insistence on the democratic dimension of the cultural policy stimu-
lates me to complement my analysis with the just-mentioned idea of 'discursive democracy.' In line with the main assumptions of Rorty's
neopragmatism, I suggest the democratization of the methods of generating
discourses so as to limit the graphically undemocratic predicament of the
present time: tiny minorities have an almost exclusive right to describe the
vast majority's rights, values, norms, loyalties, interests, access to and
distribution of goods, liberties, and freedom for recognition and self-creation.

Progress and crisis: for whom?

One of the ways to democratize discourses is to show more precisely the
identity of those who generate such discourses, and by 'identity' I mean their
cultural backgrounds, their purposes, and, most importantly, the axiological
sources to which they refer. Rorty gives us an open and honest way of doing
so. In his philosophical and literary production he does not speak to people in
the name of universal truths, objective values, and the good for everyone.
Rather, he identifies himself with the discourses generated by this plot within
the tradition of American pragmatism that can more precisely be characterized by the adjectives *Western, American, bourgeois, postmodern, liberal,
democratic, secular, intellectual*, and *urban*. Such an identification is very
telling because the discourse or discourses based upon such sources include
specific vocabularies, categories, references to values, norms, and interests that
are different or differently understood in the discourses generated by other
traditions.

Rorty explored the significance of identifying the providers of the discourses even further. For example, in the paper "Who Are We? Moral Universalism and Economic Triage," which was addressed to the UNESCO
philosophy forum in 1996, he used his neopragmatist philosophy as a tool to
answer the question, 'who are we?' Rorty resolves the meaning of the classical
question of philosophy, *What are we?* in favor of the question, *Who are we?*
The former looks for some universal features of all human beings – something, he suggests, is futile and reminiscent of metaphysics and religion. The
latter question "is asked by people who want to separate off the human
beings who are better suited to some particular purpose than other human
beings, and to gather the former into a self-conscious moral community: that
is, a community united by reciprocal trust, and by willingness to come to

fellow-members' assistance when they need it. Answers to the 'who?' question are attempts to forge, or reforge, a moral identity" (Rorty 1996, 5).

In his address he demanded not only "egalitarian redistribution of wealth" (14) but also – and this interests me most here – a discursive and narrative rearrangement of the life of different communities such as to see them as one community: "my present concern is not with predictions, either gloomy or optimistic, but rather with describing the present moral situation of the rich and lucky inhabitants of the world in terms of alternative answers to the question 'who are we?'" (10). He does not mean this question to be pre-dominantly anthropological or ethical; for him "the 'who?' question is poli-tical" (5), and this is because the involvement of 'us' in the given group of interests and purposes goes much beyond particular businesses and self-reali-zations. Our involvement in these discourses or those narratives has much to do with exercising control and domination over many other people and with participation in the course of social life. Identity, apart from other aspects, well shows the factual bonds among people, bonds that are blurred when these people identify themselves with non-human ideas and abstract values, which are, for Rorty, hidden and misleading: "There has to be *some* sense in which he or she is 'one of us,' before we start to be tormented by the question of whether or not we did the right thing when we committed perjury. So it may be equally appropriate to describe us as torn between conflicting loyal-ties – loyalty to our family and to a group large enough to include the victim of our perjury – rather than between loyalty and justice" (Rorty 2001, 223).

The democratization of descriptions and redescriptions in the presently proposed meaning is changeable and depends on the context, so it does not have the character of a lifetime declaration. Some allegiances and loyalties evolve and get transformed, and there is nothing wrong with that. However, the well-functioning democratic arrangement of discourses can prevent us from practically strengthening the non-democratic structure of power, and Rorty illustrates this in the following way: "Our loyalty to such larger groups will, however, weaken, or even vanish altogether, when things get really tough. Then people whom we once thought of as like ourselves will be excluded. Sharing food with impoverished people down the street is natural and right in normal times, but perhaps not in a famine, when doing so amounts to disloyalty to one's family" (ibid.). Hence, identification must be assisted by other forms of democratic narrating about economic inter-dependencies and political interconnections; it must also, without any doubt, be assisted by, or rather it must practically function within the framework of 'political democracy' and 'economic democracy,' as I mentioned earlier.

Rorty proposes that we should be more aware of the factually functioning social groups behind the discourses and narratives; 'factuality' refers to the purposes that these groups want to achieve, the hierarchy of values they observe, the arrangement of norms they practice, as well as the aims, loyalties, and advantages they manifest in or by their discourses. There are no special or better predisposed groups of people to provide us with a more adequate and more universal message, although there exist groups, for example, more or less definite groups of professionals – e.g., priests, philosophers, artists, politicians, scientists, economists – that think of themselves in such a way. As regards scientific language, as already mentioned, Rorty claims that it is just a useful vocabulary for certain human purposes. The status of the scientific vocabulary is closely related to the status and purposes of the groups that use this vocabulary:

> Adopting this view means replacing the choice between theological, scientific and metaphysical descriptions of the world with a choice between human purposes. But the choice of what purposes to have is almost always, in practice, a choice among groups of people rather than a choice among abstract formulae. A choice of purposes to which to devote one's life is typically a choice between actual or possible human communities: between the sort of people who have one over-riding purpose and the sort of people who have another. So, on the pragmatist view common to both Nietzsche and James, metaphysical questions are concealed political questions, questions about the group or groups with which one hopes to affiliate oneself, or which one hopes to create.
>
> (Rorty 1996, 7)

A concluding remark

Let me repeat that it is catastrophically undemocratic to accept that some tiny minorities have become the powerful generators of discourses and that they freely describe for the vast majority, through their own (the minority's) discourses, either to the majority's disadvantage or without paying much attention to what the majority want to say. Following Rorty in thinking more about the democratization of the methods for generating discourses seems to be an obvious, conclusive postulate for limiting the unwanted imposition of discourses that include values, norms, and aims that are ascribed to other groups. This is the goal at which we should, I think, work harder and more effectively. If we do not change it, the future is going to appear in such a pessimistic perspective, as Rorty puts it: "The rich and lucky people will quickly become unable to think of the poor and unlucky ones as their fellow humans, as part of the same 'we'" (Rorty 1996, 12).

References

Auxier, Randall, and Lewis Edwin Hahn, eds. 2010. *The Philosophy of Richard Rorty.* The Library of Living Philosophers. Chicago and La Salle: Open Court.

Dooley, Patrick K. 2001. "Public Policy and Philosophical Critique: The William James and Theodore Roosevelt Dialogue on Strenuousness." *Transactions of the Charles S. Peirce Society* 37(2): 162–178.

Emerson, Ralph Waldo. 1837. "The American Scholar." In *The American Scholar, Self-Reliance, Compensation*, ed. Orren Henry Smith, 21–46. New York, Cincinnati, and Chicago: American Book Co., 1911.

Emerson, Ralph Waldo. 1870. *Society and Solitude: Twelve Chapters.* A new Study Edition, with notes, philosophical commentary, and historical contextualization by H. G. Callaway. Lewiston, Queenston, and Lampeter: Edwin Mellen Press, 2008.

Franzese, Sergio. 2008. *The Ethics of Energy: William James's Moral Philosophy in Focus.* Frankfurt: Ontos.

Hook, Sidney. 1938. "The Democratic Way of Life." In *The Pragmatism Reader: From Peirce through the Present*, ed. Robert B. Talisse and Scott F. Aikin, 155–165. Princeton and Oxford: Princeton University Press, 2011.

James, William. 1906. "The Energies of Men." In *The Writings of William James: A Comprehensive Edition*, ed. John J. McDermott, 671–683. Chicago and London: University of Chicago Press, 1977.

Jewsiewicki, Bogumil. 2000. "Cheri Samba's Postcolonial Reinvention of Modernity." In *African Philosophy as Cultural Inquiry*, ed. Ivan Karp and D. A. Masolo, 215–243. Bloomington and Indianapolis: Indiana University Press.

Khalil, Elias. 2008. "Economics." In *American Philosophy: An Encyclopedia*, ed. John Lachs and Robert Talisse, 203–204. New York and London: Routledge.

Margutti, Paulo. 2013. "Pragmatism and Decolonial Thinking: An Analysis of Dewey's Ethnocentrism." *Cognitio: Revista de Filosofia* (São Paulo) 14(1): 63–83.

Putnam, Hilary. 1990. "A Reconsideration of Deweyan Democracy." In *The Pragmatism Reader: From Peirce Through the Present*, ed. Robert B. Talisse and Scott F. Aikin, 331–352. Princeton and Oxford: Princeton University Press, 2011.

Rorty, Richard. 1980. "Genteel Syntheses, Professional Analyses, Transcendentalist Culture." In *Two Centuries of Philosophy in America*, ed. Peter Caws, 228–239. Totowa, NJ: Rowman & Littlefield.

Rorty, Richard. 1989. *Contingency, Irony, and Solidarity.* Cambridge and New York: Cambridge University Press.

Rorty, Richard. 1991. *Objectivity, Relativism, and Truth: Philosophical Papers, Volume 1.* Cambridge and New York: Cambridge University Press.

Rorty, Richard. 1996. "Who Are We? Moral Universalism and Economic Triage." *Diogenes: A Quarterly Publication of the International Council for Philosophy and Humanistic Studies* 44(173): 5–15.

Rorty, Richard. 1998. *Achieving Our Country: Leftist Thought in Twentieth-Century America.* Cambridge and London: Harvard University Press.

Rorty, Richard. 1999. *Philosophy and Social Hope.* New York: Penguin.

Rorty, Richard. 2001. *Critical Dialogues*, ed. Matthew Festenstein and Simon Thompson. Cambridge: Polity Press.

Solon, Olivia. 2013. "Bill Gates: Capitalism Means Male Baldness Research Gets More Funding than Malaria." *Wired*, March 14. <www.wired.co.uk/news/archive/2013-03/14/bill-gates-capitalism>.

5 If philosophers are so smart

The metaphor of 'global economic crisis'

Maja Niestrój

Metaphors are like knots in which different philosophical problematics meet; they are intensively discussed, and sometimes run into trouble. Besides the fact that metaphors have been identified as the descriptions of things by means of words and expressions that are primarily and conventionally ascribed to something else, there is very little agreement on what metaphors factually are. When we appeal to a metaphorical expression, we talk about two things at once, two different and disparate subject matters that together give us an enriched effect. Nevertheless, when we try to analyze the issue more attentively, drawing a boundary between similarity and metaphor (e.g., *he is (like) the wolf of Wall Street; she is (like) the sun*), between a commonly used metaphor and a proper name (e.g., 'Enlightenment'), or between metaphor and scientific term (e.g., 'dark matter'), it is not an easy assignment.

The long history of writing on metaphors began with the ancient philosophers and was then extended by thinkers of almost all philosophical schools and movements, from the continental tradition, represented by Friedrich Nietzsche and Paul Ricœur, to analytic philosophy. For the latter, metaphorical expressions appear as the Gordian knot because they do not confirm truth-conditional semantics; for example, it is hard to ascribe the value 'true' or 'false' to them. Metaphors have also evoked many discussions in continental philosophy; they are intertwined with reflections on how the world appears to us and how we manifest it to others. In Nietzsche's philosophy metaphors play a crucial role: humans are immersed in metaphors, and they are even the metaphors themselves, with the meaning of their lives derived from the tension between different perspectives and drives. For Ricœur the metaphor is also something living, but in the sense that metaphors are the means to express the perception of the world. They leave the necessary open space for us to reconsider changes of perspective.

These introductory considerations show how complex the problems of metaphor can be and how much the way we understand metaphors is interrelated with other issues. An even bolder question can be posed: how much do philosophical beliefs and convictions influence the way in which we understand, classify, and assign cognitive meaning to metaphors? I claim that the explication of metaphors and their role in science will be determined not only by one's approach to the metaphorical expression itself; it will also be determined by one's attitude toward language, human cognition, and the growth of knowledge. For example, much depends on one's preconceptions about meaning and truth, or on one's chosen standpoint regarding scientific realism and anti-realism.

In my chapter I assert that metaphors are crucial for cognition and communication, and this is why they are also significant for scientific research. My convictions are mirrored by the conceptual understanding of metaphor introduced in 1980 – and developed since then by George Lakoff and Mark Johnson. According to Lakoff and Johnson, and many of their followers, metaphors are not just poetic means of expression or rhetorical figures. They are essential for human thinking, being deeply rooted in the structures of everyday language and shaping it. Moreover, their source is our direct experience, and this includes our bodily experience. Hence, conceptual theory casts metaphor in a new light and recognizes contributions from the fields of cognitive science and linguistics.

For the purpose of analyzing a specific problem regarding metaphorical expression in economic narrative, I employ the approach of Lakoff and Johnson as well as Theodore L. Brown, whose works are also based on the idea of conceptual metaphor applied to science. As regards the role of philosophers in the time of economic crisis I am also strongly inspired by the insights of Deirdre McCloskey about the narrative of economic expertise and the explanatory status of theories introduced by economists. This theoretical framework allows me to address very generally a problem regarding metaphors in the economic sciences. I will analyze in detail the metaphorical dimension of the phrase 'global economic crisis,' in an attempt to answer the question whether it is a scientific term or rather a pre-theoretical, metaphorical expression which captures a set of different phenomena. I also reflect upon the philosophical consequences of describing a given economic situation with that particular term. This study should become a trigger for a broader discussion of the role of metaphors in the social sciences, which are mainly devoted to problems of human life in its social dimension and as such have a strong influence on individuals' ways of thinking about particular communal and economic phenomena. I pose a question about the strong impact that their results and interpretations have had on the public. I argue that the choice of a metaphor is largely arbitrary, and that only some metaphors evoke creativity; others restrict the imagination or slow down the process of finding a satisfying solution, while so-called scientific terms are a kind of 'closer' – probably because they are strongly connected with laws and theories, and thus with regularities and predictability. My reflections resonate with the research led by McCloskey, who claims that the evolution from the pre-industrial to the innovative society was possible because the way of speaking about the bourgeoisie changed and the bourgeoisie as a group was socially recognized. Thus, the choice of terminology, metaphors, and stories affects indeed the plot.

First, I analyze the phrase 'global economic crisis' as it appears in selected contemporary economic literature. As mentioned earlier, the main theoretical tool for that analysis is a theory of conceptual metaphor developed for the natural sciences by Brown. The phrase will be considered in the context of some texts devoted to the problem of economic crisis and published in the years 2012–14. The main purpose is not to analyze particular uses of 'global economic crisis' but to investigate the phrase as it appears in the contemporary narrative of economic crisis. In the spirit of more speculative discussion and as a philosophical framework for analyzing the 'global economic crisis,' I remark on how the choice of metaphor influences groups and individuals and how its influence could be related to the pragmatic idea of redescription.

Conceptual metaphors in science

First and foremost, I address the problem of the *metaphorical* versus *scientific* character of the phrase 'global economic crisis.' In order to investigate it we need to take into consideration some more fundamental questions: What is the role of metaphoric expression in science? How are metaphors different from scientific vocabulary? And lastly, are 'economic crisis' and 'global economic crisis' metaphoric expressions or rather scientific terms?

Metaphor is commonly understood as the figure of speech that identifies something by means of words and expressions that are primarily ascribed to something else – a thing, a phenomenon, an activity, for example. As was already mentioned, this is a very general description that needs to be made more precise in light of a given epistemological view and even a metaphysical attitude. The exemplary philosophical issues that are directly linked to the problematic of the metaphorical components of language are: the limits and character of human cognition, the concept of knowledge, the nature of reality, and so on. Despite the fact that it is not possible to analyze or even to accommodate all those problems associated with traditional and current discussions of metaphor, it is still worthwhile to take a closer look at the issue. An achievable strategy would be to select one approach along with all its philosophical baggage and to apply it to a concrete problem. Therefore, I supplement the common understanding of metaphors with the conceptual understanding of them. The approach introduced by Lakoff and Johnson is best explained by means of paradigm examples, which show how widespread metaphors are in ordinary language and how deeply they determine the way we think, speak, and even act.

The first example is the following: *The nuclear bomb of our time is the divided banking sector and alarming number of countries with high levels of national debt.* The divided banking sector and national debt are obviously not the nuclear bomb itself, but the sense of the sentence is readable: namely, those phenomena are seen as no less dangerous and influential than a nuclear bomb. Metaphor is clearly visible here; however, this will not always be the case. An example of where it is not so clearly visible is *metonymy* – a figure of speech in which a concept is called by the name of something associated with the object to which the concept refers (e.g., 'Washington' to mean 'the Government of the United States'). According to Lakoff and Johnson, we may distinguish a whole taxonomy of different kinds of metaphors, but they have a similar cognitive-linguistic structure which responds to one scheme of mapping between the two concepts' domains. I will introduce the scheme in a more detailed way in the following paragraphs.

A second paradigm example can be shown by the following phrases: *I will attack your position, telling you that …/These allegations are indefensible/My strategy of defense is such and such.* We can see that metaphors can also be implied, rather than being expressed explicitly; they are visible in the phrase's structure, reflecting the conceptual system of their speakers.

A third paradigm example is the following: *I am up today./I am so over the moon./I am sinking into depression.* We are dealing with spatial metaphors here; namely, happiness is associated with going up, depression with falling or going down; the day that will come is ahead of us, while the past is behind. These examples show how metaphors shape and constrict our way of thinking about reality and the state of things taken objectively. They are not only present in ordinary language, but they structure our mental patterns as a result of having allowed us to successfully function in our environment.

All these paradigm examples display the philosophical burden of Lakoff and Johnson's theory, which derives from philosophical discussion of categorization, the relations between language and conceptual systems, and the tradition of ecological psychology, which investigates the ways in which concepts are shaped by human functioning in the physical and cultural environment. Having adopted Lakoff and Johnson's approach one has to accept the philosophical decisions made by these two authors. As a result, the idea of conceptual metaphor is in intellectual opposition to some contributors to the traditional Western conceptions of meaning and truth, such as Richard Montague, Saul Kripke, David Lewis, and Donald Davidson. Consequently, among those thinkers one could find natural adversaries and critics of ideas introduced in this chapter.

Unambiguously demarcating the line between metaphorical and non-metaphorical expressions is not an easy task, because, as the paradigm examples have already shown, many phrases in everyday language contain metaphorical components or at least have metaphorical origins. This is not problematic as such as long as communication between the parties involved is not disturbed. But it raises more concerns, even on a purely pragmatic level, when it comes to scientific and technical terms. Scientific vocabulary aspires to be the one that permits an adequate and intersubjective description of phenomena or events, or establishes general tendencies by means of which particular events may be explained or predicted (Hempel 1965, 139). For example, we can wonder if 'a budget gap' is a metaphor or a scientific term? If a scientific term, then we expect it to be definable in an operational way (cf. Hempel 1965, 141–46); if not, it is just a description helping us to link economic phenomena with a term understood on a daily basis – 'a gap.'

Theodore Brown took on board the problem of how conceptual metaphors work in science (including economic science) by re-examining observable mechanisms in the history of scientific development. The results of his efforts are discussed exhaustively in the book *Making Truth: Metaphor in Science.* Brown claims that the metaphorical dimension of thinking is crucial for the language of science, and metaphors are critical in the process of finding and delivering explanations (the context of justification), as well as in the inspirational phase of science when the scientists' imaginations and intuitions are conclusive (the context of discovery). The idea that metaphors stimulate the imagination and intuition brings Brown closer to Michael Polanyi, who recognized that scientists often formulate theories on the basis of hunches, being guided by dynamic visions of a hidden reality. However, Polanyi himself maintains realism to some degree, so differing from Brown.

Metaphorical genetics of 'economic crisis'

Metaphors seem to play an extensive role in the way we interpret individual experiences and in the process of relating one kind of experience to another, which is a part of scientific research. They connect and compare the source domain of literal, everyday experiences (in other words, the conceptual domain from which we draw metaphorical expressions) with the target domain. The aim of this is enlarging and enhancing the understanding of that domain, and this means the accommodation of new knowledge. Thus, metaphorical reasoning is at the very core of what scientists do when they gather observations, design experiments, make discoveries, and formulate theories and models, as well as when they communicate their results. Hence, are 'economic crisis' and 'global economic crisis' metaphors? My proposal is to analyse these two cases separately because their similarity is merely apparent. What needs to be remembered is this: my judgments – even if I've concentrated on the highest possible explanatory power of the diagnosis – remain arbitrary, and still other interpretations are possible.

I classify 'economic crisis' as a metaphor that has over time turned into a scientific term. Investigating the genetic roots of this concept by mapping between domains we may sketch the following scheme: in the source domain 'crisis,' which is well known from the non-economic world and daily experience, the following properties can be included: a dangerous and unstable situation; affecting individuals, some groups or communities, the whole society; possible negative changes; abrupt occurrence with little or no warning – and others. To the target domain will belong all the observations of the interrelated changes in the economic landscape (later called 'economic crisis'), such as: the fall of real GDP per capita; the decrease of real house and equity prices; the rise of unemployment; the increase of public debt and its imbalance with respect to current accounts. To conceptualize such a highly complex notion as 'crisis' in the economy, we map across domains, making connections between the elements of the more abstract, conceptual domain and the corresponding elements of the more concrete one. The process by which connections are made between these two disparate domains can be presented with a knowledge representation scheme (see Table 5.1).

As already noted, the economic crisis was at some stage a metaphor, but it evolved into a technical term that denotes a concrete situation or, more precisely, a class of economic and interrelated states or situations. Even if we do not have one exact definition of it, it is possible to generate intersubjective, operational definitions that constitute the basis for further communication, namely, the exchange of information among scientists or between the scientists and public opinion.

We can also understand 'economic crisis' as a taxonomical term, while seeing 'recession' and 'depression' as more precisely definable. Referring to the functional aspect of 'economic crisis' (only a metaphor taken historically), we could classify it as a Hempelian pre-theoretical term in the first phase of its development as a metaphor, which has evolved into a theoretical term. The term 'economic crisis' is commonly specified with spatial and temporal details – e.g., Indian economic crisis (in 1991), Finnish banking crisis (in the 1990s), Swedish banking crisis (in the 1990s), economic crisis in Mexico (in 1994), Argentine economic crisis (in 1999–2002). In these cases we are speaking not about terms but about proper names. We need to keep this distinction in mind.

'Global economic crisis' as metaphor

Even though we do not call 'economic crisis' a metaphor, is the phrase 'global economic crisis' a metaphor? Experts and scholars have devoted innumerable papers and books to the global economic crisis, which have been published constantly one after another. Here are a few exemplary titles from academic literature reviewed recently: *The IMF and Global Financial Crises: Phoenix Rising?*, by Joyce (2013); *Global Economic Crisis: Impacts, Transmission and Recovery*, edited by Obstfeld (2012); *The EU Economic and Social Model in the Global Crisis*, edited by Schiek (2013); *The Global Financial Crisis and the Korean Economy*, by Shin (2014) – to name a few. Despite those very suggestive titles and the impression that we are speaking about one and the same phenomenon, further explications of the topic force us to pose additional

Table 5.1 Source and target domains

Source domain – crisis	Target domain – empirical data
• a dangerous and unstable situation • affecting individuals, some groups or communities, the whole society • possible negative changes • abrupt occurrence with little or no warning	• the fall of real GDP per capita • the decrease of real house prices and real equity prices • the rise of unemployment • the increase of the public debt and its imbalance to current accounts

questions about the understanding of 'global economic crisis.' Furthermore, I argue that the global economic crisis is only a metaphor, or, according to Hempel, still a pre-theoretical term.

In the spirit of analytic philosophy we could recall the principle of compositionality, which tells us that the meaning of a complex expression is determined by the meanings of its constituent expressions. Accordingly, we need to investigate the additional term 'global' and its impact on the meaning of the whole phrase. The generally accepted meaning of 'global' is either to include or consider all the parts of the situation together or to affect the whole world. So, if a layperson hears about 'a global economic crisis,' she will think about a crisis that encompasses the whole world (understanding the world geographically, as our globe, without any exception) and that generates negative outcomes everywhere. Such an understanding of the phrase 'global economic crisis' is purely metaphorical. One could easily argue that 'global' itself as well as 'economic crisis' are scientific terms; the concept that arises out of these two notions is best presented by mapping between domains: on the one hand, the two already understood or known source sub-domains of 'economic crisis' and 'global,' and, on the other, the target domain in which we could point out all the observations associated with the phenomena of the global economic crisis.

Strictly speaking, the present economic situation, as complicated and interrelated as it is and as much as it affects many countries, is not an economic crisis that affects the whole world. 'Global' refers more to the global market (which is an abstract representation of the activities of the buying and selling of goods and services in all the countries of the world) or to the tendency toward negative growth in many (but not all) national markets. Both are represented by highly theoretical models, in which a set of hypotheses about the behavior of markets or agents is expressed as numerical predictions.

The theory of purchasing power parity (PPP) is another issue that needs to be taken into account from the point of view of the controversy connected with estimations regarding the global market. The PPP exchange-rate calculation – the economic tool impacting nearly every level of finance and investment – is controversial because of the statistical difficulties of finding comparable baskets of goods around the world. While people typically consume different goods in different countries (Europeans eat more potatoes, Iranians more rice, etc.), it is necessary to compare the costs of baskets of goods and services using a price index. Since there is no reliable way to reduce such complexity to a single number, the question arises as to the sense of PPP: what we use as the PPP exchange-rate is actually already a highly theoretical estimation that is not equally satisfying for all the purposes it is put to.

The other issues are global imbalances and tendencies in national markets. While there is still disagreement among economists over the causes of crises, especially the relative importance of various factors, the global imbalances that had been built up prior to 2007/8 are still present in any discussion. They are also the reason why any statistical estimation concerning the world as a whole remains hardly anything other than just statistics. To recall the example given by Brown: when we measure the temperature of the human body under the tongue, we expect it to be representative of the temperature of the whole body. Although the temperature can vary slightly, the value at a particular place (under the tongue) serves sufficiently as an indicator of average temperature (cf. Brown 2008, 163). As laypersons we have the same expectations of estimations of the (global) economy, but the sad truth is that there is no one such optimal place that would be representative, e.g., for real GDP growth rates in a particular year. The averages are built on other averages and estimations.

Furthermore, in comparison with former global imbalances, the current period has unprecedented features. This is the first time that capital flows go mostly from the emerging market economies (mainly Asia and the oil-exporting economies) to the advanced economies. Some sensibility and attention to possible oversimplification were shown by Schiek and Tsoukalis, who suggested that it is a kind of arrogance to name a US- and EU-based crisis the global one (Tsoukalis 2011, 25). In this context, a question arises about the distinction between the terms 'global,' 'international,' and 'national,' and about the right to call something 'global,' even if it emerged outside of national or continental borders.

The last remark about the global economic crisis concerns the way of communicating the results among economists themselves and with the public as well. Obviously, such communication takes place by means of metaphors (even high levels of metaphorical construction). For example, the thinking about and understanding of the global economic crisis (even in professional literature) is structured by the more abstract domain of illnesses: "Some [many countries] are still struggling with *deep scars* made by the crisis, and others that have been relatively less damaged are also *suffering from* stagnating global demand … . With *aftershocks* still in play, it may be premature to assess the overall impacts of the 2008 global crisis … . A sharp collapse in international trade followed, leaving *no country immune* to the sequence of economic shocks" (Obstfeld 2012, xi, 1; italics mine).

In the quoted fragment, the crisis is expressed with terminology primarily linked with illness: it has left "scares," the countries and economies "suffered" from it, none were "immune" to it, and after it, the aftershock occurred. But this metaphor has some additional impact, being rooted deeply in our everyday experiences and causing an emotional response, which, probably, also affects the merit of the discussion. So as we see, when it comes to the global crisis in economics, even the simplest questions have very complicated answers. The ideas that seem at first glance to be plainly literal, actually turn out to be metaphorical in nature. Hence, under 'global,' there are hidden: statistics, theoretical models, along with their numerical predictions, and global imbalances.

An analogous example, examined in detail by Brown, is 'global warming.' Understanding both changes in the economy and climate change involves the analysis and integration of ideas from a variety of sources and judgments about how the parts fit together to form a coherent whole. Because of the potentially enormous consequences which the global crisis (warming) can cause, the status and reliability of science is at stake here. Metaphorical expressions, especially those appearing in scientific contexts where they play a role, are mixed up together, making phrases like 'global economic crisis' a tool of persuasion in public discussion. As Brown writes: "arguments generated in the context of scientific work get translated into arguments in the larger political and social world to persuade, to support established interests, or to color public opinion" (Brown 2008, 161).

Discussion and conclusion

Actually we never think about scientific terms without reference to the theories behind them, which also ascribe nomological importance to the terms, which vindicates them epistemologically. However, such support may give the impression that those terms are more important and tell us something final about the world – we may hear an echo of discussions about determinism. It is hard to discuss laws and theories. Discussion is triggered mostly by metaphors, ambiguities that need to be clarified, and descriptions provoking our imagination. In the case of scientific terms, their seemingly fixed meanings are a kind of a closer, while in the case of metaphors, the likenesses, similarities, and analogies are a kind of 'opener' and encouragement to reconsider a given problem. That is the reason why it is important to know in which phase – pretheoretical or theoretical – a particular concept is, or, in other words, to recognize to what degree it is metaphorical. This is important for scientists and for interdisciplinary exchange, but maybe even more so for laypersons, who are more vulnerable to possible persuasion, especially when there is the appearance of scientific justification.

I propose a thought experiment that refers to the previous reflection on 'global economic/financial crisis.' Assume that we have two persons – person A and person B – who are not scientists, and were for the last thirty years in a coma, now learning about the current reality. Person A is told that the *scientific term* that describes the economic situation is 'global financial crisis.' Person B is told that the current economic reality is best described by the *metaphor* 'global financial crisis.' Which person is more likely to ask some additional questions, for example, what does the global crisis mean to her, to the economy of her country, and to the world? And shifting from philosophy to pure speculation – how will they feel, hearing about it? I could risk the answer that person A will not think about entrepreneurship at that moment. Person B probably will not either, but through her questions and the more comprehensive information given in answer to them, she could better understand the complex situation.

I mentioned this social dimension of the potential influence of chosen terminology because it can be linked with the Rortyan idea of redescription.

Metaphors leave more space for "suggesting changes in the uses of words" and "putting new words in circulation" (Rorty 2007, 124), while so-called scientific terms, with their aspiration to be intersubjective and adequate descriptions, give less. Especially in economic and social sciences a lot depends on interpretation and on a given narrative, which does not discredit the methodology or scientific character of those disciplines. This point brings me closer to McCloskey, who wrote *If You're So Smart: The Narrative of Economic Crisis* (McCloskey 1990), and ten years later, *Bourgeois Dignity: Why Economics Can't Explain the Modern World* (McCloskey 2010). Both contain the intuition that metaphors and stories largely constitute not only economic expertise but also descriptions of reality, the way individuals describe themselves and how others describe them in their social roles. These ways of describing and redescribing can be factors that shape the history of economic successes. McCloskey argues that the innovative society might have evolved thanks to growing acknowledgment of the bourgeoisie. According to her, the real revolution was in ascribing dignity and social recognition to a class that was earlier deprived of those virtues. The reason for recalling McCloskey's diagnosis in this reflection on and around metaphors is to emphasize the importance of an apparently unspectacular distinction between metaphors and scientific terms. If we grow up in a time described by the scientific term 'global economic crisis,' we are determined to be the precariat, without much possibility of redescribing ourselves. If we live in a time described by the metaphor 'global economic crisis,' we will feel that we can change this metaphor to one more useful to us.

If philosophers are so smart, what can they do in the time of economic crisis? I strongly believe that they should remain distinction- and precision-keepers. We might even quote Bertrand Russell: "The point of philosophy is to start with something so simple as to seem not worth stating, and to end with something so paradoxical that no one will believe it" (Russell 1956, 12). Making things more complicated than anyone could imagine can save us from oversimplification and ignorance and also encourage us to ask more questions. Hence, provoking and asking questions today, as it has been for ages, remains the main philosophical task.

References

Brown, Theodore L. 2008. *Making Truth: Metaphor in Science*. Urbana and Chicago: University of Illinois Press.

Hempel, Carl G. 1965. *Aspects of Scientific Explanation and other Essays in the Philosophy of Science*. London: Collier Macmillan Publishers; New York: Free Press.

Joyce, Joseph P. 2013. *The IMF and Global Financial Crises: Phoenix Rising?* Cambridge: Cambridge University Press.

Lakoff, George, and Mark Johnson. 1980. *Metaphors We Live By*. Chicago: University of Chicago Press.

McCloskey, Deirdre. 1990. *If You're So Smart: The Narrative of Economic Expertise.* Chicago: University of Chicago Press.

McCloskey, Deirdre. 2010. *Bourgeois Dignity: Why Economics Can't Explain the Modern World.* Chicago: University of Chicago Press.

Obstfeld, Maurice, ed. 2012. *Global Economic Crisis: Impacts, Transmission and Recovery.* Cheltenham and Northampton: Edward Elgar Publishing.

Rorty, Richard. 2007. *Philosophy as Cultural Politics: Philosophical Papers, Volume 4.* New York: Cambridge University Press.

Russell, Bertrand. 1956. *Logic and Knowledge: Essays, 1901–1950.* London: George Allen & Unwin; New York: Macmillan Co.

Schiek, Dagmar, ed. 2013. *The EU Economic and Social Model in the Global Crisis.* Studies in Modern Law and Policy. Farnham and Burlington: Ashgate Publishing.

Shin, Jang-Sup. 2014. *The Global Financial Crisis and the Korean Economy.* London and New York: Routledge.

Tsoukalis, Loukas. 2011. "The Shattering of Illusions – And What Next?" *Journal of Common Market Studies* 49(1): 19–44.

Part III

The economy of happiness and desire

6 Mead's bio-social theory of the Self and the economics of happiness, for a pragmatist philosophy of economics

Guido Baggio

Economists, sociologists, and psychologists have developed various theories about happiness and well-being. However, the concept of 'happiness' has not received a uniform, invariable definition. In several economic, sociological, and psychological theories and empirical studies, in fact, we find such a concept employed as a wide semantic container, implying a variety of methodological standards. Some authors use 'happiness' as synonymous with Subjective Well-being (SWB), referring to both the feeling and the state of happiness (Inglehart 1996); others consider 'happiness' as synonymous with either 'life satisfaction' (Veenhoven 2005) or 'pleasure' (appetites and self-interests) (Deci and Ryan 2001); still others, psychologists in particular, distinguish an affective component ('affection'), a cognitive component ('life satisfaction'), and SWB – the latter being defined as a "state of general well-being, synthetic, of long duration, which includes both the affective and cognitive component" (Ahuvia and Friedman 1998; Frederick and Loewenstein 1999).

In spite of the variety of definitions, almost all the above-mentioned theories and investigations make use of a hedonic approach to the concept of 'happiness,' highlighting the central role of the emotional dimension in subjects' behavioral attitudes. In the hedonic approach, happiness is the result of avoiding pain and seeking pleasure and satisfaction (Kahneman and Schwartz 1999).

In what follows, I will sketch some reflections that show how valuable a pragmatist approach to economic issues concerning happiness would be. More precisely, I will sketch an integrated account of human conduct, which may profitably contribute to the current process of rethinking the notion of the individual. The basic idea behind my proposal is that a pragmatist approach, more precisely Meadian and Neo-Meadian approaches, would offer a theoretical framework that could resolve the tension between a *hedonic* and a *eudaimonic* idea of happiness. Such a tension has often been linked to the opposition between a 'descriptivist' approach to human conduct, which pertains to how the subject actually makes decisions and acts, and a 'prescriptivist' approach, focused on how the subject should act. The overcoming of the two dichotomies – the fact/value dichotomy and the descriptive/prescriptive one – that inform the two main theoretical perspectives on happiness (hedonic/factual and eudaimonic/evaluative) as well as the two corresponding conceptions of the economic subject (rational/normative versus irrational/ emotive) can be attained through a novel understanding of the very notion of human conduct as naturally social. This would contribute to the construction of a pragmatist philosophy of economics devoted to a discussion of the notion of happiness employing a qualitative study of human interactions with the natural and social environment.[1]

Hedonic theory of happiness

The hedonic theory of happiness assumes that the achievement of pleasure is the end of human beings, based on the psychological theory of sensation. Such a theory presumes the maximization of pleasure, in terms of one's perception of being satisfied about some wants and tastes linked both to basic sensations, connected to immediate choice-satisfactions, and to deeper sensations, tied to a perception of life as a whole.[2] The first formulation of this theory dates back to Bentham's *hedonic calculus* of "experienced utility" (as Kahneman defined it), interpreted as the psycho-physiological magnitude of the individual's pleasure (Bentham 1789). After Bentham, Richard Jennings (1855) promoted an idea of economy as a science that "examines only those human susceptibilities and appetences which are similar or analogous to those which he has witnessed in the brute creation" and "only those motives which are derived, more or less remotely, from the attraction of pleasure or the repulsion of pain," by abstaining from entering "those higher paths of human conduct which are guided by morality, and by religion" (Jennings 1855, 45–46).

Stanley Jevons (1888) and Francis Edgeworth (1881) considered economics as a mathematical science, and, along the same line as physiology and the newborn psychophysics, they applied differential calculus to notions of wealth, utility, and value. As Jevons stated:

> I hesitate to say that men will ever have the means of measuring directly the feelings of the human heart. A unit of pleasure or of pain is difficult even to conceive; but it is the amount of these feelings which is con- tinually prompting us to buying and selling, borrowing and lending, labouring and resting, producing and consuming; and *it is from the quantitative effects of the feelings that we must estimate their com- parative amounts.* We can no more know nor measure gravity in its own nature than we can measure a feeling; but, just as we measure gravity by its effects in the motion of a pendulum, so we may estimate the equality or inequality of feelings by the decisions of the human mind.
>
> (Jevons 1888, 11–12)

Edgeworth explicitly appealed to the work of Fechner and Wundt to support the hypothesis that all pleasures are commensurable, and he formulates the *law of accommodation*, according to which the rate of increase of pleasure decreases as its means increase.[3]

Analogously to the reduction in psychophysics of the qualitative intensity of a sensation to the quantitative magnitude of its physical stimulus, utilitarian marginalists reduced happiness to a calculus of pleasure and pain, considering intensity and duration as the only proper dimensions belonging to feeling, and intensity of feeling as the instantaneous state that determines the degree of utility (Jevons, 65–66). They hence determined its maximization quantitatively "by purchasing pleasure, as it were, at the lowest cost of pain" (Jevons, 23) and by identifying "the physical objects or actions" with the sources of pleasure and pain (37).

The background for such an economic framework was an *a priori* methodological approach to human conduct based on the hedonistic psychological assumption that actual impulsions are the effects of 'obscure' demands for pleasure. People prefer what gives them more pleasure, and people *choose* what they *prefer* on the basis of what is *desirable* for them, namely, what is enjoyable in an exclusively 'sensorial way.' Utility is correlative to desire or want, hence, as Marshall argued,

> Economics concerns itself chiefly with those desires, aspirations and other affections of human nature, the outward manifestations of which appear as incentives to action in such a form that the force or quantity of incentives can be estimated and measured with some approach to accuracy; and which therefore are in some degree amenable to treatment by scientific machinery.
>
> (Marshall 1890, 2.2.1)

However, compared to Jevons and Edgeworth, Marshall goes one step further towards less psychologically based economics. As he argued,

> It is essential to note that the economist does not claim to measure any affection of the mind in itself, or directly; but only indirectly through its effect. No one can compare and measure accurately against one another even his own mental states at different times: and no one can measure the mental states of another at all except indirectly and conjecturally by their effects. [...] the economist studies mental states rather through their manifestations than in themselves; and if he finds they afford evenly balanced incentives to action, he treats them *prima facie* as for his purpose equal. [...] An opening is made for the methods and tests of science as soon as the force of a person's motives – *not* the motives themselves – can be approximately measured by the sum of money which he will just give up in order to secure a desired satisfaction.
>
> (Marshall, 2.2.1)

The *force* of a person's motives hence represents a shift from an economics of *sensation* to an economics of *choice*. It is not the motives that can be measured, but rather their effects, that is, "the price which a person is willing to pay for the fulfilment or satisfaction of his desire" (Marshall 1890, 3.3.1).

After Marshall, Pareto's proposal to deduce economic theories from empirical propositions about *choice* rather than about sensation, with the claim that economics is the science of logical action (letter to Laurent, January 19, 1899, in Pareto 1989),[4] offered the basis for the normative rational-agent model. Further developments of this model have assumed that individuals have *consistent* preferences, which are stable, coherent, and context-independent; that 'revealed preferences' have normative values because they are indicators of what an individual judges to be his well-being without mapping onto hedonic experiences; and that the individual is able to choose in accordance with his own conception of well-being, and therefore he has to be *free* to make his own decisions.[5] Rationality-based economics then became the mainstream paradigm until the 1980s, when new work that tested rationality assumptions found systematic deviations from orthodox theory, thus fostering a growing interest in psychologically based theories and hypotheses to test assumptions about individual rationality involved in choice processes.

Kahneman's hedonic theory of happiness

More recently, Kahneman has argued that people often do not choose what they really want and, distinguishing between Benthamian 'experienced utility' and utility as 'wantability' (concerning preferences), he has claimed that human preferences do not reflect people's interests.[6] Kahneman's descriptivist approach to human conduct suggests that human beings do not have consistent preferences and do not know how to maximize them. In particular, in an article entitled "Back to Bentham? Explorations of Experienced Utility," Kahneman (with Wakker and Sarin, 1997) presented the results of a series of studies in support of the hypothesis that the perception of pleasure concerning life as a whole is momentary, due to the fact that humans' mental capacities for remembering past affective experiences and retrieving them later are subject to systematic limitations and errors (Kahneman et al. 1997). In assuming that "experienced utility can only be understood when it is directly measured" (395), Kahneman developed a theory of total utility for the evaluation of TEOs (temporally extended outcomes). Results of surveys have shown that even if people have strong preferences about the duration of their experiences of pleasure and pain, wanting pleasure to last and pain to be brief, memory has evolved to represent the peak of an episode of pain or pleasure without serving our preferences (Kahneman 2011).

In another paper Kahneman and Krueger (2006) presented the results of surveys based on the Day Reconstruction Method (DRM) and the Unpleasant-Index (U-Index).[7] Bearing in mind the distinction between 'life-satisfaction' and 'happiness' – the former referring to our thoughts and feelings when we are thinking about our life, which occurs only occasionally (during these surveys on well-being), the latter describing feelings which we have as we live our life – the results show that people's answers are often strongly influenced by current emotional states and more general personality traits, as well as by variables that characterize the immediate context. Kahneman distinguishes two selves that influence the evaluation-process, the 'experiencing self', who does the living, and the 'remembering self', who "keeps score and makes the choices" (Kahneman 2011, 399). At the basis of the functioning of the two selves there are what he calls two systems of mind: the impulsive side of thinking, on the one hand, which acts without reflection, constituted by "effortlessly originating impressions and feelings that are the main sources of the explicit beliefs and deliberate choices," and, on the other, "the conscious, reasoning self that has beliefs, makes choices, and decides what to think about and what to do." This latter system is normally associated with the subjective experiences of agency, choice, and concentration (Kahneman 2011, 23).

Kahneman's descriptive, hedonic perspective on experienced utility and life-satisfaction has undisputed advantages. The most important is that the survey data call attention to how people feel *as* they live and not only to how they feel when they think *about* their life. From this perspective, it offers some important contributions to empirical methodological approaches to the study of everyday life topics, contributing to a better understanding of the termi-nology to use when developing surveys and experiments, as well as interpret-ing empirical data about happiness, life-satisfaction, and well-being.[8] Furthermore, the hedonic approach considers the heuristic which people use to respond to questions about their life and their errors of evaluation, when giving too much weight to some current aspects and too little to all determi-nants. It is beyond question that some available results on self-reported mea-sures of well-being may contribute to traditional welfare analysis, offering some indications about people's interests and preferences.

However, Kahneman's theory presents some limits that undermine its results. First, Kahneman often seems to confuse *pursued pleasures* with *plea-sures of achievement.*[9] For instance, patients' relief after an unpleasant experience (e.g., a colonoscopy or exposure to unpleasant film clips) is cer-tainly a pleasure, but it is a *pleasure of achievement*, that is a pleasure which appears when people have successfully overcome an unpleasant experience. As William James pointed out against Bain's philosophy of pleasure, a *pleasant act* is in itself a perfectly distinct concept from the act of *pursuing pleasure,* "though they coalesce in one concrete phenomenon whenever pleasure is deliberately pursued" (James 1890, 812). *Minimizing* the overall experience of unpleasantness as a *result* of impulse is different from *pursuing pleasure*, the latter being a *cause* for human acts. And, even if the pleasure of achievement can on special occasions become a pursued pleasure, "it does not follow that everywhere and always that pleasure must be what is pursued" (813).

Moreover, Kahneman's reductionist approach chiefly considers the psycho-physiological reactions as indices of states of stress and pleasure and identifies a person's decision-processes with the organism's reactions to sensory stimu-lations. Although one must concede the exceeding importance of bodily pleasures and pains in people's motivations to act and in their perception of well-being, the risk of such an approach is that of reducing happiness to the sum of momentary emotive evaluations, overestimating the immediate emotive, self-centered component and underestimating the intertwined long-term cognitive-affective evaluation. It is not by chance, therefore, that more recently Kahneman himself admitted that the word 'happiness' "does not have a simple meaning and should not be used as if it does" (Kahneman 2011, 398).

To sum up, the hedonic approach leaves unsolved the question of how – in a real context-dependent situation – subjects' psychological meaning of preferences would involve not only immediate hedonic pleasure but also a more complex idea of well-being, which includes both the affective and cognitive components dependent on people's relations with their social and natural environments. On this point and based on the findings of a large-scale study on the goals that young people set for themselves, Kahneman changed his mind about the definition of 'well-being.' Particularly, he admitted that it is not possible "to hold a concept of well-being that ignores what people want" and that the "goals that people set for themselves are so important to what they do and how they feel about it that an exclusive focus on experienced well-being is not tenable." Therefore, he argued, we "must accept the complexities of a hybrid view, in which the well-being of both selves [mnemonic and experienced] is considered" (Kahneman 2011, 392–93). To justify his change of heart, Kahneman concludes his reflections on well-being by admitting that "sometimes scientific progress leaves us more puzzled than we were before" (397–98).

Even if the hedonic approach overcomes the rationalistic paradigm of *homo economicus*, and, along these lines, it also highlights the limits of the arguments in favor of neo-liberal economic discourse (namely, the claim that agents generally know what is good for them and thus they should be left alone to choose),[10] it does not succeed in overcoming the individualistic, hedonistic approach that also characterizes orthodox economics.[11] More precisely, it does not give sufficient voice to happiness as a wider criterion that would gather together the many different aspects of life that people can find valuable. Such a criterion would consider first of all the psycho-social variables that co-determine human conduct (and hence choices and goals), reflecting a self-identity related to the recognition of other selves.

It follows that hedonistic aspects have to be included in a notion of human conduct aiming at reconciling the descriptive approach to human conduct with the normative approach. Instead of considering human beings as divided into two 'systems' – one referring to optimal goal-priorities, and presenting formal consistency of preferences; the other referring to the emotive human dimension as irrational and internally inconsistent but presenting the so-called 'real' character of the self – such a new perspective would consider reflexive thinking as inserted into a natural and social environment and therefore strictly intertwined with the affective-emotional aspects of human interactions. The findings of happiness research then would be considered by individuals as information to be used for improving "*their own* choices, both as private individuals and as citizen participants in collective decision-making processes" (McQuillin and Sugden 2012, 558).[12] As we shall see in what follows, such a perspective can be seen to emerge through a rethinking of Mead's social psychology, and more specifically of his bio-social theory of mind and Self.

Mead's bio-social theory of the Self and human conduct

Stressing the *innate* social dimension of human beings, Mead's social psychology (Mead 1934, 1964, 2001) proposes a complex idea of the Self as the result of mental and non-mental behavioral attitudes, the latter being the expression of human abilities to act in a social-natural environment. According to Mead, individuals acquire their identity through communication processes in which the organized community or social group gives individuals their unity as Selves. The sum of the vocal and gestural replies of others to an individual's stimuli constitute the attitude of the whole community towards the individual's behavior. Mead called such a social attitude the "generalized other," depicting it as the crystallizing of all particular attitudes into a single attitude or standpoint (Mead 1934, 90). Individuals take the general attitude towards the various phases or aspects of a common social activity or set of social undertakings in which, as members of an organized society or social group, they are engaged. As Mead argues,

> Only in so far as [the individual] takes the attitudes of the organized social group to which he belongs toward the organized, cooperative social activity or set of such activities in which that group as such is engaged, does he develop a complete self or possess the sort of complete self he has developed. And on the other hand, the complex cooperative processes and activities and institutional functioning of organized human society are also possible only in so far as every individual involved in them or belonging to that society can take the general attitudes of all other such individuals with reference to these processes and activities and institutional functionings, and to the organized social whole of experiential relations and interactions thereby constituted – and can direct his own behavior accordingly.
>
> (Mead 1934, 155)

Behind the common social activity there is a set of social primitive instincts by the nature of which the distinction between the Me and the Other is given. The instincts are social in the sense that the individual's gestural and vocal responses arise in answer to indications of various movements by other individuals in the group.[13] The early stages of these activities give rise in the individual to what are currently called human *pro-social emotions*, namely, psycho-physiological reactions to movements of other group members that induce agents to engage in cooperative behavior (cf. Bowles and Gintis 2011). The bio-social mechanism is in fact at the basis of the feeling of *sympathy*, which consists, according to Mead's definition, in taking

> a distinctively human, that is, self-conscious, social attitude toward another individual, or to become aware of him as such, is to identify yourself sympathetically with him, by taking his attitude toward, and his role in, the given social situation, and by thus responding to that situation implicitly as he does or is about to do explicitly.
>
> (Mead 1934, 300)

Sympathetic identification is here depicted as a natural process presenting both cognitive and affective aspects, since it refers to the capacities both to represent the other's intentions and beliefs (attitudes) and to share one's feelings.

Although Mead's notion of sympathy is rooted in David Hume's *A Treatise of Human Nature* and indirectly in Adam Smith's *Theory of Moral Sentiments*, in which Smith refers to sympathy as a quality of human nature at the basis of communication and social rules,[14] a more fecund parallel can be found in the current neuroscientific and neurophenomenological hypothesis on 'empathy,' related to the recent studies on mirror neurons. Empathy is generally depicted as a pre-reflexive, embodied mechanism that plays a role in understanding the intentional actions of others by ascribing meaning to their unreflective facial expressions and being able to 'read' their emotionally laden bodily attitudes (Borghi and Cimatti 2009; Gallese 2006, 2009a, 2009b; Gallese and Goldman 1998; Rizzolatti and Sinigaglia 2006).

It is worth noting that nowadays Mead's theory of gestural conversation, as the expression of an innate social dimension of human beings, is undergoing a revival among neuroscientists. Rizzolatti and Sinigaglia (2006, 48–49, 148–49), for instance, explicitly refer to Mead's work as supporting the hypothesis that the arising of human language would have had at its basis a gestural attitude linked to a preconscious mechanism for understanding the gestural attitudes of others. And McNeill (2005, 30–31) refers to what he has called "Mead's loop theory" regarding "a capacity, not present in other primate brains, for the mirror neuron circuit to respond to one's own gestures as if they belonged to someone else." Mead himself argued that

> All that is innate or hereditary in connection with minds and selves is the physiological mechanism of the human central nervous system, by means of which the genesis of minds and selves out of the human social process of experience and behavior – out of the human matrix of social relations and interactions – is made biologically possible in human individuals.
>
> (Mead 1934, 237n)

A parallel between Mead and neuroscience will therefore shed light on some topical economic issues concerning people's social attitudes. In particular it will contribute to the elucidation of two main issues with which current neuroeconomics, a new branch of BE (behavioral economics) that studies the biological basis of human economic behavior, is concerned (Kirman and Teschl 2010).[15] The first issue is epistemological: that is, understanding the process by which people take the role of the other will help to clarify what knowledge people can reasonably have about other people's beliefs, intentions, and motives. The second issue is motivational: that is, if empathetic identification leads not only to a better understanding of the other person's intentions and behavioral attitudes, this may well undermine purely self-interested choices and instead promote other-regarding behavior. Furthermore, it would again provide a good reason for reconsidering the paradigm of the economic agent as a self-interested individual (Kirman and Teschl 2010, 305). Examining in depth the bio-social basis of empathy would permit us to link the bio-psychological approach to human economic behavior to an ethical approach to it.

The Meadian pragmatist basis for (neuro)economics

Like Mead's reference to sympathetic identification, the concept of empathetic identification refers to "an individual who perfectly naturally arouses a certain response in himself because his gesture operates on himself as it does on the other" (Mead 1934, 300). Thanks to empathetic identification, an individual can comprehend the other's behavioral and expressive attitudes and interact with him through a so-to-speak *natural social-enlargement* in which the affective and cognitive dimensions are closely related,[16] without ceasing to be able to separate clearly which beliefs and feelings belong to which self. This process has its *conditio sine qua non* in the social interaction through which individuals assimilate and introject others' behavioral attitudes, and its biological support in the simulation function of mirror neurons.

However, Mead did not intend to give a reductionist interpretation of human minds, nor do I. It is difficult to trace the origin of human consciousness in brain mechanisms. *Understanding* the other's attitudes and preferences means to refer to higher cognitive abilities in which mirror neurons have a functional role. People's abilities to understand others' intentions and preferences are not identical to people's brain activation of the neural mimetic mechanism. There would be, otherwise, a specular identification, a mere imitative mirroring. After all, the notion of 'simulation' has not been given a uniform, invariable definition in neuroscience. Some neuroscientists use the concept with reference to the neural mechanism through which we understand other minds (Gallese and Goldman 1998; Goldman 1995), whereas others consider simulation as a conscious process that depends on a deliberate re-activating of some previously accomplished actions (Decety and Ingvar 1990).

Thus, a distinction should be made between a *simulation mechanism*, referred to as an embedded 'proto-intentional' mechanism of recognition of the attitudes of others (namely, a neural recognition of a co-specific's intentions),[17] and a *simulation process*, which refers to interpersonal interactions in which the individual's higher cognitive and affective abilities are involved in a process of identification with the attitudes, desires, preferences, and intentions of others.[18]

From this perspective a pragmatist empathetic identification approach would provide a sketch to adequately highlight the interdependent and reciprocally conditioning, organic relation between the self and others, generally attributed to the empathetic attitude. The simulation process, in fact, mediates between our ability to share meanings about actions, intentions, feelings, and emotions and the empathetic identification that allows us to put ourselves in another's shoes and attempt to interpret, more or less correctly, other people's beliefs, intentions, and motives.[19]

Identity and agency

From this perspective, too, the pragmatist approach to empathetic identification would also contribute to a sketch of an integrated account of identity and agency that would overcome the tension between a descriptive and a normative approach to human conduct, and in particular between self-preference and other-regarding preferences. The experiences that persons live through and their closeness to other people occur in relation to what we saw Mead calling the 'generalized other,' namely, the "organized community or social group which gives to the individual his unity of self" (Mead 1934, 154). The attitude of the 'generalized other' is the attitude of the whole community, namely, the common *ethos* which gives unity and consistency to the person's *identity*. As Mead argues,

> It is in the form of the generalized other that the social process influences the behavior of the individuals involved in it and carrying it on, i.e., that the community exercises control over the conduct of its individual members; for it is in this form that the social process or community enters as a determining factor into the individual's thinking.
>
> (Mead 1934, 155)

The community's identity is hence embedded in the self as a co-determining factor of his valuating processes of preferring and choosing. People's social attitudes, which in part contribute and in part are subject to a community's *values* (often incommensurable values),[20] offer the basis for empathetic identification through which private, subjective preferences are potentially shareable.

Amartya Sen would probably agree with Mead's explanation of the Self as following particular rules of conduct. Indeed, Sen has also pointed out that the Self's identity is generated in a community and is strictly related to rule-based conduct (Sen 1985b). More precisely, discussing the nature of the behavioral foundation of economics, Sen tackled the problem of 'identity,' stressing that "community, nationality, class, race, sex, union membership, the fellowship of oligopolists, revolutionary solidarity, and so on, provide identities that can be, depending on the context, crucial to ourselves" (Sen 1985b, 348). A person's identity and concept of his own welfare – he continues – can be influenced by the position of others in ways that may involve identifying with others. This means that the pursuit of self-goals may well be compromised by consideration of the goals of others in the group with whom the person has some sense of identity.[21] The recognition of interdependence with others' goals may suggest to the individual "certain social rules of behavior" that are not necessarily of intrinsic hedonic value, but nonetheless "of great instrumental importance in the enhancement of the respective goals of the members of that group" (Sen 1987, 85).[22] As he argues,

> One of the ways in which the sense of identity can operate is through making members of a community accept certain rules of conduct as part of obligatory behavior toward others in the community. ... [A]cceptance of rules of conduct toward others with whom one has some sense of identity is part of a more general behavioral phenomenon of acting according to fixed rules, without following the dictates of goal-maximization.
>
> (Sen 1985b, 349)

In support of his thesis Sen refers to Adam Smith's idea, expressed in his *Theory of Moral Sentiments*, that there are some general rules of conduct that have been fixed in our mind by *habitual reflection* and are of great use in correcting misrepresentation of self-love concerning what is appropriate to do in our particular situation (Smith 1759, 160). According to Sen, there would also be a "natural selection" argument in favor of such behavioral modes, leading to their survival and stability, as well as an evolutionary influence that works in a direction quite different from self-satisfaction (Sen 1985b, 350; see also Sen 1977 and 1973, 252–53).

From a Meadian perspective one could say that the self's behavioral attitudes toward others show interdependence between communal-goals and self-goals at the core of social acts, without implying either the identification between self-interest and the interests of others, or, on the contrary, the idea that communal-goals are the product of a pure sentiment of altruism. Habitual reflection is in fact based on the embedded ability to learn social *habits*, namely, social rules of action.[23] Habits result from the action of natural selection, consisting in a process of empirical generalization through which habits became normative.

This suggestion would offer also an explanation of Sen's distinction between *sympathy* and *commitment*. The former corresponds "to the case in which the concern of others directly affects one's own welfare" (Sen 1977, 326) and is egoistic, for the pursuit of one's own utility may be helped by pleasure from others' pleasures and pain from others' pain. On the contrary, *commitment* is concerned with breaking the link between a person's welfare and his choice of action through anticipations of welfare states. Commitment is hence concerned with the ethical dimension of behavior, with the intrinsic importance of the role of agency and the influence that this role has on the person's evaluation of what is *valuable*. As Sen puts it, "man is a social animal and his choices are not rigidly bound to his own preferences only … . An act of choice for this social animal is, in a fundamental sense, always a social act" (Sen 1973, 252–53). It is possible that "people may be induced by social codes of behaviour to act *as if* they have different preferences from what they really have" (Sen 1973, 258) and then that their choice may be guided by various motives, the pursuit of personal well-being being only one of them (Sen 1985a, 188).

Since agency roles concern a person's evaluation of motives that are different from personal preferences, the mixture of motivations makes it hard to gain an insight into a person's well-being on the basis of the observation of his behavior (Sen 1985a, 188). As Sen puts it, there are some unresolved questions concerning economic approaches like the 'revealed preference' approach (Samuelson 1948; Little 1949), which attempts to explain revealed preferences with reference only to behavior observations.[24] Sen criticized this approach in a paper on "Behaviour and the Concept of Preference." In particular he examines the philosophy behind the approach of revealed preference and the interpretation of underlying preferences, arguing that a person "may not have a connected preference pattern and in terms of observation it is difficult to distinguish such incompleteness from indifference." What is of interest in the *interpretation* of the revealed preference theory lies in the skilful use of the assumption that "behaviour reveals preference" and not, despite claims to the contrary, in explaining "behaviour without reference to anything other than behaviour" (Sen 1973, 258).[25]

Now, Sen's arguing that behavior *reveals* preferences, rather than *explains* behavior, is close to Mead's account of social behaviorism as "simply an approach to the study of the experience of the individual from the point of view of his conduct, particularly, but not exclusively, the conduct as it is observable by others" (Mead 1934, 2).[26] The external act is a part of the process that has started within. However, Mead would have also argued that the individual expresses his preferences in terms of the behavior of the whole social group of which he is a member, "since his individual acts are involved in larger, social acts which go beyond himself and which implicate the other members of that group" (Mead 1934, 6–7). Such an approach is particularly concerned with subjective experiences, namely, the "inner phases" of social acts, but "works from the outside to the inside instead of from the inside to the outside, so to speak, in its endeavour to determine how such experience does arise within the process" (Mead 1934, 8). This point implies that if a person lives in a community that promotes a culture of egoistic rule-governed behaviors, he will quite likely act referring mainly to self-regarding preferences.

For a pragmatist philosophy of economics

A pragmatist approach to economic issues would have important potential applications in socio-economic research. A *Pragmatist Philosophy of Economics* would in fact contribute to developing further a new theoretical approach to economics that would complement the present debate about individualistic *versus* social theories of economic behavior. More specifically, the theoretical framework of a pragmatist philosophy of economics would offer a wider perspective on human economic behavior and decision-making processes. Emerging developments from this proposal would strengthen at once the principled commitment to freedom of choice and the case for the quest for individual happiness. Each individual's welfare, generally seen in orthodox economics as subsumed under the general heading of formal rationality and in BE as the maximization of self-pleasure or minimization of self-pain, reveals from a 'Meadian' perspective the instrumental role of social behavioral patterns and socio-cultural environment (social group, community, nationality, race, sex, and now more and more social media) in the orientation of behaviors, as well as identity and perception of well-being of the self. There is, hence, no sharp distinction between personal and ethical dimensions.

More generally, showing that features of social situations can have massive effects on individuals' behaviors, a pragmatist philosophy of economics aims to offer a better understanding of people's choice processes and behavioral architecture, applied to many domains of private and public action. Consistent with this, I envisage also a new perspective concerning the links between economics and ethics. This approach to economics aims at offering a suitable framework for overcoming the technical/ethical dichotomy, as well as the *poiesis/praxis* dichotomy of economic efficiency *versus* ethical 'oughtness.'

As it is well known, pragmatists have rejected the dichotomy between ethical reflections and scientific reflections. Both Mead and particularly Dewey denied the view of ethical values as a product of deductive reasoning. Rather, they considered values as the product of behavioral attitudes that individuals acquire in social interactions, or, as Mead would say, "taking the role of the others." The fact/value dichotomy is hence a false dichotomy, the result of an old distinction – rooted in philosophical reflection – between the particular and the universal, between the contingent and the necessary. However, since values are pragmatic values of behavior expressed in social practices, the parameters that are considered criteria for determining what happiness is, are also the product of determined social-cultural contexts that allow a greater comprehension of reality and ideality. After all, it is not by chance if the economic crisis we are experiencing is now dramatically highlighting the fallacy of the 'neutrality' claimed by economists and politics when picturing world social situations. In particular, the dramatic dichotomy – a *real* dichotomy this time – between the tragic social situation of crisis and the technical objectives (fiscal compact, balance, statistical projections) at the basis of political, economic choices of governors, renders explicit the values behind them. In other words, the claimed neutrality of economists and policy technicians invoking an abstract free market ideal is an explicit value-assumption legitimating rule-governed behavior, namely, egoistic and individualistic, self-preferencing behavior.

The pragmatist philosophy of economics model would thus have a socio-economic impact by offering some insights in favor of 'individual's social well-being,' addressing some hypotheses on how we can optimally use social-ties mechanisms to implement good social practices. This suggestion has important implications also on theoretical contributions that pragmatist philosophy of economics can offer to the recently born behavioral public economics. The sheer complexity of modern life undermines arguments for rigid mandates or for dogmatic neo-liberal laissez-faire. Potential applications would concern also sciences of education, for a social-ties, human behavioral model could offer some practical insights for pedagogical reflections on how to promote some good practices.

With its decisive understanding of the inextricable link between thinking and acting at the basis of the human capacity for inquiry and of social experience as the common ground for the verification of ideas, pragmatism offers a very specific contribution to the development of the scientific method of inquiry, stressing the social and economic value of scientific research. It would hence be possible to overcome the distinction (McCloskey 1985, 159–62) between a purely philosophical methodology and a practicing economic (that is, scientific) methodology.

Notes

1 See among others Dasgupta 2001; Nussbaum and Sen 1993. Khalil (2004) and Klamer (2003) advanced some interesting insights on the potential fruitful interactions between Dewey's focus on value matter and analysis in economic contexts. See also Dreon 2015.
2 Cf. Lewin 1996; Bruni and Sugden 2007.
3 As Bruni and Sugden (2007, 152–53) pointed out, the law of accommodation is close to the notion of *hedonic adaptation*.
4 Cf. Bruni and Sugden 2007, 154ff.
5 Cf. McQuillin and Sugden 2012.
6 The reference is to Fisher 1918.
7 DRM combines elements of experience sampling and time diaries (Kahneman et al. 2004) and is designed to facilitate emotional recall. The U-index measures the proportion of time an individual spends in an unpleasant state (Kahneman and Krueger 2006, 19–21).
8 The distinction between happiness and life-satisfaction, for example, came to Kahneman during a survey, posing the question on life-satisfaction (Kahneman 2011, 499n).
9 William James moved the same critique to Bain's pleasure-philosophy (James 1890, 812–13).
10 In line with this perspective, behavioral economists proposed approaches of 'soft paternalism' (or 'nudge theories'), which seeks mechanisms that protect individuals from choices that could produce immediate benefits but long-term costs, as, for example, self-destructive practices. Cf. Camerer et al. 2003, 2007; Thaler and Sunstein 2008. On the soft paternalistic approaches, see McQuillin and Sugden 2012, 559–62.
11 It is not by chance, I think, that behavioral economics (BE) has seen its main implementation in financial research, where choice processes seem to be totally

disconnected from the social context and motivated by *bias* of almost totally subjective, and often self-alienated, projections.

12 McQuillin and Sugden are here referring to the work of Loewenstein and Ubel (2008).
13 On this point see the recent studies of Panksepp (1998).
14 According to Hume sympathy is a disposition to shared sentiments, to participate in the emotional life of others and by communication to form general rules to pursue. Sympathy is in fact a principle of human communication and man's drive to better his condition. Through sympathy individuals partake of the satisfaction of every one that approaches them, taking satisfaction for their esteem (cf. Hume 1739, 2.2.5). Smith, who further elaborated Hume's use of sympathy to explain economic phenomena, considered sympathy an individual's "fellow-feeling with any passion whatever," which may arise from "the view of a certain emotion in another person," but not "from the view of the passion, as from that of the situation which excites it" through the imagination (Smith 1759, 1.1.1).
15 On the more general topics of urgent interest across neuroscience and philosophy from the perspective of pragmatism, see Shook and Solymosi 2014.
16 Cf. Bower 1983. Giusti and Locatelli (2007, 11) pointed out that Mead is among the first authors to introduce the cognitive element into the affective meaning of 'empathy.'
17 Cf. Gallese 2009b. The concept of 'proto-intention' refers to Damasio's concept of 'proto-self' (Damasio 1999, 170ff.), which is the biological preconscious function that pre-exists to the self-feeling. Like the proto-self 'proto-intention' is a function arising through the interaction between neural signals and social and natural environment stimuli.
18 On this point, it would be possible to find out some potential connections to the use of neuron mirrors and the paradox Khalil highlights about the rise of divergent processes from the same neuron mirrors' activation (Khalil 2011).
19 For further developments on this point see Baggio 2016.
20 On this point see Klamer 2003.
21 Also, James's concept that the social self is a constituent of the Self would be useful here for finding some analogies between Sen's and pragmatists' ideas. However, a full discussion of James's psychology is beyond the scope of this chapter.
22 Cf. Sharma and Sharma 2010; Max-Neef 1987; Max-Neef and Ekins 1992.
23 'Habit' has to be identified with mental attitudes and feelings which characterize in part each individual's behavioral dispositions. In particular, according to Peirce, "Intellectual power is nothing but facility in taking habits and in following them in cases essentially analogous to, but in non-essentials widely remote from, the normal cases of connections of feelings under which those habits were formed" (Peirce 1891, 169).
24 Such an approach is based on 'logical behaviorism,' which defined sentences referring to mental events as 'nonsensical' and promoted a reductionist approach to psychology based on the observability of human behavior. Revealed preference theory has taken this approach as a reference (Samuelson 1948; Little 1949), while claiming to explain "behaviour without reference to anything other than behaviour" (Little 1949).
25 On this point see also Lewin 1996 and Bruni and Sugden 2007.
26 It is worth noting that Barbalet (2008) has compared Sen's distinction between sympathy and commitment with the Jamesian complex-self.

References

Ahuvia, A. C., and D. C. Friedman. 1998. "Income, Consumption, and Subjective Well-Being: Toward a Composite Macromarketing Model." *Journal of Macromarketing* 18: 153–168.

Baggio, G. 2016. "Sympathy and Empathy: G. H. Mead and the Pragmatist Basis of (Neuro)Economics." In *Pragmatism and Embodied Cognitive Science*, ed. R. Madzia and M. Jung, 183–208. Berlin: De Gruyter.

Barbalet, J. 2008. "Pragmatism and Economics: William James' Contribution." *Cambridge Journal of Economics* 32: 797–810.

Bentham, J. 1789. *An Introduction to the Principles of Morals and Legislation*. Kitchener: Batoche Books, 2000.

Borghi, A., and F. Cimatti. 2009. "Embodied Cognition and Beyond: Acting and Sensing the Body." *Neuropsychologia* 5: 763–773.

Bower, G. H. 1983. "Affect and Cognition." *Philosophical Transactions of the Royal Society B: Biological Sciences* 302: 387–402.

Bowles, S., and H. Gintis. 2011. *A Cooperative Species: Human Reciprocity and Its Evolution*. Princeton and Oxford: Princeton University Press.

Bruni, L., and R. Sugden. 2007. "The Road Not Taken: How Psychology Was Removed from Economics, and How It Might Be Brought Back." *Economic Journal* 117(516): 146–173.

Camerer, C. F., M. Bhatt, and M. Hsu. 2007. "Neuroeconomics: Illustrated by the Study of Ambiguity Aversion." In *Economics and Psychology: A Promising New Cross-Disciplinary Field*, ed. B. S. Frey and A. Stutzer. Cambridge, MA: MIT Press.

Camerer, C., S. Issacharoff, G. Loewenstein, T. O'Donoghue, and M. Rabin. 2003. "Regulation for Conservatives: Behavioral Economics and the Case for 'Asymmetric Paternalism'." *University of Pennsylvania Law Review* 151(3): 1211–1254.

Damasio, A. R. 1999. *The Feeling of What Happens: Body and Emotion in the Making of Consciousness*. Boston, MA: Harcourt.

Dasgupta, P. 2001. *Human Well-Being and Natural Environment*. New York: Oxford University Press.

Decety, J., and D. H. Ingvar. 1990. "Brain Structures Participating in Mental Simulation of Motor Behavior: A Neuropsychological Interpretation." *Acta Psychologica* 73: 13–24.

Deci, R. M., and E. L. Ryan. 2001. "On Happiness and Human Potentials: A Review of Research on Hedonic and Eudemonic Well-Being." *Annual Review of Psychology* 95: 542–575.

Dreon, R. 2015. "The Aesthetic, Pleasure and Happiness, or: Why Freedom Is Not Enough." *Pragmatism Today* 6(1): 6–21. <www.pragmatismtoday.eu/summer2015/02%20Dreon.pdf>.

Edgeworth, F. 1881. *Mathematical Psychics*. New York: Kelley, 1967.

Fisher, I. 1918. "Is 'Utility' the Most Suitable Term for the Concept It Is Used to Denote?" *American Economic Review* 8(2): 335–337.

Frederick, S., and G. Loewenstein. 1999. "Hedonic Adaptation." In *Well-Being: The Foundations of Hedonic Psychology*, ed. D. Kahneman, E. Diener, and N. Schwarz, 302–329. New York: Russell Sage Foundation.

Gallese, V. 2006. *Corpo Vivo, simulazione incarnata e intersoggettività: una prospettiva neuro-fenomenologica*. In *Neurofenomenologia*, ed. M. Cappuccio, 293–326. Milan: Bruno Mondadori.

Gallese, V. 2009a. "Motor Abstraction: A Neuroscientific Account of How Action Goals and Intentions Are Mapped and Understood." *Psychological Research* 73: 486–498.

Gallese, V. 2009b. "Mirror Neurons, Embodied Simulation, and the Neural Basis of Social Identification." *Psychoanalytic Dialogues* 19: 519–536.

Gallese, V., and A. I. Goldman. 1998. "Mirror Neurons and the Simulation Theory." *Trends in Cognitive Science* 2: 493–501.

Giusti, E., and M. Locatelli. 2007. *L'Empatia integrata: analisi umanistica del comportamento motivazionale nella clinica e nella formazione.* Rome: Soveria Multimedia.

Goldman, A. I. 1995. "Simulation and Interpersonal Utility." *Ethics* 105(4): 709–726.

Hume, D. 1739. *A Treatise of Human Nature*, ed. L. A. Selby- Bigge. Oxford: Clarendon Press, 1896.

Inglehart, R. 1996. "The Diminishing Utility of Economic Growth." *Critical Review* 10: 508–531.

James, W. 1890. *Principles of Psychology.* Chicago: Encyclopaedia Britannica, Inc.

Jennings, R. 1855. *Natural Elements of Political Economy.* London: Longman, Brown, Green, and Longmans.

Jevons, W. S. 1888. *The Theory of Political Economy.* London and New York: MacMillan.

Kahneman, D. E. 2011. *Thinking, Fast and Slow.* New York: Farrar, Straus & Giroux.

Kahneman, D. E., and A. B. Krueger. 2006. "Developments in the Measurement of Subjective Well-Being." *Journal of Economic Perspectives* 20(1): 3–24.

Kahneman, D. E., and N. Schwartz, eds. 1999. *Well-being: The Foundations of Hedonic Psychology.* New York: Russell Sage Foundation.

Kahneman, D. E., A. B. Krueger, D. A. Schkade, N. Schwarz, and A. A. Stone. 2004. *The Day Reconstruction Method (DRM): Instrument Documentation.* <http://sitemaker.umich.edu/norbert.schwarz/files/drm_documentation_july_2004.pdf> (web page no longer available).

Kahneman, D. E., P. Wakker, and R. Sarin. 1997. "Back to Bentham? Exploration of Experienced Utility." *Quarterly Journal of Economics* 112: 375–405.

Khalil, E. L., ed. 2004. *Dewey, Pragmatism, and Economic Methodology.* London: Routledge.

Khalil, E. L. 2011. "The Mirror Neuron Paradox: How Far Is Understanding from Mimicking?" *Journal of Economic Behavior and Organization* 77(1): 86–96.

Kirman, A., and M. Teschl. 2010. "Selfish or Selfless? The Role of Empathy in Economics." *Philosophical Transactions of the Royal Society B: Biological Sciences* 365: 303–317.

Klamer, A. 2003. "A Pragmatic View on Values in Economics." *Journal of Economic Methodology* 10(2): 191–212.

Lewin, S. B. 1996. "Lessons for Our Own Day From the Early Twentieth Century." *Journal of Economic Literature* 34(3): 1293–1323.

Little, I. M. D. 1949. "A Reformulation of the Theory of Consumer's Behaviour." *Oxford Economic Papers*, n.s., 1(1): 90–99.

Loewenstein, G., and P. A. Ubel. 2008. "Hedonic Adaptation and the Role of Decision and Experience Utility in Public Policy." *Journal of Public Economics* 92: 1795–1810.

Marshall, A. 1890. *The Principles of Economics.* Amherst, NY: Prometheus Books, 1997.

Max-Neef, M. 1987. *Desarrollo a escala humana.* Montevideo: Nordan.

Max-Neef, M., and P. Ekins. 1992. *Real-Life Economics: Understanding Wealth Creation.* London: Routledge.

McCloskey, D. 1985. *The Rhetoric of Economics.* Madison: University of Wisconsin Press.

McNeill, D. 2005. *Gesture and Thought*. Chicago: Chicago University Press.

McQuillin, B., and R. Sugden. 2012. "Reconciling Normative and Behavioural Bconomics: The Problems to Be Solved." *Social Choice Welfare* 38: 553–567.

Mead, G. H. 1934. *Mind, Self, and Society*, ed. Charles W. Morris. Chicago: University of Chicago Press.

Mead, G. H. 1964. *Selected Writings*. Chicago: Chicago University Press.

Mead, G. H. 2001. *Essays on Social Psychology*, ed. M. J. Deegan. New Brunswick, NJ: Transaction Publishers.

Nussbaum, M., and A. Sen, eds. 1993. *The Quality of Life*. Oxford: Clarendon Press.

Panksepp, J. 1998. *Affective Neuroscience: The Foundation of Human and Animal Emotions*. Oxford: Oxford University Press.

Pareto, V. 1989. *Lettres et correspondances*. Vol. 30 of *Oeuvres complètes*. Geneva: Droz.

Peirce, C. S. 1891. "The Architecture of Theories." *Monist* l(2): 161–176.

Rizzolatti, G., and C. Sinigaglia. 2006. *So quel che fai*. Milan: Raffaello Cortina.

Rorty, R. 1979. *Philosophy and the Mirror of Nature*. Princeton: Princeton University Press.

Samuelson, P. A. 1948. "Consumption Theory in Terms of Revealed Preference." *Economica*, n.s., 15(60): 243–253.

Sen, A. 1973. "Behaviour and the Concept of Preference." *Economica*, n.s., 40(159): 241–259.

Sen, A. 1977. "Rational Fools: A Critique of the Behavioral Foundations of Economic Theory." *Philosophy & Public Affairs* 6(4): 317–344.

Sen, A. 1985a. "Well-being, Agency and Freedom: The Dewey Lectures 1984." *Journal of Philosophy* 82(4): 169–221.

Sen, A. 1985b. "Goals, Commitment, and Identity." *Journal of Law, Economics, and Organization* 1(2): 341–355.

Sen, A. 1987. *On Ethics and Economics*. Oxford: Basil Blackwell.

Sharma, S., and M. Sharma. 2010. "Self, Social Identity, and Psychological Well-Being." *Psychological Studies* 55(2): 118–136.

Shook, J. R., and T. Solymosi, eds. 2014. *Pragmatist Neurophilosophy: American Philosophy and the Brain*. London and New York: Bloomsbury Academic.

Smith, A. 1759. *The Theory of Moral Sentiments*, ed. D. D. Raphael and A. L. Macfie. Oxford: Oxford University Press, 1976.

Thaler, R. H., and C. R. Sunstein. 2008. *Nudge: Improving Decisions about Health, Wealth and Happiness*. New Haven: Yale University Press.

Veenhoven, R. 2005. "Happiness in Hardship." In *Economics and Happiness: Framing the Analysis*, ed. L. Bruni and P. L. Porta, 243–266. Oxford: Oxford University Press.

7 The hegemony of finance

Recognition and the capture of desire

Henry Kelly

Culture is the way through which subjects access the world in order to obtain understandings and to access other subjectivities. It is also the semiotic framework of symbolic mediation through which the life-world is structured. This chapter will examine the impact of neo-liberal financialization upon the semiotic and sociocultural dispositive. It will be maintained that the process of financialization can be understood as one by which the financial sector of the economy was able to shift the framework of symbolic mediation to its advantage and in doing so was able to alter recognition relations in a fashion that increased its perceived valuation. The rise to hegemony of finance has had both material and symbolic impacts that affect society in different ways. In the material sphere it filters subjects towards those activities that are profitable to its interests, in addition to imposing symbolically a semiotic framework that colonizes the life-world of subjects, by seeing all cultural difference as a question of historical accident and efficiency concerns. This tendency leads to different orders of symbolic mediation being collapsed into the logical dimension of what is economically valuable.

Financialization will be viewed as a process that, by pathologizing recognition relations, is able to allow the financial sphere to impose itself upon other spheres as a superior order of standing. This causes culture to lose its richness, and this loss has an impact upon and diminishes the aesthetic and ethical life of the community and the lives of people.

The chapter will begin with a brief sketch of the historical background to financialization and its main features: chiefly the rise of the financial sector to a position of hegemony both materially and symbolically. This sketch will be followed by the introduction of the theoretical framework through which this *problematique* will be analyzed: the recognition ethics of Axel Honneth accompanied by the work of Laurent Thévenot and Luc Boltanski on orders of standing. After having characterized the manner in which financialization can be taken to pervert and capture the desire of subjects, the article will conclude with a discussion of how this state can be overcome. Insight on this matter will be taken from the Italian autonomist tradition, above all the work of Mario Tronti.

Origins of financialization

The rise to hegemony of finance is closely associated with the neo-liberal phase of global capitalism. Beginning in the 1970s state policy has followed, for the most part, neo-liberal arguments which advocate the de-regulation of the economy, including the financial sector. Such doctrines maintain that the market is more efficient when there is no state intervention, and any attempt at regulation will tend to skew the market towards special interests which may capture the state. The deregulation camp argues that removing any barriers to financial innovation and activity will assist the overall growth of the economy by allowing investment and capital to flow towards the most profitable business initiatives.

This assertion has proven to be a fallacy with respect to the global financial crisis and perhaps more significantly its aftermath, demonstrating that the true spirit of financialized capitalism is rentier behavior.

A consequence of deregulatory policy and the increased freedom of capital to circulate, along with financial innovations, has been so-called financialization, which can be seen as the separation of financial returns from labor and the material base of the economy. Such a form of economic activity is highly unstable, and has been viewed from a Keynesian-Minskian tradition as leading to inevitable crisis. From these perspectives a crisis will arise when overly optimistic expectations readjust to the fundamentals of the economy. Such crises, along with the initial process of financialization, are undesirable because, in addition to the negative welfare effects of rapid economic reversals, they bring about a lack of confidence in the financial sector which renders it difficult for it to fulfill its role.

There is a risk of state[1] intervention being captured by certain interest groups, leading to powerful lobbies being favored by the regulatory framework, new entrants being penalized and the consumers of goods and services losing out. The key point is that even so-called free markets, with little or no state interventions, can and normally do experience a similar process with the rise of hegemonic monopolies, which are able to manipulate the market and public policy in their favor. The argument that free markets and deregulation remove value judgements from the economic sphere itself stems from a meta-theoretical doctrine. Richard Peet (2011) and Greta Krippner (2011) both demonstrate the political nature of the move to a financially centered economy. More abstractly the move towards a finance-led regime may be seen to accompany a transition to a world increasingly centered on the rapid transmission of images. A material basis or at least a material condition of the possibility for the current extent of financial transactions is the rapid and global spread of Internet communications technologies.

The necessity of recognition

Axel Honneth's work on struggles for recognition can provide insight into the mechanisms whereby arguments are used to capture discursive space. In "The Struggle for Recognition" Honneth reconstructs Hegel's *Phenomenology of*

Spirit and with it a tripartite division of ethical life. Subjects are posited as only obtaining self-confidence, self-respect, and self-esteem through an intersubjective phenomenology of the self (Honneth 1996, 94). In the sphere of the family subjects are recognized and loved in a manner that fosters self-confidence, in the sphere of the state subjects are recognized as autonomous beings in a manner that fosters self-respect, and in the societal sphere what is particular about subjects, namely, their individual contributions to the abstractly defined goals of society, are recognized, allowing them to attain self-confidence (Honneth 1996, 121).

It is the societal sphere and the form of recognition that takes place within it that are of interest for the current analysis. Subjects attain self-confidence when society recognizes the value of their individual contributions to the collective goals that society pursues. It is having their contributions valued and recognized by others that allows subjects to be confident about their own value for society.

Given the abstract nature of societal goals in the modern era, an interpretative framework is required to mediate between the concrete contributions and talents of individuals and broad societal goals (Honneth 1996, 129). For Honneth a struggle for recognition is the process by which groups and individuals that believe they are misrecognized attempt to convince broader society of the value of their contributions by symbolic and material means. Honneth maintains that all economic remuneration is a consequence of the ability of groups within given professions to capture the semantic frameworks and grammars of recognition in such a way that their contributions are viewed as more socially valuable and are accordingly awarded a higher amount of material remuneration (Honneth 2001, 52–54).

The nature of recognition relations in the societal sphere and the character of the economic distribution that flows from it have become hegemonically structured. Honneth's analysis argues for a pluralization of ideas of the good and what is taken to be valuable, which would allow a broader range of lifestyles to be recognized and therefore remunerated.

Honneth's work can be supplemented by that of Thévenot and Boltanski on 'orders of standing.' They argue that there are different orders within which different attributes are acknowledged and social esteem obtained. The problem is when one order, at present that centered on economic value and success in the commercial and financial sectors, is able to impose itself vertically on the others (Boltanski and Thévenot 2006 [1991]). Adam Smith's (1983) *Lectures on Rhetoric and Belles Lettres* follows in a similar vein. In this relatively neglected text Smith explains his famous comment about the eternal desire of man to truck and barter. This desire is a consequence of man's search for social esteem by his peers, and for Smith the activity that is most highly esteemed is rhetorical ability. The ability to convince one's interlocutors is achieved in the most quantifiable and materially visible manner in the market place (Kalyvas and Katanelson 2001). The ability to convince others to one's advantage, or, returning to Honneth, the ability to manipulate the semantic and semiotic bridge in such a way as to demonstrate favorably one's contribution to the goals of society, is highly esteemed.[2] This framework tends to focus on mutual recognition between peers in a society, the contemporary economy is such that the concept of value has been pathologized by the hegemony of the interests of finance capital, leading to a capture and perversion of subjects' desire for recognition. Instead of being able to feel self-esteem due to one's peers recognizing one's contributions, subjects tend to seek recognition on capital's terms.

The capture of desire

An interesting point of departure when examining the nature of concrete recognition relations is Graham Cassano's synthesis of Veblen and Hegel in "Symbolic Exploitation and the Social Dialectic of Desire." Cassano takes recognition to have been pathologized by desire invested vertically in the desire for the Master's desire. He articulates a need to destroy traditional sovereign patterns of desire that ensnare agents. Instead, a counter-hegemonic culture of solidarity should be constructed that rejects the normative systems of status distribution associated with pecuniary capitalism: instead of seeking recognition from the dominant classes there would be self-recognition on the part of the laboring classes. For Veblen, systems of conspicuous consumption lead to the value of consumed articles being based solely on how they are regarded by the other. Desire is not something internal: it is a social force that accompanies the metaphorical internalization of the self by the other, and, following René Girard, only another's desire can produce desire. The Self engages in conspicuous consumption in order to captivate the other. He/she attempts to emulate the other's own desire (Cassano 2009). Subjects retain their good name when they accept the hegemonic perception of reality's properties that is posited by the power of the other's desire. This semiotic epistemology depends on the perception of the privileged, which is itself the outcome of struggle. For Cassano it is the commoner's desire that invests the ruling class with prestige that in turn legitimates their exploitation. By affiliating with the Master, by desiring the Master's desire, the socialized subject receives compensation for his/her symbolic labors.

In this analysis subjects obtain a form of second-order recognition that prevents them from seeking true mutual and reciprocal recognition: their fear of losing the extant recognition which they receive from conforming with the dominant in society, prevents them from attempting to overhaul structures of exploitation. This failure reduces both the self-esteem and the self-respect of agents in a subaltern position. Their selection of forms of self-realization is pathologized by their captivation by the master's desire, which in turn reduces their autonomy as agents and their self-respect.

Similar conclusions could be obtained from Peter Fleming's study of modern motivational practices in the workplace, in "Authenticity and the Cultural Politics of Work." Fleming departs with the statement that historically employment has been a time when workers forego their true values and feelings. This process led social criticism to focus on the dehumanizing effects of the corporation, which engendered a form of temporary death during working hours. Yet recently employees have been encouraged to be authentic in the workplace. For Fleming this encouragement is the pivotal reference point from which to understand motivation and productive performance. When workers bring their whole selves to the workplace, an untapped reserve of creativity is made available and the innovative abilities and ingenuity of workers can be exploited (Fleming 2009, 1–15). In the contemporary economy, value creation depends on the manipulation of images that convince consumers of a firm's integrity. This perspective is idealist rather than materialist about economic value. The standard and dominant interpretation of exchange value is marginalism, whereby the value of a good or service is equated with its price, which is given by the marginal demand for it. Fleming sees value as being the product of symbolic mediation and creative activity. The value behind a good is its concept, what it is seen as representing. The creative sectors of post-Fordist capitalist economies concentrate on producing and developing the images and interpretative structures that enable goods to be valued above their production cost. What is occurring with the discourse of authenticity is not the recognition of the full personhood of employees, but rather a technology of appropriation that draws on the social life of the commons, which capital needs in order to reproduce itself. This process can be seen by the way in which emphasis is not placed upon worker initiative with greater task discretion, but rather on authentic displays of identity normally reserved for non-work (Fleming 2009, 36–55). The issue is that of a consumerist selection of a lifestyle to adopt: the production of identity is fitted into archetypical stereotypes, with these demands to be authentic being much more likely to fall upon the lowest-ranked workers rather than on senior management. The externalities of production are often offloaded onto workers' family lives.

Autonomists see capitalists parasitically turning to non-work to shore up an accumulation process that cannot reproduce itself alone. It requires life and the life of the commons as an ontological root.

As in Cassano's work the identity or desire of subjects is captured and perverted by the dominant. Instead of simply accepting the abstract labor input of employees, an attempt is made to appropriate the whole self and blur the boundary between work and non-work. Employees rather than being recognized as valuable beings in their own right have their personalities put to use to create value for the firm.

The problems described by Cassano and Fleming are different from the misrecognition and disrespect described by Honneth but have similar outcomes in the inability of subjects to develop complete, practical relations to self. For Cassano the desire of subalterns is twisted by their wish to be recognized by those in dominant positions: they select the consumption choices (following Veblen) but also, by extension, modes of being which the master takes to be acceptable. Their desire for the master's desire impedes subjects from pursuing their own path to a meaningful form of self-realization. Subjects require recognition to be confirmed in themselves, but the structure of power relations has pathologized the process, so that subalterns (slaves) only desire the recognition of the master. This cycle can be broken by the realization that subalterns can recognize each other. For Fleming subjects are encouraged to be authentic in an attempt to extract more out of them during their time at work, and this instrumental use of the depths of personality can interfere with the internal identity of subjects.

Franco Berardi's book, *The Soul at Work*, follows similar themes. It examines the manner in which in post-Fordist forms of production, or what Berardi calls semiocapitalism, the mind, language, and creativity become the primary tools for production. In *'operaismo'* (workerism), alienation is defined as the relationship between human time and capitalist value. It is a sense of loss felt by consciousness when faced with an object in the context of capital's domination. The working class is no longer conceived as a passive object of alienation but with the ability to actively refuse, an act that is capable of building a community, starting from the estrangement of its own interests from those of capitalistic society, which Berardi sees as a necessary condition for the construction of any ultimately human relationships (Berardi 2009, 21–25). In Cassano's terms the working class needs to free itself from its desire for the capitalist's desire before it can reach true recognition relations.

Labor has to become more uniform from a physical and ergonomic point of view with the shift to computer-driven office work at the same time that it has become more differentiated and specialized with respect to the content it develops. Every hour of labor imputed by different workers has come to have highly divergent productive values. Abstract labor has been pushed to its extreme as it has lost residual materiality and concreteness. High-tech workers have come to consider labor as the most essential part of their lives, the opposite of the case of the industrial worker. Under traditional capitalism 'enterprise' meant innovation and creativity while 'labor' meant repetition of prescribed tasks. In a post-industrial society these two have become less clearly divided. At highly cognitive levels workers see their labor as an enterprise where they can spend the best part of their energy, independent from the economic and juridical conditions they experience. Enterprise becomes the center towards which desire is focused as the object of economic and psychological investments. Creative, innovative, and communicative energies are invested in the labor process.

The work of Berardi and Fleming highlights the fundamentally plastic and liquid nature of value in contemporary post-Fordist economies. Although they both focus on the labor-process side of economic relations, their conclusions are equally true for capital and finance components of the economy. The production of value is chiefly dependent on the manipulation of images and the creation of a semiotically based series of conceptions.

Drawing on the work of Honneth, the ethical value of economic contributions is dependent on how the semantic-mediating framework assesses such contributions in the context of the mediating framework. Finance, in capturing this framework, has been able to impose its conception of value.

Financialization's central element is the circulation of financial instruments that are valued far in excess of their material, concrete bases in the real economy. Derivatives act as symbols for wealth and in doing so beget more wealth, until the cycle collapses with a rapid reversal of expectations.

The hegemonic force of capital is able to capture the desire of the workers for recognition and use it for its own material and symbolic ends, materially by using the workers desire for recognition as a means to extract surplus-value and symbolically by controlling the mediating framework of the life-world.

The form of symbolic hegemony that accompanies neo-liberal financialization is more far-reaching and insidious than other, previous forms of verticalized recognition, in that it is able to take control of the very idea of the valuable. Rather than simply manipulating the semiotic framework which mediates between concrete practices and abstract ideas of the common good, it replaces any other conception of the good with its sole idea of the good, monetary value. Rather than making an appeal to how its output contributes to more pluralistic values that are held in society, money becomes the sole measure of worth. The chief success of finance capital has been to interrupt any other social valuation and to offer its material manifestations (money, commodities, institutional hier-archies) as the means through which social relations are imagined and negotiated (Haiven 2011, 103). Financialization not only perverts recognition by directing it vertically towards a Master-like Totality, rather than allowing mutual recogni-tion among peers, it also perverts the whole process by fetishizing the object, money, which comes to replace the face of the Other and concrete social inter-action. In the terms of De Angelis, "capital seeks not merely to accumulate sur-plus value but to impose economic value as the singular hegemonic measure of all social theory" (De Angelis 2007). Ethical life along with deeper aesthetic values are lost through the search for recognition and the creation of the prac-tical relation to self of self-esteem and one's contribution to the collective good in terms of monetary output. In this sense finance has captured recognition to such an extent as to replace the whole mechanism of interpersonal recognition with recognition by a Totality given to those with money.

Materially, finance's dominance exerts a twofold effect on the economy, directing productive energies away from activities that have a use- or life-value (Noonan 2011) to those that aid the endless accumulation of capital. This is done by shifting the desire of workers towards the sectors that finance holds to be important and more directly through the banking system by financing only certain types of enterprise (Peet 2011).

The potential for autonomy and peer recognition

The solution to this social and economic malaise that autonomists propose is the refusal of work, where the multitude withdraws from salaried work and denies its constructed subjectivity as a proletariat (Berardi 2009, 74–107).

Mario Tronti's essay the "Strategy of Refusal" argues for a Copernican inversion (Eden 2012) in the manner in which relations between capital and labor are viewed. Rather than departing from the primacy of capital, as orthodox Marxist analyses have done, Tronti maintains that it is labor and the worker who bring capital into being. While the capitalist is the 'employer' (*datore di lavoro*), the worker is the 'employer capital' (*datore di capitale*). Workers bring capital into being not only by selling their labor but also by bringing about the class relation.

This perspective leads to economic organization being seen as dependent upon the compliance of the workers. Capital is able to maintain its position of dominance only through the use of institutionalized political power and, perhaps more significantly for the post-Fordist phase of capitalism, by affecting the desire of workers. As the previous section on recognition relations outlines, subjects require recognition in the spheres of the family, the state, and society in order to develop fully practical relations to self. Honneth's reconstruction of the societal sphere focuses upon the relation of self-esteem, where what is particular about each individual, his or her contribution to the collective goals of society, is recognized. The vague and abstract nature of these goals in modern societies makes necessary a mediating framework between concrete practices, talents, and employment in a given sector and the general goals.

Capital, and in particular, finance capital, has been able to capture the mediating framework. This phenomenon leads to those skills and professions that best serve the interests of financial capital becoming more highly valued and obtaining a correspondingly higher level of remuneration. This can be seen in the relative decline and de-professionalization of much of the industrial sector, at least in the Western world, and a shift towards financial employment.

As workers desire recognition in order to achieve self-esteem and to feel valuable to society, they are drawn towards those sectors of the economy that are most highly esteemed. While there remains to some extent a civically orientated element in the nature of societal recognition, this has decreased with the increasing concentration and growing impact of the mass media. A crucial component of imposing a conception of the valuable is the control of the means of symbolic mediation. Subjects require recognition, but if one interest in a society is able to reach a position of hegemony the recognition relations become pathologized. Instead of obtaining recognition for their contribution to society, subjects become recognized for their contributions to the interests of finance capital. Orders of standing, distinct communities of value lose their horizontal and pluralist configuration. Subjects' desire for recognition becomes captured by the Master (capital), and they are dependent on its goodwill for their well-being.

This development has both material and symbolic effects. In the material sphere it leads to economic activity being shifted towards particular sectors, namely, those where surplus-value can be best extracted by the hegemonic interest and away from others. In the case of finance capital this has been economically damaging because its activities are highly unstable and can exert a direct impact on other production through the transmission mechanism of the banking sector. Symbolically the capture of the framework of symbolic mediation serves to reduce the richness of the life-world: instead of a plurality of diverse interpretations of what is valuable in the civic, ethical, and aesthetic fields, a narrow focus on economic value prevails. This can lead to the dominance of instrumental reasoning accompanied somewhat paradoxically by the absence of any meaningful *telos*.

If capital is taken to perform the role of Master in pathologized recognition, it follows that labor fulfills the role of Slave. Yet the Master is dependent upon the Slave, as his/her position is only relational. This echoes Tronti's depiction: capital is dependent upon labor, but labor is not dependent upon capital. This is because labor has the possibility of extricating its invested desire from the recognition relation with capital and attaining peer recognition in the commons. On the other hand, the analogous option does not appear open to capital, although financialization has been viewed by some (Teixeira and Rotta 2012) as an attempt by capital to render itself autonomous from labor and material production. This effort is accompanied by an increasing focus upon the immaterial economy, an economic reality governed by the creation and manipulation of images rather than the production of tangible goods and services. Autonomist writers have contextualized this phenomenon as a response by capital to the increasing mobilization and organization of workers in the initial post-war period. Capitalists started to dismantle the spaces that allowed workers to become aware of their own subjectivity and replace them with an individualized, liquid economy. Although capitalists have been somewhat successful in this goal, the shift to immaterial production is accompanied by heightened instability. The exchange value of material goods has a tangible base in the cost of the raw inputs and the labor time required to produce them. In the case of immaterial goods and services, the most extreme example of which is finance and financial derivatives, there is no tangible basis for price formation. This leads to highly volatile economic situations as the price of goods and services comes to depend entirely upon expectations. Financial assets ultimately depend upon tangibles, which in turn depend on labor both for production and consumption.[3]

Finance's rise to hegemony is clearly linked to an attempt by capital to extricate itself from being entwined with labor. This effort is clearly contradictory, as the crisis has shown, yet this has not eliminated the fiction. As Haiven writes, "crises are the result of the necessary failure of capital's self-representation in price, its chronic inability to accurately assign value to social goods and cooperation" (Haiven 2011, 112). The profits made by financial institutions even following the global financial crisis are much larger than those made in industry, agriculture, or other services. After the crisis, finance has come to depend on being bailed out through the tax system, and the intervention of government as an intermediary has allowed the crisis and separation from productive work to be overcome. Governments instead transfer the fruits of workers' labors to the financial sector in the form of state aid. This at least formally is dependent upon the democratic consent of the governed. They must then view finance as being of such importance to the economy that it is worth sacrificing all of production for its well-being. This social superiority which the financial sector has been assigned must according to Thénevot and Boltanski be justified by a perceived special contribution to the social good, but as the effects of the global financial crisis and recession accelerate and worsen this becomes increasingly hard to justify. The financial sector, rather than making an especially valuable contribution to society and the economy, is, through bank bailouts and the austerity packages necessary to allow the banks to survive, draining the material well-being from the economy. This provides an excellent opportunity for society to dis-invest both its income and its desire from seeking hegemonic recognition from the Totality and to realize that the solution to current problems, both in the economy but more fundamentally in remedying anomie and social disintegration, lies in a freeing of desire and imagination. Peer recognition in the commons presents the opportunity to escape from a colonized life-world and to achieve a form of ethical life in one's communities. An empirical example of this logic is the spread of time banks and community currencies, which seek to replace the dichotomous and anonymous nature of economic activity into production and consumption for accumulation with the circulation of labor in communities. These schemes, which for the most part remain rudimentary and in their infancy, remove money from the economic transaction and symbolically free the participants from the colonizing logic of capital. They free economic activity and production from the necessity of having to obtain capital apart from the tools needed for the work to be done, and in doing so help to elucidate the ability of labor to free itself from capital.

Notes

1 I am using 'state' loosely; this applies equally to inter-state bodies on a regional or global level.
2 It is not the contribution one makes through commerce that is esteemed by Smith, but on a metalevel, the ability to convince others of the value of that contribution.
3 In the case of real estate, the value of the existing house stock only depends on people being able to afford it, or at least have a credit line.

References

Berardi, Franco. 2009. *The Soul at Work: From Alienation to Autonomy.* Los Angeles: Semiotext(e).
Boltanski, Luc, and Laurent Thévenot. 2006. *On Justification: Economies of Worth*, trans. Catherine Porter. Oxford: Princeton University Press.

Cassano, Graham 2009. "Symbolic Exploitation and the Social Dialectic of Desire." *Critical Sociology* 35(3): 379–393.

De Angelis, Massimo. 2007. *The Beginning of History: Value Struggles and Global Capitalism.* London: Pluto.

Eden, David. 2012. *Autonomy: Capitalism, Class and Politics.* Farnham: Ashgate.

Fleming, Peter. 2009. *Authenticity and the Cultural Politics of Work: New Forms of Informal Control.* Oxford: Oxford University Press.

Haiven, Max. 2010. "The Financial Crisis as a Crisis of Imagination." *Cultural Logic*, pp. 1–23.

Haiven, Max. 2011. "Finance as Capital's Imagination." *Social Text* 29(3): 93–124.

Honneth, Axel. 1996. *The Struggle for Recognition: the Moral Grammar of Social Conflicts.* Cambridge: Polity.

Honneth, Axel. 2001. "Recognition or Redistribution? Changing Perspectives on the Moral Order of Society." *Theory, Culture & Society*, 18(2–3): 43–55.

Honneth, Axel. 2012. *The I in We: Studies in the Theory of Recognition.* Cambridge: Polity.

Kalyvas, Andreas, and Katznelson, Ira. 2001. "The Rhetoric of the Market: Adam Smith on Recognition, Speech and Exchange." *Review of Politics*, 63(3): 549–579.

Krippner, Greta R. 2011. *Capitalising on Crisis: The Political Origins of the Rise of Finance.* London: Harvard University Press.

Noonan, Jeff. 2011. "Use Value, Life Value, and the Future of Socialism." *Rethinking Marxism* 23(1): 117–134

Peet, Richard. 2011. "Inequality, Crisis and Austerity in Finance Capitalism." *Cambridge Journal of Regions, Economy and Society* 4: 383–399.

Ricœur, Paul. 2007. *The Course of Recognition.* London: Harvard University Press.

Smith, Adam. 1983. *Lectures on Rhetoric and Belles Lettres.* Oxford: Clarendon.

Teixeira, Rodrigo Alves, and Tomas Nielsen Rotta. 2012. "Valueless Knowledge-Commodities and Financialization: Productive and Financial Dimensions of Capital Autonomization." *Review of Radical Political Economics* 44(4): 448–467.

Tronti, Mario. 1971. *Operai e capitale.* Turin: Einaudi.

8 Deep capture

The hidden role of rationalizations, psychology, and corporate law, and what philosophy can do about it

Marcin Kilanowski

What do we owe to constructivism? It does allow us to see that we are part of certain relations, that the construed descriptions of the world in which we are involved are to serve the interests of particular groups privileged over others, and that the categories of truth, rationality, or universality are often utilized in order to discipline others and keep some mouths shut. The ranks of constructivists include Richard Rorty (hopefully he would not deem such a label an offense). In his works on the primacy of democracy over philosophy, Rorty suggests that we depart from philosophy as the search for truth and turn toward democracy and freedom (Rorty 1991b). He does not state, however, or he does so not explicitly enough, that in a democracy, it is no longer truth that wins, but the stronger or more numerous opinion. Truth does not win, for in the light of the failure of centuries past, the pursuit of truth is being suspended. There are no longer any standards of rationality that can be adopted while choosing between better or worse attitudes, for there is no reference point with respect to which we could proceed with such an assessment. What we are left with, then, are different narratives, which compete with each other. But still the problem is that such a change does not lead to freedom and solidarity, as Rorty would wish.

Rorty chooses democracy over philosophy, for he believes that it is a more certain path toward solidarity, understanding, and communication between cultures and ourselves. Democracy also means an environment more suitable for sensitivity toward the other, as well as sentimental education instead of education based on principles, rules, and laws (Rorty 1993). The former, Rorty claims, allows the protection of another human being and his or her needs to a greater extent than existing regulations concerning human rights based on universal values and truths. Presenting such a vision of a path toward solidarity, he does not discern, however, a number of other elements: the power game, which is constantly in the making, and which often wins out, and the rationalizations that each of the parties uses in a more or less conscious way, though, most of the time, without being aware of it at all. One can have the impression that Rorty's philosophy follows Platonism much more than he himself acknowledges. According to this, if we become aware of the fact that we have hurt, we shall hurt no more; if we understand that we have excluded, we shall abandon our old ways, get to know each other better, and begin to forge the bonds of solidarity. In other words, once we come to know something, we shall start acting in accordance with it. But such a line of thinking does not acknowledge all the other processes that occur at that time and that may lead us, often without our being aware, into a wholly different direction.

In this chapter, what I strive to do is prove, with the use of specific examples, that even though the power game and rationalizations do not refer to the category or value of truth (which would undoubtedly please Rorty), they do refer to freedom and profit. However, if the game and rationalizations do indeed facilitate them, it is the case only with respect to some people, while others are still faced with enslavement and exploitation. This issue shall also be touched upon. It will become clear that it is not which categories we choose as our reference points, but how we use them; however, the very fact of using them is hardly acknowledged. We are not aware of this, for we live our lives following numerous rationalizations, indicating and proving that our categories, values, or beliefs lead us in this or that direction and that this is simply the way it has to be.

The starting point for further deliberations concerns the environmental disaster that happened at the Deepwater Horizon platform in the Gulf of Mexico in 2010, and which was caused by the actions of British Petroleum (BP), a company basing its code of conduct on values such as freedom and profit.[1] Though not the only example, this will make it clear that a change of the reference point, i.e., one category or one value in the place of another, does not diminish existing suffering, exploitation, and coercion. Some values or categories are simply replaced by others, which proves that it does not matter which values or categories these are, just as it does not matter whether we justify them by referring to the universal, or to the local, the temporary, the communal, as Rorty preaches. The outcome can be the same, regardless of which categories or values we rely on. No greater solidarity is to be achieved, solidarity which was Rorty's wish. The anticipated effects are not to occur. The only thing that is to change is the group of influence, i.e., some are to replace others, and corporate law legitimizes such a change by means of the rationalizations that it follows and reproduces.

The drive for profit: the case of BP

We all care about the environment. While we segregate trash, politicians win Nobel Peace Prizes for green policies, and big businesses – in this case, BP – constantly reassure us that they are environmentally conscious and that they create "responsible operations at every BP operation."[2] However, this would be too simplistic a description. Unfortunately, caring for the environment has not been BP's priority for years, its peak being perhaps 2010, when we witnessed the oil spill in the Gulf of Mexico. During all the years of the company's operations, there have been many such incidents on their drilling fields, and the environmental concerns raised by the employees changed little in the company's conduct. And all that we happen to know about the incidents is based on articles and independent investigations, their contents being more than alarming: apparently, on BP's premises, the fact that rusty pipelines, tanks with cracks, and old safety cups were constantly in use was nothing out of the ordinary.[3]

Why did BP not react? What we have found out is that those who raised these concerns, like Mr. Sneed, who was among the authors of critical reports,[4] were questioned by the company, "scolded by supervisors," and threatened with dismissal. The company reported 99% compliance with safety regulations when, in fact, there was 80% non-compliance. But, apparently, keeping up appearances was most important. The company still pledged good intentions and repeated slogans about responsibility for the environment, and even after the BP Deepwater Horizon oil spill, it was named "runner-up for Openness and Honesty."[5] How was that possible? Mostly due to the drive for profit: profit that, as corporate law preached, justifies corporate actions and should be the only concern of corporations (Friedman 1962, 133). And those in charge of corporations, as the corporate law school book says, should maximize the profit. Following this line of argument, it is up to corporations to decide which course of action is appropriate: it is not to be decided by, for instance, the courts, which do not have ample knowledge, as was stated in the case *Shlensky v. Wrigley.*[6]

Rationalizations, dispositions, and blame

Most of the time, corporate law is conceived in terms of protecting shareholders. Corporate lawyers, CEOs, and board directors – like those of BP – constantly try to reassure us that this is the only constituency they are obliged to serve. But another perspective is clear here, and this is a perspective broadly discussed in academia and much present behind the majority of business transactions. The issue at stake is what to do with legal regulations that still constrain us from realizing any business idea that comes to mind. In accordance with such a perspective, no one cares about the shareholders here: it is all about profit, and the case of *Kamin v. American Express* clearly shows whose profit it is.[7] What is at stake most of the time, under the cover of protecting shareholders, is the profit of those running the companies. However, apart from generating profit as such, corporations also produce the rationalization according to which the drive for profit is good because it is done for the benefit of shareholders, which in actual fact is not necessarily the case.

One might say the story of protecting shareholders is similar to the story of the need for unconstrained individual activity. Both were often used as smokescreens – rationalizations – backed with reference to values such as profit and freedom. And references to both profit and freedom often appeared and still appear together, as in the case of corporate law with, for example, its duty-of-care test, wherein the 'reasonableness' of a business decision is measured in the light of one's freedom to act and the goal he or she should have in mind, which is maximizing the profit.[8] Reference to profit and freedom has also helped construct smokescreens for everything that has seemed incongruous to the one right world-view. Our Western culture, imbued with rationalistic philosophy, is abundant in stories of various rationalizations being generated, helping to justify the oppression of infidels, heretics, slaves, criminals, women, the unemployed, or the homeless.[9] For centuries, we have heard that 'they were born to be like that' – naturally undeveloped, insane, or just lazy – and that they have deserved their place in society. The worst part is that those who live by these rationalizations are 'good, ordinary people' responding to market stimuli, an interpretation of the Bible, made up 'scientific data,' or, as Max Weber has pointed out, the Protestant concept of success, according to which he who works will be rewarded.[10] This is why Hannah Arendt talks about "the banality of evil," which does not just come and go but approaches slowly and is reproduced in the course of various actions. This is what social psychology points to as well.

According to social psychology, reproduction appears thanks to the interaction between situations of which we are a part and our dispositions of which we are not conscious.[11] Sometimes a little rationalization is enough to exploit the disposition of a teacher or a mechanic to continue administering electric shocks, as in the Milgram experiment.[12] This has been the power of all the regimes of the twentieth century: to rationalize inequality, i.e., why some are at the bottom while others are on the top, according to people's dispositions. But ideologies have not come to an end. The drive for profit, in the name of the wealth of shareholders and no matter at what cost, is greater than ever (see Chen and Hanson 2004). Our times are dominated by the ideology of wealth maximization, but, in fact, it produces wealth only for some and rationalization for everybody.

We are 'good people' who do not see that we are doing wrong by pressing one button of Milgram's electric shock box after another. What guides us is our disposition to rationalize and comply, to follow easy explanations of causal relations and simplistic understandings of various situations, which are pushing us in a direction of which we are often not aware. If we come to see that the outcome of our actions is something that we did not quite expect, we blame the situation, not recognizing that it would not have had such a significant effect if we had seen our own role in the whole process – in allowing the dispositions to control us, in creating and following various rationalizations. As soon as we start rationalizing – building simplistic and coherent explanations and taking things for granted – we are less and less able to see the other forces that guide us: our implicit motives, attributions, presumptions, and images of the world that have replaced the real world of other human beings.

Fighting for freedom

Coming back to the case at issue, it can be said that, in light of the above, corporations' leaders, managers, and directors are not bad people; they are 'good people too.' They often say, as BP does now, that it was the rig's owner and operator, Transocean, that was to blame, or it was the fault of the employees "not following BP's own procedure," taking "shortcuts and risks."[13] If these employees had just worked better, or if they had just paid more attention, the oil spill would not have happened. CEOs rationalize and blame the situation on others, not seeing that it is their own disposition that blinds them to their own role in the way catastrophic events unfolded, and this blindness is caused by the drive for profit and "meeting performance targets" to present "shiny statistics" – sometimes by making them up – to keep up with competitors, because this is what the 'free market requires' and what corporate law supports by regulations.[14]

What is crucial in this context is the free market, as well as individual freedom within its borders. They cannot be questioned and must be protected from critics, the enemy it is necessary to combat. There is a long tradition of corporate interests taking precedence in such cases. The way was prepared long ago and can be exemplified by Louis Powell's (the future Supreme Court Judge) "Confidential Memorandum," calling to "Fight Back" when the way corporations function is questioned. According to his report, everyone is to play a role in this battle: the American Chamber of Commerce, lobbyists, lawyers, academics, textbooks, media, and politicians. As corporations were told, "there should be no hesitation in attacking the Naders, the Marcuses and others who openly seek destruction of the system ... nor should there be reluctance to penalize politically those who oppose it."[15] All the resources are supposed to be used to fight for and rationalize the interests of corporations by telling the story of a free America, in which "the contraction and denial of economic freedom is followed inevitably by governmental restrictions on other cherished rights" (Powell 1972, 7). There was just one perspective that was supposed to survive, only one that people should believe. This was that profit is what we should cherish and that consumption is what we should focus on, without being aware of the consequences it has on our lives and the environment. Furthermore, what was also always at stake was our individual freedom.

As we can observe on the basis of Powell's example, the goal of corporations was to fight criticism coming from society, against the attempts of the government to regulate business, against the threat of losing profits – all of that in the name of preserving the free market and individual freedom of choice, of one right vision of the economy, of human activity and what counts as a good life – and it could be said that the goal was achieved with the victory of the free market over the centrally planned one. But was it really a victory? Is corporate capitalism different from a centralized communist economy? If we go down Hayek's list of what leads to serfdom, we see that the criteria are also fulfilled in the way the corporate world functions (Hayek 2004), thanks to the present legal rules (in the USA this is primarily the Delaware law). In communism, everything belonged to everybody but was governed in a centralized way. Similarly, today's corporations, which belong to every shareholder, are governed in a centralized manner, whereby the majority shareholder can have a say in the functioning of the corporation, although most of the time it is the directors' duty to balance the different interests of shareholders.[16] Of course, the argument goes that there is a difference, because being a shareholder is a voluntary activity, and everyone can still sell his assets. But can we really leave the corporate world? We will always feel the consequences that the BP profit-maximization philosophy brought upon us – the polluted environment – whether we are shareholders or not. The question is: is this the 'free market' and the free world that we wanted?

The disposition – can we change it?

The present form of the market is praised because "an organization's internal governance affects its performance" and this leads to "success" (Allen and Kraakman 2003, 3). But now it is obvious whose success this is. Milton Friedman's analysis, according to which the free market is governed by an 'invisible hand,' which will create more wealth for everybody, has not materialized.[17] The divisions in economic standing are growing rapidly, and ecological disasters happen more and more often. But we still follow what he said, and it does not matter which political leaning we are inclined towards. Friedman is praised by those previously in government (Bush) and by those at present (Summers). He is also praised in academic works, for "facilitating individual efforts to create wealth is wise public policy," even though their authors admit that wealth "is not always deployed to advance total human welfare" (Allen and Kraakman, 2), though this is not the business of corporations.

And where are we now? We behave as if we were taking part in Milgram's experiment and we 'shock' people at home and abroad, ourselves, our children, and future generations by acting harmfully without thinking about the consequences of our actions, but following rationalizations about the 'drive for profit' and unconstrained individual freedom. We ruin other people's personal and social lives, destroy possible relations of trust and friendship, and devastate families, when, in the name of profit, they are evicted from their homes because they are not able to pay the mortgage.[18] We also ruin both their and our own health by allowing environmental pollution, upheld by the activities of corporations such as BP. Of course, the standard answer would be that people have a choice, that they are free. Those people could just work harder and their lives could be different. They could pay more attention at work and secure their position, like Mrs. Pritchard in *Francis v. United Jersey Bank*.[19] They are the ones to blame if something goes wrong, just as they are responsible for their own lives. But by giving such an answer, we will continue to 'shock' them as well as ourselves, because what we do to others sooner or later has consequences for us.

One cannot be satisfied with this answer when thinking critically. The answer to the question why these people were not able to direct their lives differently will point to their disposition. They blamed the situation, instead of blaming themselves or others who created the conditions for a future crisis, exploitation, or harm done to other people. And we sometimes start realizing the processes of which we are a part and which we shape by our action or inaction. However, most of the time it is after and not before the harm is done. Can we change that? We can propose reforms in the legal system. In the case of the oil drilling industry, we can propose excessive liability caps for energy exploration activities, increase the availability of non-economic damages, and levy heavy new energy taxes, but the industry itself is resistant to all of these propositions. As we can read in a US Chamber of Commerce letter, "Congress should resist the rush to act on legislation" because that will be too much of a burden on corporations and their profits. Companies would "be unable to afford insurance to cover the liability risk." Moreover, awarding damages is "entirely subjective," and courts would not be able to evaluate cases in the correct way.[20] In short, the Chamber believes that the best thing is to leave corporations alone. By that, it follows what Powell has taught: oppose any governmental restrictions and regulations, because what matters is maximizing profit and unconstrained freedom to act.

It is not only the Chamber of Commerce that has reacted to the attempts to regulate. In Louisiana alone there were "72 oil and gas lobbyists, 25 chemical industry lobbyists and 43 lobbyists for the chamber of commerce and business groups."[21] All of them worked through seven environmental lobbyists, two of whom also lobbied for Chevron. This is Powell's strategy in action. Moreover, regulations are also opposed by 'political contributions.' Donations often run into the millions and keep politicians' critical thinking switched off.[22] Even Nature Conservancy, a non-profit group, accepted millions in cash and was on the BP International Leadership Council. Conservation International also received millions.[23]

We can say that such contributions are not appropriate, and CEOs will admit that too, when faced with the data. As in the case of BP, they will point to the 2002 "policy to stop making corporate donations anywhere in the world" that they have implemented after years of making donations.[24] But it did not stop after 2002. Who was responsible for that? Again, it is an inadequately trained employee who was not prepared for the job who is to blame. However, corporations and their directors are acting appropriately, and if someone in the corporation acts negligently, the corporation should not be the one to blame. They would have to 'neglect cavalierly' to be held responsible, according to *Graham v. Allis-Chalmers Manufacturing Co.*[25] They would have to ignore "either willfully or through inattention obvious danger signs of employee wrongdoing," but they will certainly say that they did not know.[26] Ultimately, we can speak about the 'deep capture' of attempts to regulate and the 'deep capture' of knowledge of those independent NGOs that cooperated with BP and did not prevent the oil spill from happening again. Striving for profit was preserved through various acts and rationalizations. Individual choice, free of governmental encroachment, was protected. The blame was passed to the guilty ones as before, to the employees, to the situation, or to the lack of knowledge.

The way out – critical education?

Executives continue to prosper. After all, the BP executives were not held accountable for the oil spills in the Gulf of Mexico, California, and Texas, and some were promoted despite these accidents. But the government is trying. The National Oil Commission has pointed out systematic failures across the whole industry. Senator Bob Graham said that after Deepwater Horizon there is a chance to overcome the "ideological preference for less government."[27] But even if the government succeeds in one case, the problem prevails. The problem of the reproduction of a "culture of coziness," the problem of agencies such as the Minerals Management Service being "friendly with those it regulated," will still remain (Rousseau 2012; Dewey 1991a; Popper 1945). Such problems can easily appear in different sectors.

One can say that the problem is our naïve thinking about ourselves that causes us to be dispositional, which, as some believe, is totally rational. It limits our capacity to see what causes our actions and what consequences they have. That could change, or so we are told, if our education focused on critical thinking instead of teaching how to memorize and repeat. From Rousseau to Popper and Dewey, we see constant criticism of the old educational system.[28] Such a system leaves us unprepared when old 'truths' can no longer be applied, and if applied, it, in effect, creates harm and the loss of opportunities. The unquestioned position of such 'truths' not only in law, economics, and social and political sciences, but also in natural sciences, shapes our approach toward the world, which is constantly changing. We face new problems and are not able to deal with them (Arendt 1968; Berlin 1958; Unger 2002; Rorty 1994). We follow old patterns of thinking supported by rationalizations, and we try to apply well-memorized laws of necessity instead of the law of shifting considerations.

The solution lies in education. We need to learn that knowledge is fallible and that it should be revised when the circumstances change. In other words, we should be open toward revision of our knowledge and the 'truths' we follow. We should not be taught that something is good or evil, because we often have a hard time in describing what is good or evil, when we are heroes and when we are monsters. Instead, we should teach how to question and how to be critical toward what we see and what we have at our disposal. We should teach how to be independent in thinking, remembering that we are entangled in various relations that form us, just as we form them. Such an education should be an ongoing endeavor that does not stop within the school walls but continues in our daily life. All of this will help us to stop repeating and reproducing rationalizations that serve to preserve the status quo. Moreover, criticism and openness, as Berlin, Arendt, Unger, and Rorty believe, may help to awake our imagination to the issue of how to change the present conditions for the better (Rorty 1989, 8). It may help to wake up our energy and push toward engaging in the public discourse and becoming responsible for it. This can lead to the establishment of forms of cooperation, keeping in mind that our well-being is linked with the well-being of others.

Rorty, however, goes further and says that in order for that to happen, we have to stop searching for the absolute truth, ultimate knowledge, and one model of rationality, because we have not found them despite our long search, and it seems pointless to continue.[29] We should replace our desire to reach such a final truth and certainty and redesign our educational system in a way that is not constructed around such categories. He believes that this is a pre-condition for the growth of solidarity, compassion, and responsibility. But, as we were able to see on the basis of the BP case, though not only this case, a change of the reference point did not change behavior. Instead of fighting for the truth, as many entities did in the past, BP and other corporations fight for profit and freedom. Moreover, they are often aware of the localized nature of their approach, proving that it does not matter whether we justify our choices by referring to something absolute and universal, or by referring to group beliefs or interests, as in the case of shareholders' interests, which they feel obliged to protect. Moving from universalism to constructivism does not change much: only those who are in power change. Some groups replace others, but the outcome is the same. Constructivism does not free us from the politics of the use of power and does not necessarily lead to dialog and solidarity.

To sum up: toward honesty

We need education and a society that supports the free exchange of ideas, one in which no single idea would be considered as final and no knowledge would be fixed. Thanks to such education, we could start building a society that could respond to coming disasters, a society driven not only by financial profit but also by responsibility for the well-being of its members, one which would not accept that progress requires us to drill and the air or water to smell of oil. In such a society, thanks to the education based on critical thinking, we could better prevent future 'deep captures' and the next Deepwater Horizon oil spill.

But one might ask whether that is indeed possible. Can education broaden our horizons, our consciousness, and free us from rationalizations, as well as from our dispositions? Answering in the affirmative would mean that we could free ourselves from the power game, from the structures of power, from those that try to make their interest ours, by creating rationalizations for everyone, but which profit only the few. We could finally feel responsible for our own lives and the lives of others, and such responsibility would not be imposed on us through legal or social regulations, but would be shaped by real relations that connect us all, through which we can see that we start and end in others, just as they start and end in us (Rorty 1991a, 197). A more in-depth answer to the question of education posed above should be shaped by everyday action, not being afraid of new challenges; however, one issue is already clear: blaming 'truth' or the search for truth and praising con-structivism, by teaching us about our ethnocentrism, as Rorty does, is not going to facilitate dialog, peace, and solidarity (Kilanowski 2017). Getting rid of the concept of truth and rationalizations that were created by reference to that concept is not going to stop the development of new rationalizations, which can be created by reference to such categories as freedom or profit, as presented in this chapter.

This analysis allows us to see that it does not matter whether we refer to the category of truth, freedom, or profit. What matters is how we use such concepts. Accusing 'truth' of not allowing us to reach for more freedom or profit, or, vice versa, blaming the search for freedom or profit as a threat to discovering the truth, is missing the point that, whatever we do, it does not matter if we appeal to these or those concepts or values, if they are absolute and universal, or if they are developed through history. What matters is how we use them, which shows that we are the ones who decide what to do and not to do with them. Valuing truth, freedom, or profit and searching for them is not synonymous with creating any significant danger, as long as we are humble and we understand that we make mistakes.[30] There is a difference between believing in one objective truth, searching for it, and being certain that one knows it and believing that truth should not be questioned anymore.[31]

Acknowledging that we make mistakes seems to be the most difficult part. It seems that most of the time we prefer our rationalizations to the difficulties that arise during the process of thinking critically. And even if sometimes we recognize that what we do is not right, we do not want to be honest with ourselves, because on the flip side of being honest and trying things on our own lies the possibility of making gains and following these or those rationalizations in order to support our decisions. If we could become honest with ourselves, we would see that there is no truth, freedom, or profit in the long run, and sometimes not even in the short run, if we exploit or harm others, if we "shock" them as in Milgram's experiment. By doing that to others, we do it to ourselves, although we have a hard time seeing it, even now five years after the BP oil spill, when we await another ecological disaster in the Chukchi Sea.

Notes

1 The Deepwater Horizon oil spill, also called the BP oil spill or the Gulf of Mexico oil spill, was an oil spill in the Gulf of Mexico that took place for three months in 2010. It was the largest accidental marine oil spill in the history of the petroleum industry. The spill resulted from an explosion at the Deepwater Horizon rig. The explosion killed eleven men working on the platform and injured seventeen others. After three months, the leak was stopped, but only after it had released 780,000 m^3 of crude oil into the water.

2 Since 2007 BP has worked to implement an operating safety system to create "responsible operations at every BP operation," as stated by Toby Odone, a company spokesman. (Lustgarten and Knutson 2010).

3 Lustgarten and Knutson say: "A 2001 report noted that BP had neglected key equipment needed for an emergency shutdown, including safety shutoff valves and

gas and fire detectors similar to those that could have helped prevent the fire and explosion on the Deepwater Horizon rig in the gulf."

4 Lustgarten and Knutson say: "Instead of receiving compliments for his prudence, Sneed – who had also complained that week that pipeline inspectors were faking their reports – was scolded by his supervisor, who hadn't inspected the crack but believed it was superficial, according to a report from BP's internal employer arbitrators."

5 In her article, Natalya Sverjensky (2010) says: "even as recently as May 2010, determined long before the Deepwater rig exploded, BP was named runner-up for the 'Openness and Honesty' reporting category at the Corporate Register's 2010 CR Reporting Awards."

6 *Shlensky v. Wrigley*, 237 NE 2d 776 (Ill. App. 1968), is a case in which the Court accepted the discretion of the board to determine how to balance the interests of stakeholders. It represents a shift away from the idea that corporations should only pursue shareholder value. In *Shlensky v. Wrigley* a challenge was brought by shareholders against the director's decision. The shareholders questioned the decision of the Chicago Cubs' president, who refused to install field lights for night games at Wrigley Field. The president argued that it was good for residents in the surrounding neighborhood not to be disturbed at night and that the late-night games would disturb those who wanted to sleep. This meant that night games could not be organized and that there would be lower profits for shareholders. In its ruling, the Court affirmed the director's decision. The president was not liable for failing to maximize returns to shareholders. The decision of the president was not contrary to the best interests of the corporation and the shareholders because there was no fraud, illegality, or conflict of interest in making that decision. The court followed the argumentation from the case *Davis v. Louisville Gas and Electronic Co.*, 16 Del. 157 (1928), which stated that the directors are elected to make decisions and unless there is sign of fraud, the decision should be accepted as final, and that the judgment of the directors of the corporation should be considered as formed in good faith, meaning that the decisions that they make should be assumed to be for the benefit of the corporation.

7 *Kamin v. American Express*, 383 N.Y.S.2d 807 (1976), is a case in which Howard Kamin and a minority shareholder filed a shareholder derivative suit against American Express and its officers after allegedly they negligently issued a dividend to be paid out to stockholders in the form of shares of Donaldson, Lufkin, and Jenrette, Inc. (DLJ). They argued that the dividends were a waste of corporate assets in that the stocks of DLJ could have been sold on the open market, saving American Express about $8 million in taxes. The court decided that it would not interfere with the decision of a company's directors unless there was evidence of fraud or dishonest practice. For the court, the suit was only based on a disagreement with the company's business decisions. The court held that issues of policy and business management were better left to the judgement of corporate management.

8 Under United States corporate and business association law (Delaware law and Revised Model Business Corporation Act), the duty of care is part of the fiduciary duty of directors toward the corporation. The director is obliged to act in accordance with good business judgment and to use ordinary care and prudence when making business decisions – the care an ordinary person would use under similar circumstances. Other aspects of fiduciary duty are duty of loyalty and duty of good faith. Directors' decisions are typically protected under the business judgment rule, so long as they do not breach their duties or the decision does not lead to a loss. If such a breach occurs, the director will not be protected under the business judgment rule, and he or she will be required to show the entire fairness of the transaction.

9 Not only do they produce rational arguments, but also rationalizations, and these are two quite different things.

10 Isaiah Berlin points to "good ordinary people" who are responsible for the slaughter of individuals, and to the simple ideas in which they believed (Berlin 1958, 28). As an example of 'made-up scientific data' driven by politics and not by serious scientific inquiry, one might consider mass sterilization programs in Nazi Germany. "Good ordinary people" also supported euthanasia ('mercy killings') as a program implemented to kill German infants and children regarded as a burden on national resources, and later applied to persons who were 'unproductive.' Between 1939 and 1945 a total of 200,000 people were killed with the support of pediatricians, psychiatrists, family doctors, and nurses, with a body of 'scientific' literature supporting such actions. For more on the subject, see Friedlander 1995, Kevels 1985, and Michalczyk 1994. Regarding the analysis of the Protestant conception of success, see Weber 2010.

11 For more on the expression and concept of 'the banality of evil,' see Arendt 2003. In her book, Arendt explains that Eichmann was neither a fanatic nor a madman, but an average human. He was following orders and was more concerned with his own interests and personal advancement than with ideology. She does not question that he was anti-Semitic, although that was less important than his stupidity.

12 The Milgram experiment was conducted by Stanley Milgram, a professor of psychology from Yale University. In that experiment Milgram tested obedience to an authority figure who asked subjects to act against their personal conscience. Milgram first described his research in an article in the *Journal of Abnormal and Social Psychology* and later in 1974 in his book *Obedience to Authority: An Experimental View* (Milgram 1974).

13 In "Safety and Cost Drives Clashed as CEO Hayward Remade BP," Tony Hayward (BP CEO) insists that BP has turned a page on safety. BP's spokesman Andrew Gowers has also said, "BP's absolute No. 1 priority is safe and reliable operations." However, some think that the cost-drive affects safety. As Ross Macfarlane, a former BP health and safety manager on rigs in Australia, who was laid off in 2008, says, workers had "high incentive to find shortcuts and take risks." He added that "you only ever got questioned about why you couldn't spend less – never more." Of course, BP vigorously denies putting savings ahead of safety (Chazan et al. 2010).

14 "Placement on awards and rankings allows companies to keep up with their competitors and produce annual reports with shiny statistics and nice pictures. But they don't bring us nearly as close as needed to building the low-carbon, sustainable economies of the future" (Sverjensky 2010).

15 The author of Powell's Memo is Lewis Powell. A corporate lawyer and member of the boards of eleven corporations, Powell wrote a confidential memo in 1971 to his friend Eugene Sydnor, Jr., the Director of the US Chamber of Commerce. Not too long afterwards, he was nominated by President Nixon to the US Supreme Court.

16 Since *Shlensky v. Wrigley*, 237 NE 2d 776 (Ill. App. 1968), and *AP Smith Manufacturing Co. v. Barlow*, 98 A.2d 581 (N.J. 1953), the balancing of stakeholder interests has been left to a director's business judgment. The ruling of this case suggests that *Dodge v. Ford Motor Co.*, 170 NW 668 (Mich. 1919), no longer represents the law in most states. In *Dodge* the Michigan Supreme Court held that Henry Ford owed a duty to the shareholders of the Ford Motor Company while operating his business. The Court held that his actions should benefit his shareholders rather than the community or employees. What may seem to be a change in the law may also be an indicator that even though *Dodge* was interpreted as embodying the principle of 'shareholder value' in companies, in fact in *Dodge* or *Shlensky* directors were really protecting company value from being disseminated outside the company, protecting it from the decisions of owners (as in *Dodge*) or shareholders (as in *Shlensky*).

17 Friedman defends profit-making and Adam Smith's idea of 'the invisible hand of the market' against critics. However, the difference is that he only applies it to corporations and rejects any moral responsibility – unlike Smith – on the part of corporations. They are obliged only to compete openly and not to deceive or to act fraudulently. Placing any other responsibility on corporations "shows a fundamental misconception of the character and nature of a free economy." He then adds: "In such an economy, there is one and only one social responsibility of business – to use its resources and engage in activities designed to increase its profits so long as it stays within the rules of the game, which is to say, engages in open and free competition, without deception or fraud" (Friedman 1962, 133).

18 Such a situation took place in the United States during the Great Recession, which began with the subprime mortgage crisis and resulted in homes being worth less than the mortgage taken out on them. The resulting significant number of foreclosures led to a slump in consumer spending and an erosion of the financial strength of banking institutions and other parts of the economy.

19 In *Francis v. United Jersey Bank*, 87 N.J. 15, 432 A.2d 814 (N.J. 1981), the Supreme Court of New Jersey dealt with the case of a family-owned business that operated as a reinsurance broker. Mrs. Pritchard, a grieving widow who was drinking heavily, was a director who never became involved in the business. She was sued by the trustee in bankruptcy for breach of her duty of care. The court rejected the idea that a director could be a 'dummy director,' serving merely as an ornament. Mrs. Pritchard's business was a reinsurance business in which the practices of holding other peoples' money in a trust-like situation required greater care from the directors. Given Mrs. Pritchard's total lack of involvement and failure to monitor the managers, the court found her negligent for nonfeasance.

20 A letter from the US Chamber of Commerce regarding legislation related to the Gulf of Mexico oil spill was sent on July 21, 2010, to the members of the United States Congress by R. Bruce Josten, Executive Vice President for Government Affairs of the US Chamber of Commerce.

21 As Josh Harkinson (2010) says: "According to Louisiana's lobbying database, the state has 72 oil and gas lobbyists, 25 chemical industry lobbyists, and 43 lobbyists for chambers of commerce and business groups. There are only seven environmental lobbyists (two of whom also lobby for Chevron) and two lobbyists for fishing interests."

22 A more in-depth presentation of the issue of financing political parties and an approach to changing this can be found in Lessig (2012).

23 Joe Stephens (2010) says that "BP has been a major contributor to a Conservancy project aimed at protecting Bolivian forests. In 2006, BP gave the organization 655 acres in York County, Va., where a state wildlife management area is planned. In Colorado and Wyoming, the Conservancy has worked with BP to limit environmental damage from natural gas drilling."

24 Carol D. Leonning (2010) says: "BP said on its website 'In 2020 BP changed its policy to stop making corporate donations anywhere in the world.' But many of the groups that received BP's money said they were unaware of this code and prohibition on political contributions. Allan Zaremberg was a director of a tax-exempt political organization, known as a 527, which received a $3 million BP donation in 2006 for its work. It was the largest known single amount the firm has given to a political group."

25 *Graham v. Allis-Chalmers Manufacturing Co.*, 41 Del.Ch. 78, 188 A.2d 125 (Del. Supr. 1963), was a derivative lawsuit against the directors for breach of fiduciary duty. The shareholders argued that the directors were liable for price-fixing violations of antitrust laws because they did not have a monitoring system that would have allowed them to uncover the illegal activity of the employees. The Delaware Supreme Court found the question of whether a corporate director has become

liable for losses to the corporation through neglect of duty depends on whether he or she refused or neglected cavalierly to perform the duty of a director, or has ignored "either willfully or through inattention obvious danger signs of employee wrongdoing." This case established the Graham Standards, which basically impose a duty of inquiry on the directors only when there are obvious signs of employee wrongdoing.

26 Graham was optimistic about the likelihood of proposals actually going somewhere in a Republican-controlled House. His full statement was: "I believe that this issue and the searing impact that Deepwater Horizon has had on the conscience of America is such that it will override an ideological preference for less government, less government intrusion" (Sheppar 2011).

27 Brian Naylor discusses the "culture of coziness" (Naylor 2011). He also gives an example: "Investigations before and after the Gulf spill found the agency quite friendly with those it regulated. In Louisiana, oil companies offered football tickets and hunting trip invitations to MMS inspectors."

28 Such a situation happens due to our education not preparing us to face the problems of today's world but also, as Isaiah Berlin points out, due to the fact that the sphere of 'knowledge' is occupied by experts protecting their sphere of influence (Berlin 2013).

29 Dewey says that we learn to be responsible persons through 'a give and take' relation (Dewey 1991b, 195).

30 Even if we can see the truth, we might be far from understanding it, as happened in the case of the Apostles, who tried to understand the teachings of Christ and constantly failed.

31 In 2015, the Obama administration granted conditional permission to Royal Dutch Shell to begin drilling in the Chukchi Sea. However, the equipment and procedures of the corporation are far from ensuring that the process will be safe. That is why Nick Jans says: "Drilling for oil in the Chukchi Sea will still be a catastrophe waiting to happen. Yet, instead of learning from BP's example in the Gulf of Mexico, Shell's corporate hubris remains intact, and the government seems content to let big oil have its way once again" (Jans 2015).

References

Allan, William T., and Reinier Kraakman. 2003. *Commentaries and Cases on the Law of Business Organization*, 4th ed. New York: Wolters Kluwer.

Arendt, Hannah. 1968. *Between Past and Future: Eight Exercises in Political Thought.* New York: Viking Press.

Arendt, Hannah. 2003. *Eichman in Jerusalem: A Report on The Banality of Evil.* London: Penguin Classics.

Berlin, Isaiah. 1958. *Four Essays on Liberty.* Oxford: Oxford University Press.

Berlin, Isaiah. 2013. *The Crooked Timber of Humanity: Chapters in the History of Ideas*, ed. Henry Hardy. Princeton: Princeton University Press.

Chazan, Guy, Benoit Faucon, and Ben Casselman. 2010. "Safety and Cost Drives Clashed as CEO Hayward Remade BP." *Wall Street Journal* (Eastern edition), June 30.

Chen, Ronald, and Jon Hanson. 2004. "The Illusion of Law: The Legitimating Schemas of Modern Policy and Corporate Law." *Michigan Law Review* 103(1): 1–148.

Dewey, John. 1991a. *Human Nature and Conduct.* Vol. 14 of *The Middle Works of John Dewey, 1899–1924*, ed. Jo Ann Boydston. Carbondale: Southern Illinois University Press.

Dewey, John. 1991b. *Individualism, Old and New*. In *The Later Works of John Dewey, 1925–1953*, vol. 5: *1929–1930, Essays, The Sources of a Science Education, Individualism, Old and New, and Construction and Criticism*, ed. Jo Ann Boydston. Carbondale: Southern Illinois University Press.

Friedlander, Henry. 1995. *The Origins of Nazi Genocide: From Euthanasia to the Final Solutions*. Chapel Hill: University of North Carolina Press.

Friedman, Milton. 1962. *Capitalism and Freedom*. Chicago: University of Chicago Press.

Harkinson, Josh. 2010. "BP – Beyond Prosecution: How the Oil Industry and Chamber of Commerce Convinced La. Lawmakers to Go Easy on BP." *Mother Jones*, June 30.

Hayek, Friedrich von. 2004. *Road to Serfdom*. Chicago: University of Chicago Press.

Jans, Nick. 2015. "Arctic Disaster Awaits Us." *USA Today*, May 27.

Kevels, Daniel J. 1985. *In the Name of Eugenics: Genetics and the Uses of Human Heredity*. Cambridge: Harvard University Press.

Kilanowski, Marcin. 2017. "Truth, Universality or Dialog? Reflections on Richard Rorty's Response." *Ekonomia i Prawo* [Economics and law] 16(1): 47–57.

Leonning, Carol D. 2010. "Despite BP Corporate Code, Firm Has Made Political Contributions." *Washington Post*, June 29.

Lessig, Lawrence. 2012. *Republic, Lost: How Money Corrupts Congress – And a Plan to Stop It*. New York: Grand Central Publishing.

Lustgarten, Abrahm, and Ryan Knutson. 2010. "Reports at BP over Years Find History of Problems." *Washington Post*, June 8.

Michalczyk, John, ed. 1994. *Medicine, Ethics and the Third Reich*. Kansas City, MO: Sheed & Ward.

Milgram, Stanley. 1974. *Obedience to Authority: An Experimental View*. London: Tavistock.

Naylor, Brian. 2011. "Drilling Oversight Agency Faces 'Troubling' Obstacles." *NPR*, April 19.

Popper, Karl R. 1945. *The Open Society and Its Enemies*. London: Routledge.

Powell, Lewis F., Jr. 1972. "Confidential Memorandum: Attack on American Free Enterprise System." *Washington Report* 11, no. 23 (October) (US Chamber of Commerce, Washington, DC).

Rorty, Richard. 1989. *Contingency, Irony, and Solidarity*. Cambridge: Cambridge University Press.

Rorty, Richard. 1991a. "Moral Identity and Private Autonomy: The Case of Foucault." In *Essays on Heidegger and Others*. Cambridge: Cambridge University Press.

Rorty, Richard. 1991b. *Objectivity, Relativism, and Truth*. Cambridge: Cambridge University Press.

Rorty, Richard. 1993. "Human Rights, Rationality, and Sentimentality." In *On Human Rights: The Oxford Amnesty Lectures*, ed. S. Shute and S. Hurley. New York: Basic Books.

Rorty, Richard. 1994. *Consequences of Pragmatism: Essays 1972–1980*. Minneapolis: University of Minnesota Press.

Rousseau, Jean-Jacques. 2012. *The Basic Political Writings*, ed. Donald A. Cress. Hackett Publishing Co.

Sheppar, Kate. 2011. "Did We Learn Anything From BP Oil Spill?" *Mother Jones*, January 12.

Stephens, Joe. 2010. "Nature Conservancy Faces Potential Backlash from Ties with BP." *Washington Post*, May 24.

Sverjensky, Natalya. 2010. "Beyond Petroleum: Why the CSR Community Collaborated in Creating the BP Oil Disaster." *EC Newsdesk* (Ethical Corporation), August 2.

Unger, Roberto M. 2002. *False Necessity: Anti-Necessitarian Social Theory in the Service of Radical Democracy.* New York and London: Verso.

Weber, Max. 2010. *The Protestant Ethic and the Spirit of Capitalism.* Oxford: Oxford University Press.

Part IV
The efficiency of markets

9 Pragmatic theory of information and the efficient market hypothesis

From philosophical ideas to traders' behavior analyses

Agnieszka Hensoldt

What is the use of philosophy in times of economic crisis? In what way and in what sense (if any) can philosophers help us to cope better with our lives in these times? Most answers to these questions see the role of philosophy as critique, critique that is a way to improvement. This critique can be a critique of ideology, calling into question fundamental assumptions of the existing economic and social order. As such, every critique of this kind is always ideology itself, and it is usually based on an ethical discourse employing more or less explicitly concepts such as (in)justice or (in)equality. Thus, its legitimacy is questionable. The philosophical critique of an economic or social order can also take the form of a critique of language, i.e., the form of exposition and analysis of how the use of certain concepts (rather than some others) influences our understanding of the world. A critique of language may seem on the surface to be more objective and less dependent on or even independent of our personal ideological choices. However, this is only a guise. As there is no objective or universal conceptual scheme (as Hilary Putnam would say), or no universal language game (as Ludwig Wittgenstein would say), we can only expose some connections between ways of speaking and forms of life, but even this exposition is always made from a certain point of view and with regard to certain purposes.

What are the conclusions then? Every attempt at a critique of this kind risks being called illegitimate, as it may always raise questions about its foundations, e.g., "why should we accept this rather than other hierarchies of values?" What such an attempt at critique may look like in practice could have been witnessed by those who followed Polish public discussions on the place and role of philosophy in the Polish educational system this spring. On the one side there were defenders of economic calculations and profitability; on the other, defenders of education for open-mindedness, critical thinking, and self-consciousness. As it was easy to predict, the arguments of the two sides did not meet, even in the sense that they could start using a common conceptual scheme. We should not feel surprised by such a situation, as it is hardly possible to introduce concepts such as open-minded and critically thinking citizens into a discourse where the concept of economic profit narrowly construed (and also considered in a short run) is the central category.

Why have I mentioned this discussion? This is – in my opinion – a good example of the social and psychological fact that even the most nuanced and sophisticated arguments may not be found worth hearing (or reading) when a listener (or a reader) is not potentially interested in the point of view of the argumentation. (I intentionally do not mention the acceptance of other values; I mean only a weaker condition, which is easier – but very often still hard – to fulfill.) It is not my intention to say that this kind of philosophical critique is useless – quite otherwise, it may provide very interesting analyses, but they are interesting for philosophers, sociologists, social theorists, and even for some economists, but not for those who are able to draw any practical consequences from these analyses.

My contribution is less ideologically engaged. This chapter is devoted to a rather technical application of philosophical ideas, namely, Charles Sanders Peirce's theory of cognition, its application to the general pragmatic theory of information, and, further, to analyses of market efficiency. I shall argue here that pragmatist ideas (in particular Peirce's ideas) concerning the process of human cognition may be helpful in conceptualizing buyers' and sellers' behaviors in various markets.

My chapter is organized as follows. First, I offer a pragmatic theory of information proposed by E. D. Weinberger (2002). I will concentrate on its general assumptions, conceptual background, and general aims rather than on detailed mathematical solutions. Second, I argue that Weinberger's theory of pragmatic information is in fact the heritage of Peirce's views on human cognitive patterns. Third, I point out further applications of Weinberger's theory of information and Peirce's reflections on human cognition to economic analyses of market behavior.

Weinberger's theory of information

The fundamental assumption of Weinberger's theory of information is that "the practical meaning of information stems from its usefulness in making an informed decision" (Weinberger 2002, 107). Weinberger's main aim is to formulate "a quantitative definition of pragmatic information in a general setting that is unique in satisfying certain plausible postulates." Thus he builds a model which 1) allows us to compare and measure in some ways the information value (content) of given messages and 2) satisfies this pragmatic assumption.

The model that Weinberger proposes includes the following aspects of situations with message transmissions.

The most important element of Weinberger's model is a decision-maker *D*. This is a crucial characteristic of a pragmatic theory of information. (In non-pragmatic theories the central category is usually a message with its various attributes.) Information is valuable first of all from the point of view of a receiver, and what is more important, this point of view is closely connected to decisions that have to be taken or will have to be taken. It has to be mentioned here that a decision-maker in Weinberger's model does not have to be human: "[it] could also apply to an animal, a person, or even a number of people jointly making decisions," and also to an artificial system capable of "decision making" (Weinberger, 109).

The process of decision-making consists in choosing among a set of alternatives $\{a_1, a_2, \ldots a_M\}$. These alternatives are not yet actions – in cases of humans we may think of them as rules of action or ideas about how to act. They can also be thought about as habits of mind or habits of action. I will elaborate on this aspect later.

Each of these potential choices leads to an outcome, so we have also a set of outcomes $o \in O = \{o_1, o_2, \ldots o_N\}$. A decision-maker finds some of them more desirable than others. Accordingly, she/he/it will prefer some alternatives (leading to preferable outcomes) to others. Yet not every action leads to an outcome that has been expected or predicted by the actor. Weinberger gives a few examples of possible reasons for this indeterminacy:

- the mapping from the a's to o's is not deterministic,
- D has imperfect information about which of the o's is, in fact, the best,
- D is unable to process the available information optimally,
- D is unable to guarantee that the decision made is the one actually implemented, possibly because of 'environmental noise,' e, etc.

(Weinberger, 108)

As there is no guarantee that choosing a certain a will result in a given o, in Weinberger's model each a is attributed with a set of pairs, in which the first element is an outcome o, and the second one, the respective probability of reaching a given outcome $q = (q_1, q_2, \ldots q_N)$.

What happens when D is presented with a new message m? The best that D can do is to update the respective selection probabilities to $pm = (p_{1|m}, p_{2|m}, \ldots, p_{N|m})$ in such a way that the probability of a superior outcome is increased. Of course, it may happen that D is unable to process the received information optimally (does not understand it, cannot see any connection between the information and D's aims, etc.) and then the distribution of probabilities stays unchanged.

What should attract our attention is that the distributions of probabilities discussed here are not objective in any sense or empirically established: they are results of more or less subjective estimations by D.

Let us now proceed to the definition of the pragmatic information itself: "The pragmatic information, $I_M(p;q)$, of the message ensemble M is the information gain in going from q to p_m, averaged over all messages $m \in M$" (Weinberger, 108). As we have seen, pragmatic aspects of this theory of information are connected mainly to the assumption that if we want to estimate properly what the value of a given message is, we need to consider the point of view of a receiver, and the notion of a receiver is interpreted particularly pragmatically in Weinberger's theory. A receiver is not just a subject of cognition whose state of knowledge might be changed by a new message (like, for example, in Floridi's theory) but is first of all a decision-maker and an actor. This requires widening the concept of a receiver by attributing to a receiver a few important abilities: the ability to recognize one's aims, the ability to choose ways to achieve a given aim, and finally the ability to undertake purposeful actions.

The level of informativity, however, is not estimated on the basis of results of actions, or at least not done directly. According to Weinberger's definition of pragmatic information, what is estimated is "the information gain in going from q to p_m," i.e., the difference in distributions of probabilities, and these distributions, as it has just been mentioned, are established rather subjectively, not on the basis of any empirically verified rate of success (in a statistical sense of this expression). Of course, this 'subjectivity' is not completely empirically-free: probabilities are estimated on the basis of messages, and the source of messages is the environment. The nature of a message may vary (as Weinberger states, "[it] may be the output of some process"), including reactions of the environment to D's actions.

Though Weinberger calls his model "the theory of pragmatic information," none of the pragmatist thinkers are mentioned in his paper. He refers to a few authors of theories of information, mainly critically (Shannon, Grassberger, Crutchfield, Young, Standish). The only philosophical thinker whose ideas Weinberger cites in a positive context and whom Weinberger treats as a predecessor, in some sense, is Aristotle. Weinberger invokes Aristotle because of his theory of causation and particularly the concept of final causation, which "implies purposeful action" (Weinberger, 116). The application of this concept to the description of the organic (non-human) world has been criticized since the seventeenth century (Francis Bacon, Baruch Spinoza); however, Weinberger argues that acceptance of this kind of explanation can be fruitful.

Although Weinberger does not invoke any pragmatist thinkers, I shall argue that the pragmatist (philosophical) ideas were a source of inspiration for his theory and that most of these ideas come from one author, Charles S. Peirce.

The role of Peirce's ideas as a source of interesting conceptualizations and attitudes is naturally different from Aristotle's ideas. Aristotle holds that every change has its final causation; thus he shows that actions of non-human beings can be regarded as purposeful actions – this is what Weinberger finds inspiring. Peirce's interests concern first of all human beings, yet he is the author of an idea equally (if not more) important for Weinberger's theory, namely, the idea that, to estimate the value (in a very wide sense of the term) of a sign or a message, one must consider how assuming that this message is true would change one's actions. When there is no change the meaning of this new sign does not differ from the total meaning of acknowledged beliefs – so Peirce would say. In Weinberger's theory such is the situation in which the informativity of a message is zero: "no pragmatic information accrues from processes in which the probabilities of the outcomes are preserved" (Weinberger, 110).

Peirce's role in the foundation of the pragmatic theory of information

What are recognized as one of Peirce's important contributions to the pragmatic theory of information are his papers on logical comprehension and extension; yet they will not be the subject of my interest here. In my view these papers present Peirce's ideas concerning cognition and inquiry that find their application in Weinberger's theory. The exposition of these ideas we can find in Peirce's papers starting from 1877: "The Fixation of Belief" (1877), "How to Make Our Ideas Clear" (1878), and "The Doctrine of Chances" (1878).

In "How to Make Our Ideas Clear" Peirce for the first time (in print) formulates the pragmatist maxim:

> Consider what effects, which might conceivably have practical bearings, we conceive the object of our conception to have. Then, our conception of these effects is the whole of our conception of the object.
>
> (EP1.132)[1]

This first formulation is not of much use to us here, mainly because it is taken from a paper devoted to logical characteristics of concepts, and a decision-maker D (in Weinberger's model) does not have to have any conceptualizing abilities. However, when we look at later versions of the maxim of pragmatism, which are (at least in Peirce's opinion) more precise, we find formulations much closer to Weinberger's assumptions, for example, this one in the 1903 *Lectures on Pragmatism*, Lecture VII:

> the maxim of pragmatism is that a conception can have no logical effect or import differing from that of the second conception except so far as, taken in connection with other conceptions and intentions, it might conceivably modify our practical conduct differently from that second conception.
>
> (EP2.234)

Generally, these formulations of pragmatist ideas, which say more about cognitive patterns, would be more helpful. For example, the close connection between what is acknowledged as true and actions is shown by Peirce in the following short and relatively clear sentence: "Our beliefs guide our desires and shape our actions" ("The Fixation of Belief," 1877, EP1.114). This pragmatist idea in this sentence is expressed in such a general way that it gives wide possibilities for interpretation: in both Peircean and Jamesean style, it can be applied also to a theory of information. This view is probably close to what Weinberger has in mind when he calls his theory of information "pragmatic."

Yet, it is not my aim here to give the impression that in Peirce's papers one can find sentences that one can fit to anything. On the contrary, my point is that Peirce's account of human cognitive behavior, expressed in "The Fixation of Belief," is based on the same common-sense intuitions that have to be included in any pragmatic information theory. These are the convictions that:

1   The value of our beliefs (or received messages) can be estimated in the short run only in relation to our actions based on these beliefs or messages.
2   The truth is a very important feature of our beliefs, but its usefulness as a validating factor is at least limited, because in some cases (in fact, in most cases) it is not possible to ascertain *a priori* whether information is true or not.
3   This rejection of truth as a validating factor and the stress instead on the role of actions (and their successfulness) do not have to mean that we are taking a completely subjective point of view. Peirce is convinced (and that is why his stance is such a useful starting point, for example, for Weinberger) that comparing results of actions with expectations and changing our beliefs so that we could satisfy these expectations as much as possible, will finally provide us with true beliefs. According to Peirce this procedure is the only way of allowing 'the external reality' to influence and shape our knowledge.

It has to be stressed here that without this assumption of the existence of "external permanency," which influences us all "according to regular laws" (EP1.120), and the two previous assumptions, no model of pragmatic information could be built (and it would be absolutely impossible to apply such a model to, e.g., biological evolution, as Weinberger does). Thus "the practical bearings" mentioned by Peirce have to be of general validity and cannot be interpreted as widely as, for example, in James.

Another contribution of Pierce in setting the foundation for pragmatic information theory is his conceptualization of actions in a state of uncertainty. Peirce's famous analysis of the case of drawing a card from two packs of mixed red and black cards ("The Doctrine of Chances," 1878; EP1.147) seems to be a simpler case of Weinberger's model of pragmatic information. Peirce visibly has a problem applying the concept of probability to this situation, as he is convinced that using the concept of probability makes sense essentially in application to infinite sets.

> An individual inference must be either true or false, and can show no effect of probability; and therefore in inference to a single case considered in itself, probability has no meaning.
>
> (EP1.147)

In these last words Peirce apparently takes into consideration only the strictly logical meaning of the concept of probability. Nevertheless, he describes a thought experiment in which a man has to draw a card from one of two packs, one containing 25 red cards and 1 black, the other one, 25 black cards and 1 red. Drawing a red card means being transported to eternal felicity; a black one, being consigned to everlasting woe. Knowing the relations between the numbers of red and black cards in each of the two packs, the person making this choice would probably use simple reasoning and choose the pack with 25 red cards. What Peirce stresses in his analysis is the fact that this choice is not a guarantee of a happy end, and thus, according to Peirce, this is a proof of the worthlessness of reason applied to cases involving probability. Whether we agree with Peirce's final conclusion or not, it has to be admitted that Peirce provides us with a situation wherein an actor sees the relation between his/her actions and the results of those actions as probabilistic and the actor can estimate the probability of success in relation to his/her choices. This was an ingenious and original analysis at that time: we can find nothing similar either in Leibniz's logic of probabilities (i.e., *De arte combinatoria*) or in J. S. Mill's logic of induction.

Peirce's conception of habit of mind

Although Weinberger's theory of information is based only on very general presuppositions concerning processes of cognition (both human and non-human), some more specific findings and assumptions concerning human processes of cognition might be useful (and even necessary) when the model is applied to the interpretation of concrete cases. I have mentioned above Peirce's ideas of pragmatic meaning, as well as his conceptualization of actions in a state of uncertainty, yet in my opinion there is one more very important contribution that Peirce makes to studies of human cognition, which can be inspiring here: this is his thorough investigations of human habits. What in Weinberger's model is called a set of alternatives might be interpreted, as earlier noted, as habits of mind or habits of action.

According to Peirce, habit is "a general law of action, such that on a certain general kind of occasion a man will be more or less apt to act in a certain general way" ("Minute Logic," 1902; CP2.148). Most of human actions and reasonings are the results of following previously established habits. Nonetheless, such does not mean that we think and act in a completely mechanistic way. Peirce distinguishes between self-controlled habits and those which cannot be controlled. This second group is called (in Peirce's terminology) 'instincts' ("Minute Logic," 1902; CP2.170). What is interesting from the point of view of the theory of cognition, or any kind of moral theory, are self-controlled habits. Habits of this kind are developed by induction: "Certain sensations, all involving one general idea, are followed each by the same reaction; and an association becomes established" ("The Law of Mind," 1892;

EP1.327–28). Thus they are always subject to critique as well as to change. In one of his later papers, entitled "Pragmatism" (1907), Peirce holds that a critical approach is the crucial feature of self-controlled habits:

> in calling a habit "self-controlled," I do not mean that it is in the power of the man who has it to cast it off [...]; for we well know that he has no such power, – but what I mean is that it has been developed under the process [...] in which critical feelings as to the results of inner or outer exercises stimulate to strong endeavors to repeat or to modify those effects.
>
> (EP2.431)

In this passage Peirce emphasizes not only a critical attitude but also the fact that we do not have full control even over self-controlled habits. The example that he uses to illustrate this phenomenon concerns decorating one's house. Peirce's point is that one cannot give up a habit of trying to render one's house beautiful. Whether Peirce is right or not in this matter, this example shows that the indispensable part of each habit is purpose. (Let us notice that this is exactly mirrored in Weinberger's model, in which every element of a set of alternatives is connected to sets of outcomes via distributions of probabilities, and this is not a simple causal connection but rather a teleological one: an alternative is chosen always with regard to a preferable outcome. What is more, Weinberger stresses the significance of the concept of purposeful action for his theory.)

Although ideas about how to achieve a given purpose are changeable, the purpose itself most likely is not. In Peirce's example the purpose is rendering one's surroundings beautiful, a purpose which might be rejected, for some people with smaller, for others with greater difficulty. However, there are human purposes that can hardly be rejected, and I do not mean here only those resulting from basic human, biological needs. What they are depends mostly on cultural context. In modern Western societies the pursuit of profit broadly defined should be counted among them. In nearly all kinds of economic theories, including the eldest (such as Adam Smith's and David Ricardo's), an example of such a fixed purpose is that all market players seek to profit. This is also the fundamental assumption that is essential in various attempts to apprehend market 'forces' and 'mechanisms.'

Applications of Weinberger's theory of information and Peirce's approach to human cognition to economic analyses of market behavior

In Weinberger's paper there is just a one-sentence mention of the possible application of his theory to the 'efficient market hypothesis' (EMH). This reference should be understood as a kind of shorthand, as it is hard to imagine in what way the pragmatic theory of information could help in verifying or falsifying EMH.

In finance the 'efficient market hypothesis' asserts that financial markets are 'informationally efficient,' making the achievement of excess returns in the long run (theoretically) impossible.

In various forms of EMH, the first thing that is conspicuous is that its subject – like in pragmatic theory of information and Peirce's theory of cognition – is the relation between information, ideas of action, and results of action. In the EMH case, 'information' means, of course, 'market information on traded goods/assets'; 'action' means 'buying or selling at a certain price,' and 'results' means 'profits and losses.' And this is the sense in which Weinberger's theory may be applied to conceptualizing and even formalizing these various relations.

Markets may be efficient (in the EMH sense) to varying degrees. Accordingly, three levels of efficiency are distinguished.

The weak form of EMH says that prices on traded assets (e.g., stocks, bonds, or property) already reflect all past publicly available information. The semi-strong form of EMH claims both that prices reflect all publicly available information and that they instantly change to reflect new public information. According to the strongest version of EMH, prices instantly reflect even hidden or 'insider' information.

What is important here is the question, what kind of information received by an agent might allow a receiver to earn excess returns? – i.e., what kind of information allows one to make an accurate and possibly unique prediction of changes in market prices? When we formulate this question using the concepts of Weinberger's model, we find out that it concerns the kinds of messages in which pragmatic information is more than zero; i.e., what change in the distribution of probabilities will increase the probability of a superior outcome? As we can see, the strong form of EMH claims that there is no such information:

> the 'efficient market hypothesis' that undergirds essentially all of modern finance is succinctly, but precisely stated as the claim that the pragmatic information of previous price histories is zero.
>
> (Weinberger, 116)

One of the important questions of modern economy has been whether financial markets are 'informationally efficient' as EMH asserts. The definitive answer to this question (if there is any) is outside the interest of this chapter; nonetheless, it has to be mentioned here that

1   the EMH claims have been disputed both empirically and theoretically (by behavioral economists) since the late 1960s. Empirical evidence has varied (depending on times and markets); however, it has generally not been supportive of strong forms of EMH (Nicholson 1968; Basu 1977; Rosenberg et al. 1985).
2   Behavioral psychology analyses of traders' behavior in stock markets have generally not supported EMH, because they show that people are not so rational as it is presupposed by EMH, e.g., individuals either employ hyperbolic discounting or have inclinations to herd behavior (e.g., Tversky and Kahneman 1974; Kahneman and Tversky 1979; Thaler 1994).

3   If we take a more 'philosophical' perspective, it turns out that it is not even possible to say whether (when and where) the EMH assertions are right, because to verify the EMH claim that in the long run excess returns are impossible, one would need to say what level of returns is abnormal for a given market and what is average.

4   Maybe it is not important whether and to what extent the EMH claims are right. However, it is important what people (individual investors, stock managers, economists, etc.) think about it, as there have been quite numerous claims (made by economists) that (blind) belief in EMH is responsible for the late 2000s financial crisis, that people were too confident about the rationality and self-healing powers of markets and hence underestimated the dangers of asset bubbles breaking (e.g., Milner 2009; Nocera 2009).

If our analysis so far has been correct, then first, one can apply Weinberger's model of pragmatic information to analyses of relations between information coming from various sources, traders' decisions, and results of traders' actions (this is possible when the pragmatic value of at least some kinds of market information is other than zero). What might be particularly promising is the model's pragmatic and probabilistic character. It makes a decision-maker the central category, and this is not an average, always-rational trader but a person (or a group of people, or even a computer software) with its limits, mental habits, and various biases. Even if a decision-maker is not a human in a strict sense of the term (but a computer software), it is a human product, so it follows rules established by its (human) creators. If the rules are in some cases inappropriate, so will be the algorithms and the whole software. Good examples of faulty results following from inappropriate rules are claims (mentioned above) that the late 2000s financial crisis was the result of various assumptions (made by people consciously or unconsciously) that turned out to be wrong or at least inappropriate, considering the contemporary financial market mechanisms. And it does not matter whether they were individual people making traders' decisions, people in brokerage houses, or computer programs. What is important here is that a significant proportion of these actors acted on wrong assumptions or assumptions which turned out to be wrong.

If we are to 'translate' what we just described into the concepts of Weinberger's model, we should say that the final result was not a preferable outcome. Differing reasons might be given for this (again expressed in the concepts of Weinberger's model):

1   the decision-maker chose a wrong a_i from a set of alternatives because he/she/it had imperfect information concerning the relation between a_i and possible outcomes, e.g., the probability of preferable outcomes turned out to be much lower;

2   although the decision-maker chose a right a_i (concerning the corresponding distribution of probabilities) but unfortunately a non-desirable outcome was realized, its probability for realization was low; or

3   the decision-maker is not able to estimate which outcome is in fact the best from the point of view of its interests and – what becomes visible *post factum* – thus chooses a wrong outcome and obviously an a_i from a set of alternatives that leads to this outcome with the highest probability.

In fact, all these three scenarios might be useful in a description of the same situation – everything depends on which interpretation is considered to be the most useful. The first two interpretations, though they might look different in theory, are in fact the same in practice. As the distributions of probabilities are results of more or less subjective estimations made by a decision-maker, there is no way of discovering 'the real' distribution of probabilities and thus of discovering a potential mistake in its estimation.

The third interpretation seems distinctly different from the first two. How useful it might become depends on how precise we would like to be in describing a decision-maker's aim. If he/she/it just tends toward the biggest possible returns, it is generally not possible to choose the wrong outcome: the only risk that may arise here is the risk of choosing a wrong alternative. On the contrary, if the aim is to be described more precisely (e.g., to earn a 25% return in a year), it might happen that the very decision to establish a concrete aim will turn out to be wrong.

From the point of view suggested in this chapter the most useful interpretation seems to be the first one, namely, that a wrong a_i has been chosen and the result of the undertaken actions is at least non-preferable. This viewpoint seems to be the most inspiring if Peirce's conception of habit is to be applied to analyses of traders' behaviors in the terms of Weinberger's model.

Second, mathematical or computational modeling based on Weinberger's theory may become not only a source of knowledge but also a tool for exploring and denouncing unhealthy market mechanisms and market players' behaviors; e.g., messages with relatively low pragmatic information change traders' actions in a great measure, and vice versa.

Third (and last but not least), this is a good moment for coming back to origins, namely, to the philosophical ideas. Even if Peirce's ideas of pragmatic meaning and his conceptualization of actions in a state of uncertainty have not directly influenced Weinberger's theory, Weinberger's theory of pragmatic information is in fact the heritage of Peirce's views on human cognitive patterns. It is based on the assumptions that might be considered (by Weinberger) the core of a very general pragmatic attitude, but in fact they are an essential part of Peirce's doctrine. Yet in my opinion there is one more very important contribution by Peirce to studies of human cognition, which can be useful if application of Weinberger's model to concrete cases is needed: this is Peirce's thorough investigations into human habits of mind. Combined with his views on meaning they can be very inspiring in attempts to explain human behavior (including trading behavior) – e.g., the tendency toward conservatism or toward revolutionary behavior – as well as in looking for reasons for rapid changes in patterns of one's behavior. Such explanations are part of the field of psychological research, but I believe that philosophical investigations, in particular those inspired by pragmatist thought, also might shed original light on these matters.

The usual public reaction to various financial crises is to search for those who are responsible. Those willing to have their say in such discussions often believe in one of two options: either the entire responsibility lies with the financial institutions, or these are common people (common investors) who should have been more rational. The aim of this analysis is not to resolve this dispute but to examine critically these kinds of suggestions regarding people's irrationality. What is more, the very concept of rationality will not be the subject of this analysis because either, first, this would require thorough and long examination (which definitely is beyond the scope of this chapter), or, second (and more importantly), those defenders of rationality do not refer to any special conception of rationality: rather, they mean choices that would turn out (*post factum*) more adequate in a given situation.

Now let us return to the original question: could people have been more rational? If we translate this doubt into the terminology of Weinberger's model, we will ask: could they have chosen another alternative? This does not help a lot, but if we look for an interpretation of this question in Peirce's terms, we receive another question: could they have changed their habits? Peirce's remarks on the nature of habits can become our starting point in attempts to answer this latter question. According to Peirce, at least some of our habits cannot be totally rejected: they can be at most modified. The habit of pursuing profit seems to be one of them. It is really hard to imagine that some market players in modern Western societies one day may stop acting with regard to profit maximization.

One can object that every profit level is related to its proper level of risk. That is true and this fact is mirrored in Weinberger's model in an elegant way. It might be said that recognizing the acceptable level of profit is the very essence of the problem. Yet the level of risk – the same as 'distribution of probabilities' in Weinberger – is not objective, and what is worse, its true extent is known always *post factum*. The question why more rational decisions have not been made is usually a form of covert criticism that too high a risk has been accepted. Nonetheless, if we invest or take credit at a lower level of risk, we usually have to agree to less profit or higher costs. To do so one has to have reasons – applying Peirce's terminology – to modify one's habits in those aspects that are subject to self-control, and those aspects are established by induction. These modifications are the "results of inner or outer exercises [or experiences which] stimulate to strong endeavors to repeat or to modify those effects" ("Pragmatism," 1907; EP2.431). In modifications of habits where experience is lacking, it is no surprise that one reverts to what one used to do or to what others do. It is not easy (and very often it is not possible) to reject 'proofs' of induction. Reasoning not based on some information coming from induction (experience) or deduction, is not – strictly speaking – reasoning. Peirce calls the process of looking at things in a novel way (that is, of inventing a hypothesis) 'abduction.' Commenting on the nature of induction, he hinted that "the matter of no new truth can come from induction or from deduction ... . It can only come from abduction; and abduction is, after all, nothing but guessing" ("On the Logic of Drawing History from Ancient Documents Especially from Testimonies," 1901; CP7.219).

What lessons can we learn from this analysis in respect to the 'efficient market hypothesis'? What psychologists call 'herd behavior' is an integral part of human cognitive processes. Peirce called it in a more elegant way the "human inclination to conservatism." The ability to not 'follow the herd' is not a common gift, nor is the ability to invent new hypotheses. In the discussion of whether the EMH claims are right or not, neither Weinberger's theory of information nor Peirce's reflections on human processes of cognition (and habits of mind) are supportive of the strong form of EMH: it does not give even a hint regarding how prices could instantly reflect hidden or 'insider' information, i.e., how anything unknown could influence traders' behaviors and thus market prices.

Acknowledgments

The research project has been financed by the Polish National Science Centre on the basis of decision no. DEC-2012/07/B/HS1/00310.

Note

1 I quote from the *Collected Papers of Charles Sanders Peirce* (Peirce 1931–58), with the usual abbreviation 'CP' and followed by the volume and paragraph number, and from *The Essential Peirce: Selected Philosophical Writings* (Peirce 1992–98), as 'EP', followed by volume and page number.

References

Basu, S. 1977. "Investment Performance of Common Stocks in Relation to Their Price-Earnings Ratios: A Test of the Efficient Markets Hypothesis." *Journal of Finance* 32: 663–682.

Kahneman, D., and A. Tversky. 1979. "Prospect Theory: An Analysis of Decisions under Risk." *Econometrica* 47(2): 263–292.

Milner, B. 2009. "Sun Finally Sets on Notion That Markets Are Rational." *Globe and Mail*, July 3. <www.theglobeandmail.com/globe-investor/investment-ideas/features/taking-stock/sun-finally-sets-on-notion-that-markets-are-rational/article1206213/> (retrieved January 31, 2015).

Nicholson, F. 1968. "Price-Earnings Ratios in Relation to Investment Results." *Financial Analysts Journal* 24(1): 105–109.

Nocera, J. 2009. "Poking Holes in a Theory of Markets." *New York Times*, June 5. <www.nytimes.com/2009/06/06/business/06nocera.html?scp=1&sq=efficient%20market&st=cse&_r=0> (retrieved January 31, 2015).

Peirce, C. S. 1931–58. *Collected Papers of Charles Sanders Peirce*, ed. C. Hartshorne and P. Weiss (vols. 1–6), and A. W. Burks (vols. 7–8). Cambridge, MA: Harvard University Press.

Peirce, C. S. 1992–98. *The Essential Peirce: Selected Philosophical Writings*, 2 vols., ed. N. Houser and C. Kloesel. Bloomington: Indiana University Press.

Rosenberg, B., K. Reid, and R. Lanstein. 1985. "Persuasive Evidence of Market Inefficiency." *Journal of Portfolio Management* 13: 9–17.

Tversky, A., and D. Kahneman. 1974. "Judgement under Uncertainty: Heuristics and Biases." *Science* 185: 1124–1131.

Thaler, R. H. 1994. *Quasi Rational Economics*. New York: Russell Sage Foundation.

Weinberger, E. D. 2002. "A Theory of Pragmatic Information and Its Application to the Quasi-species Mode of Biological Evolution." *BioSystem* 66: 105–119.

10 The relativity of transaction costs

Liu Mu and Kenneth W. Stikkers

'Transaction costs' is the central notion of new institutional economics (NIE). Ronald Coase (1937) first proposed this concept, but he confined it only to the market economy. With the rise of NIE, the notion of transaction costs has been applied to many other fields, such as jurisprudence, politics, history, etc., and to research involving every type of economic system. While the transaction cost paradigm has had great success in some respects, it has been misused as well. One finds that 'transaction costs' is used to explain everything, but there has been a failure to indicate the boundary of its explanatory power. The immense explanatory power of transaction costs is prone to a lack of falsifiability, thus turning the theory into a tautology.

One of the major reasons for this situation is that the question of whether transaction costs are universal or relative for human society has not been properly considered. From a longitudinal perspective, the question is whether transaction costs exist throughout human history, or are they just a product of specific historical stages, while from a latitudinal perspective, the question is whether transaction costs exist in all societies and cultures, or are they only peculiar phenomena within certain societies and cultures. The reason why the transaction cost paradigm has been misused is because the universality of transaction costs is considered self-evident. The goal of this essay is to reveal the conditions for the existence of transaction costs. It is meaningless to discuss transaction costs without considering these conditions.

Transaction costs and bounded rationality

Narrow transaction costs include only costs concerning market transactions. Thus, transaction costs will not exist if there are no economic transactions between individuals or groups. In its development, however, NIE has expanded the concept of transaction costs beyond this narrow definition. Steven Cheung (1992), for instance, defines transaction costs as the costs that are unlikely to exist in a Robinson Crusoe economy. Therefore, all costs stemming from interpersonal actions belong to transaction costs. Economic transactions are merely one form of interpersonal interaction. Hence, since society is the totality of interpersonal interactions, there are large transaction costs in every society. However, since it would be misleading to call the costs in this broader sense 'transaction costs,' Cheung instead often calls them 'institutional costs.' He believes that institutional costs are universal and are the generalized transaction costs that occur in every society.

New institutional economics adopts the bounded rationality hypothesis rather than the completed rationality hypothesis adopted by neoclassical economics. According to this hypothesis although they desire to be rational, people are not hyper-rational, because it takes time and resources for an individual to obtain information, and their ability to process information and make plans is limited (Cheung, 3). As a result of bounded rationality, economic transactions are full of uncertainty, which inevitably causes transaction costs. New institutional economics tends to regard bounded rationality as a feature of an unchangeable, universal humanity, and therefore its inescapable conclusion is that transaction costs are universal and to be found through all stages of history and in all societies. To some degree, new institutional economists are followers of Thomas Hobbes and tend to presume that there was a state of nature before the appearance of society. Since everyone is self-interested, conflicts may erupt during the pursuit of scarce resources, and as a result of bounded rationality, interpersonal actions cause large transaction costs. The purpose of various institutions, such as law and morality, is to reduce these costs. The natural state of the Hobbesian jungle is regarded as self-evident. In this situation, all individuals, because their interests are mutually conflicting, must be suspicious and jealous of one another and be confronted with enormous uncertainty regarding their external environments. If individuals shared the same interests, then the uncertainty of interpersonal actions would disappear and bounded rationality would lose its basis.

However, is the Hobbesian jungle the logical starting point for every society? Or, is it a product only of specific historical conditions, in which it appears to be self-evident? In the view of NIE, the bounded rationality hypothesis is a major correction to the completed rationality hypothesis and brings economics closer to the real world, and it must be regarded as an important theoretical breakthrough. Max Scheler, a leading German social philosopher of the early twentieth century, who significantly influenced German economic thinking in the rebuilding of Germany (Stikkers 1987) points out, however, that the practice of life and theories are closely united in wedlock: "Thus a theory supports a practice which was itself the origin of this theory" (Scheler 1961, 142). Therefore, the real meaning of the bounded rationality hypothesis can be understood only in the context of the practices of modern social life and not as a universal phenomenon.

Scheler further observes that in traditional communities (*Gemeinschaften*) persons do not exist as independent and self-interested individuals but rather "are united by blood, tradition and history" (166). In this situation the 'individual' is integrated into the collective: "everyone knows and feels that the community as a whole is inherent in him – he feels that his blood is the blood which circulates in the community" (165). The basic principle of morality is 'solidarity,' whose inherent tendency is to "extend 'responsibility' as far as possible beyond the limits of the individual person" (142): "we should feel we participate in all guilt" (141). "The attitude underlying this notion is one of horror at the very appearance of evil, no matter who brings it about, and delight in the appearance of the good. The destiny of all mankind, indeed of all spiritual persons is always felt to be implicated in both phenomena" (142). Since personal and collective interests merge, conflicts of interests among individuals do not exist, and a notion of rationality as the servant of individual interests, in the sense that orthodox economics assumes, is unknown. Furthermore, relationships among individuals "used to be the natural continuity and permanence of a disposition of love and trust," and "[t]he requirement of binding 'promises,' of agreements to be concluded, was felt to be an insult" (Scheler, 157). Others' thoughts and feelings need not be surmised but are experienced directly. There is no uncertainty during interpersonal interaction stemming from distrust, and therefore bounded rationality and transaction costs are not generated from it in such communities. Conflicting interests, suspicions, and indifference are not felt, and therefore individuals do not pay a price for interaction with others. In such communities, it is impossible for institutions to be understood as tools for reducing transaction costs.

The moral principle, however, has changed radically in modern society (*Gesellschaft*). As Scheler notes, one of the major characteristics of modern morality, resulting from the lack of feelings of solidarity which one finds in traditional communities, is "to limit responsibility as much as possible, to reject all guilt for the acts of 'others'" (Scheler, 142). Lacking solidarity, modern morality confines the individual to himself, and he is responsible only for his own behavior. One deems only oneself trustworthy, and others cannot be trusted: "if one thinks and feels that other people, everything else being equal, 'have evil designs,' one will naturally refuse responsibility for others' acts" (142).

With the rise of modern distrust, solidarity has been replaced by suspicions and indifference. Therefore, one always finds information incomplete, others opportunistic, and the outside world uncertain. Only in this case does the individual deeply experience the limits of his own rationality. Hence, high costs must be paid for transactions with others: "The merchant's fear of being cheated has become the basic category of the very perception of others" (Scheler, 143).

Thus, the bounded rationality hypothesis and transaction cost paradigm are merely products of the experiences of modernity. They are correct only with respect to modern society, but NIE regards them as applicable to every society and every historical stage. New institutional economics believes that institutions, such as morality and customs, are tools that can be used to reduce transaction costs, and transaction costs are logically as well as historically prior to all societies and cultures. As a matter of fact, however, transaction costs are merely a product of only specific moral principles and social structures and are not universal. In short, NIE has cause and effect reversed.

Transaction costs and value propositions

Like various other economic costs, transaction costs are a kind of opportunity cost. This means that transaction costs are a product of the allocation of scarce resources among alternative uses and are prices paid for achieving some particular ends. A 'transaction cost,' however, must be understood either as a cost proper or as a kind of sacrifice. Scheler distinguishes the two concepts: sacrifice involves the abandonment of some good belonging to a qualitatively lower level of value for a good belonging to a higher level of value when the two goods and their corresponding values conflict with each other. By contrast, if two goods are not acknowledged as corresponding to qualitatively different levels of value, then foregoing the one good for the other is merely to bear an opportunity 'cost' and to pay a 'price' for the preferred good. For example, when one prefers steak over salmon, because one anticipates that the former will provide a greater quantity of pleasure than the latter, one only pays an opportunity cost by foregoing the latter for the former. If one, however, foregoes some immediate pleasure, such as eating steak, for the sake of one's health, one sacrifices something of a relatively lower level of value, namely, pleasure, for the sake of a relatively higher value, namely, life. The value of life is of a qualitatively higher order than pleasure and is not merely equivalent to some quantity of pleasure. Likewise, if one foregoes one's life for a value that one experiences as higher than that of life, such as justice or love, one *sacrifices* one's life for that value and is not merely paying some opportunity cost for it. Therefore, the concepts of 'cost' and 'price' pertain only to goods of the same qualitative level of value and are governed by the normative, calculative principle that a good bearing a value of smaller quantity ought to be abandoned for the good bearing value of greater quantity, when the two goods conflict with each other.

Modern society, especially in its economic thinking, Scheler argues, does not recognize any hierarchy among values but, through its notion of 'utility,' brings all goods down to the same qualitative level of value: everything is seen as having some 'price,' making it quantitatively comparable to everything else. This phenomenon is one of '*ressentiment*,' a notion which, Scheler notes, Friedrich Nietzsche had already introduced and described: out of weakness and an inability to achieve those values that one secretly acknowledges as higher than what one is able to achieve, one drags down those things manifesting such higher values to one's own lower level of achievement. For example, out of one's weakness to achieve spiritual greatness, one belittles those things manifesting spiritual greatness by dragging them down to the level of utilitarian calculation and putting a price on them. Art becomes just one more commodity for consumption or 'investment'; university students who are drawn to those activities manifesting spiritual values, such as art, literature, history, philosophy, or religion, are often ridiculed, because such activities are seen as unable to generate much income and hence as impractical, rather than admired for their transcendence of the mundane values measured by money. Indeed, modern morality, as manifest in market economies, denies the spiritual values of persons, Scheler proclaims, both in theory and in practice: the old notion of a 'right to life,' stemming from such spiritual values, has given way to the notion of 'earning a living.' Human life, reduced to 'human resources' and 'human capital,' is a cost of production, which, like all other costs, is to be minimized, and hence it must justify itself – be 'earned' – in accord with its ability to create objects of market, utility value (Scheler, esp. 158–62).

The value propositions of modern society are shaped largely by *ressentiment*, as Scheler describes, and are located predominantly at those lower levels that lend themselves to prices, and the attention of economics to opportunity costs stems from this modern tendency. The notion of opportunity costs recognizes no differences between levels of value: only those benefits accruing from various uses of some good can be compared quantitatively.

This conclusion also applies to transaction costs. The existence of a transaction cost means that some positive value has been abandoned in order for the transaction to occur. Therefore, discussion about transaction costs is meaningful only among subjects whose value propositions pertain to the same value-level. Hence, if two societies hold value propositions belonging to different levels of value, their transaction costs cannot be compared directly. Value propositions change with changes in social systems. Therefore, it cannot be determined whether such changes increase or decrease transaction costs. This point, however, is overlooked by NIE.

New institutional economics understands institutions from a functional perspective, and, since transaction costs are frictions in economic activities, the major function of institutions, according to NIE, is to reduce uncertainty and transaction costs. Therefore, the criterion for measuring the performance of institutions is the extent to which they reduce transaction costs. However, the precondition for measuring and comparing different institutions is that those institutions subscribe to the same value propositions, so that things of the same kind may receive the same evaluation. While the foregoing of a certain kind of thing in society A is viewed as a price, the foregoing of the same kind of thing in society B should also be viewed as a price. It is meaningful to talk about the change of transaction costs only if they are measured by the same criterion, that is, in accord with the same level of value. Similarly, something can be found 'better' or 'uglier' only if the criteria for 'good and evil' or 'beauty and ugliness' remain constant during the process of comparative evaluation. Otherwise, the change of criterion can make the evaluated objects 'better' or 'uglier,' even if they themselves have not changed. Institutional change reduces transaction costs or economic development increases overall transaction costs in a meaningful way only if basic value propositions remain constant. For the transaction costs of good x to change, the quality (or meaning) of x must remain unchanged; otherwise it is meaningless to talk about changes in quantity. Yet, value propositions do change in the long run.

New institutional economics distinguishes two sorts of institutions: informal and formal institutions (North 1990). The former include moralities, customs, ideologies, etc., and thus, value propositions are an important part of informal institutions. Empirically, value propositions change continuously throughout history, and values differ across various societies. Therefore, the meanings of transaction costs vary with time and place, and it is meaningless to summarize the overall changing trend. From this observation one can see the logical contradiction implied in NIE: on the one hand institutions, including value propositions, are regarded as tools devised to reduce transaction costs. For example, according to Justin Lin (1989), ideology is a tool to simplify decision-making. Therefore, value propositions are logically posterior to transaction costs. On the other hand, however, since specific value propositions are the precondition for transaction costs, they seem prior to transaction costs. In short, NIE, here again, reverses cause and effect.

Discussion of changing transaction costs is meaningful only with respect to the same value proposition, or value-level. In the context of modern market economy, basic value propositions remain stable, so the discussion of how institutional changes influence the quantity of transaction costs is very useful. This is Coase's great contribution to economics (see Coase 1960). However, if one discusses this question from the perspective of an entire history, under the hypothesis that the basic value propositions of mankind remain unchanged, and thereby forces the specific value propositions of modern Western society upon all stages of history and all societies, as new institutionalists do, one would be guilty of Eurocentrism in economics.

The attention to transaction costs derives from economics' emphasis on efficiency. Since transaction costs are viewed as noise in a market economy and interfere with economic efficiency, the function of institutions is to reduce them. However, if one generalizes this conclusion to the whole history of mankind and assumes that all institutions throughout human history derive their origin from efforts to reduce transaction costs, one makes an unreasonable assumption, namely, that all societies, no matter what their ways of life and living standards are, regard economic efficiency as their highest aim and economic well-being as their highest value. This assumption is precisely the result of the *ressentiment* that has shaped the value propositions of modern society. For many cultures the value of economic welfare is relegated to the relatively lower portion of their order of values: they experience certain spiritual values, such as the value of honor and holiness, as much higher than and as worth the sacrifice of economic values, such as wealth and efficiency. Modern societies, however, seem incapable of recognizing and achieving such higher, spiritual values, and so they are haunted by value-delusion and *ressentiment* and regard economic welfare as the highest if not the only value: for them everything has a monetary price and hence nothing is honorable, sacred, or holy. Therefore, other cultures and stages of history are inevitably misunderstood and viewed as 'undeveloped.'

This Eurocentric prejudice takes two specific forms: some economists believe that all societies attain efficiency, while others argue that inefficiency is the norm throughout history. Cheung (1992) holds the former and deems that rent dissipation is inevitably minimized under given constraints. This means that existing institutions are always the most efficient of all conceivable ones, under the given constraints. Since mankind always achieves its goals successfully under specific circumstances, the thought that some institutions are superior to others is self-contradictory. This seeming relativism, which identifies institutions with their functions, is nothing but contemporary absolutism.

North (1981) holds the latter view and believes that inefficient institutions are more frequent in human history than efficient ones. He, too, thus assumes that all societies pursue the same thing, 'economic efficiency,' but most of them do not succeed very well. Both of these two seemingly antithetical viewpoints are based in the *ressentiment* that overlooks the differences in value propositions between various societies.

It is meaningless to say that a society is economically unsuccessful or inefficient, when it holds certain spiritual values to be higher than those of economic welfare and is thus relatively indifferent to the latter. Hence, every society should be evaluated on its own criteria in research concerning its economy. It is not enough merely to 'identify' certain transaction costs. What matters is that these transaction costs are 'felt' by the concerned subjects as relative to their own value propositions. The economist should not speak for them but ought to allow them to speak for themselves.[1] New institutional economics wrongly measures all societies with the criteria of modern society, which it wrongly assumes to be universal.

Transaction costs and scarcity

Transaction costs are a kind of opportunity cost, which means that transaction costs are imaginable only in a world of scarcity. Scarcity means that, relative to human desires, which economists generally assume to be infinite, resources are always finite, and so selection is necessary. New institutionalist economists follow those of the mainstream in assuming that infinite desires are part of universal human nature and, therefore, that mankind is destined never to overcome the scarcity of resources (e.g., Robbins 1935 [1932], 13).[2] The hypothesis of 'economic man' is based upon this concept of scarcity: scarcity restricts human desires, and so rational choice is necessary. Thus, the concept of 'transaction costs' presupposes that human desires are universally infinite and hence that scarcity is also universal. Moreover, since institutions are considered as tools for reducing transaction costs, all of them are products of scarcity.

Is it possible that scarcity exists only in specific stages of history and in specific cultures? Are means always scanty compared with ends? Mainstream economics fails to raise such fundamental questions. If scarcity is only the product of specific historical or cultural contexts, opportunity costs, including transaction costs, would be only relative rather than universal, as new institutionalists, along with mainstream economists, assume.

For the purposes of this essay, one counterexample is sufficient to illustrate that scarcity is not absolute. Hunting-gathering economies of the Stone Age are just such a counterexample. The formalism of economic anthropology argues that its economic man hypothesis is applicable even to hunting-gathering economies. Therefore, mainstream economists view the aboriginal economy as nothing but a primitive version of modern capitalist economy. As a result of infinite desires and low productivity, the ability of Stone Age people to satisfy their desires is inevitably limited. Therefore, compared with modern economies, hunting-gathering economies are necessarily much more troubled with scarcity and extreme poverty.

However, as the distinguished economic anthropologist Marshall Sahlins shows, Stone Age society is "the original affluent society" (Sahlins 1972): "all the people's material wants are easily satisfied" (1). The reason why affluence is achieved is not improvement of productivity, but a very low level of desires. Therefore, hunters can be "free from market obsessions of scarcity" (2).

Sahlins demonstrates that scarcity has no relevance to the Stone Age economy. The reason why formalistic economists have misunderstood the economy of Stone Age people is that it considers scarcity to be ontological and universal. However, scarcity is actually a result of the gap between ends and means. Hence, "Having equipped the hunter with bourgeois impulses and paleolithic tools, we judge his situation hopeless in advance" of the empirical evidence (Sahlins, 4). Resources that are regarded as scarce in modern society, are not scarce at all for Stone Age people. All kinds of materials needed in production and living, such as stone, bones, wood, and fur, are abundant and can be obtained directly. People's demands can be easily satisfied, and therefore natural resources are not scarce. Contrary to what many economists and others believe, hunting-gathering economy is not exhausting, and time for leisure is not scarce: Stone Age people have plenty of leisure time (Sahlins, 17–21).[3] Standing outside of such an economy, one might imagine that the hunters' desires are confined to the lowest level of productivity. However, if one enters into their society, one finds that suppressed desires do not exist. In this case, the discussion about efficiency is meaningless because efficiency becomes a problem only if resources are scarce. If scarce resources are reasonably and fully utilized, efficiency will be achieved. Otherwise, inefficiency and waste will take place. However, if resources exceed desires and all needs can be easily satisfied, resources will be by no means fully utilized and will not need to be rationally allocated. Then the difference between economy and waste will disappear.

Hunters have no idea of building wealth, and saving is not a virtue. If poverty is understood as one's subjective experience of one's living conditions and not merely a quantity of material wealth, hunters are by no means impoverished. In hunting-gathering economies, resources are not scarce, and the choice between different goals is unnecessary. So, there are no transaction costs, and people do not experience the pains caused by the foregoing of positive values. Labor is not distressing, and the time spent on it is not regarded as a cost. In order to look for food, hunters migrate all year round. However, instead of being tired and bored, they experience their journeys as meaningful and fulfilling. When what one does is full of meaning and value, one does not experience anything as a 'cost' or 'price.' As a result of not experiencing opportunity costs, one cannot experience transaction costs as well. In such societies there are also many informal institutions, but one reverses cause and effect when attempting to explain them with transaction costs, as do the new institutionalists. With the development of modern market economy and ever-increasing human desires, scarcity has come to reign supreme, and "insufficiency of material means becomes the explicit, calculable starting point of all economic activity" (Sahlins, 4). Only with the development of unlimited desires can opportunity and transaction costs be deeply felt, and hence those concepts are not universal but only relative to those societies that do not know how much is enough (Skidelsky and Skidelsky 2012) or what money cannot buy (Sandel 2012).

Notes

1 The prominent classical institutionalist economist Daniel W. Bromley makes a similar point, drawing especially from American pragmatism: judgments about economic policies must address the '*felt*,' real-world concerns of actual citizens and not just the abstract considerations of '*homo economicus*,' such as 'Pereto optimality' (Bromley 2006, 150).

2 As Hilary Putnam (2002, 54, 60, 74) and others (Stikkers 2015) have noted, Robbins perhaps did more than any other economist to cement the notion of 'scarcity' into the very definition of economics. As he wrote:

> Here we are, sentient creatures with bundles of desires and aspirations, with masses of instinctive tendencies all urging us in different ways to action. But the time in which these tendencies can be expressed is limited. The external world does not offer full opportunities for their complete achievement. Life is short. Nature is niggardly.
>
> (Robbins 1935, 13)

This condition, which Robbins takes as 'natural' and universal, is, as Sahlins (1972) shows, only relative to those cultures that encourage their members to want always more.

3 Benjamin Franklin had already observed of Native Americans, "almost all their Wants are supplied by the spontaneous Productions of Nature, with the addition of very little labour, if hunting and fishing may indeed be called labour when Game is so plenty … . they have few but natural wants, and these easily supplied." By contrast, "with us are infinite Artificial wants, no less craving than those of Nature, and much more difficult to satisfy" (letter to Peter Collinson, May 9 , 1753, in Franklin 1987, 470–71).

References

Bromley, Daniel W. 2006. *Sufficient Reason: Volitional Pragmatism and the Meaning of Economic Institutions*. Princeton, NJ: Princeton University Press.

Cheung, Stephen. 1992. "On the New Institutional Economics." In *Contract Economics*, ed. L. Werin and H. Wijkander, 48–65. Oxford: Basil Blackwell.

Coase, Ronald H. 1937. "The Nature of the Firm." *Economica* 4(16): 386–405.

Coase, Ronald H. 1960. "The Problem of Social Costs." *Journal of Law and Economics* 3(1): 1–44.

Franklin, Benjamin. 1987. *Benjamin Franklin: Writings*, ed. J. A. Leo Lemay. New York: Library of America.

Lin, Justin. 1989. "An Economic Theory of Institutional Change: Induced and Imposed Change." *Cato Journal* 9(1): 1–33.

North, Douglas. 1981. *Structure and Change in Economic History*. New York: W. W. Norton.

North, Douglas. 1990. *Institutional Change and Economic Performance*. New York: Cambridge University Press.

Putnam, Hilary. 2002. *The Collapse of the Fact-Value Dichotomy, and Other Essays*. Cambridge: Harvard University Press.

Robbins, Lionel. 1935. *An Essay on the Nature and Significance of Economic Science*, 2nd ed. London: Macmillan.

Sahlins, Marshal. 1972. *Stone Age Economics*. New York: Adline de Gruyter.

Sandel, Michael J. 2012. *What Money Can't Buy: The Moral Limits of Markets*. New York: Farrar, Straus & Giroux.

Scheler, Max. 1961. *Ressentiment*, trans. William W. Holdheim, ed. Lewis A. Coser. New York: Free Press of Glencoe.

Skidelsky, Robert, and Edward Skidelsky. 2012. *How Much Is Enough? – Money and the Good Life*. New York: Other Press.

Stikkers, Kenneth W. 1987. "Max Scheler's Contributions to Social Economics." *Review of Social Economy* 45(3): 223–242.

Stikkers, Kenneth W. 2015. "Economies of Scarcity and Acquisition, Economies of Gift and Thanksgiving: Lessons from Cultural Anthroplogy." In *Value and Values: Economics and Justice in an Age of Global Interdependence*, ed. Roger T. Ames and Peter D. Hershock, 214–228. Honolulu: University of Hawai'i Press.

Part V
Looking beyond the crisis

11 A pragmatist model of transforming urban inequalities

Creating livable cities in a time of crisis

David W. Woods

> The pragmatists replace the model of the planner as an *expert* offering truthful *advice* to the public (compulsion) with that of the planner as a *counselor* (persuasion), who fosters public deliberation about the *meaning* and *consequences* about relevant plans with those who will bear the burden and enjoy the benefits of *purposeful change*.
>
> (Charles Hoch, *What Planners Do*, 1994: 294)

Since the September 15, 2008, economic crash, the world has seen times of human suffering and uncertainty on multiple levels – economic, social, ecological, and existential – that have led to a crisis in cities worldwide. This crisis focusing on cities has further exasperated the already widening inequalities between income groups (wealthy versus low-income, with the middle class being squeezed out of the worlds' largest cities), as well as growing inequalities in social capital, which enables individuals and groups to expand their horizons; in ecological capital (potable water for all citizens, not just those who can purchase it, as well as clean air, accessible parks, and open spaces); and in existential capital, which allows for the belief in oneself and hope in the future. In this chapter, I will argue that planning scholars need to undertake a more nuanced analysis of inequalities in cities, to present a pragmatist model of transformation that draws from Dewey, Mead, Habermas, Green, Fung, and Woods, and to apply this model to the three architectures (social, built, and ecological).

George Herbert Mead's context-specific, radical transformation-focused insights about how to achieve a deeper, social democracy date from the late years of the nineteenth century, before the beginning of his close partnership with the famous pragmatist philosopher John Dewey. These insights include the idea that local urban activism is the most effective way to foster wider social change. Since the early 1960s, leading urban planners, philosophers, sociologists, and other political theorists have developed Mead's original insight, producing a considerable body of scholarship on the effectiveness of participatory and deliberative democracy as a tool for transforming communities through empowering local civic leaders and other citizens to influence public decisions, both in the United States and in other nations. Dewey would point out that achieving this goal requires individual and civic investment in a long-term process of educating citizens in more deeply democratic habits of community living. Mead and Robert E. Park (Park et al. 1925) would add that it also requires adapting our existing institutions to respond to the inputs of more deeply democratic individuals and communities. This will not be easy, because empowerment changes power relations.

Important recent works in transformative social theory that combine Mead-inspired ideas and methods from Jürgen Habermas on deliberative democracy and from John Dewey on democratic citizen participation have become effective and influential guides for scholars and activists. Over the last twenty years, considerable scholarship has focused on participatory democracy *and* deliberative democracy, at times using the terms interchangeably. This is not a distinction of theory versus practice, but of emphasis on an active public role in shaping public policy or on deliberative means of assuring that all are respectfully heard.

Citizen participation beyond the franchise is not necessary for ordinary bureaucratic decision-making on matters like whether an applicant for a land-use permit has submitted all necessary documents, or for ordinary representative decision-making on issues like whether to grant a variance to allow a new restaurant to use a portion of a public sidewalk for outdoor seating in a business zone in which this is already common practice. However, in post-disaster contexts of deciding whether to rebuild a city neighborhood or a village park, citizen participation can contribute to social healing. In making long-range plans, including budget planning (Baiocchi 2003), dispersed and diverse citizen-embedded knowledge and values can make plans more effective as well as more achievable. In these and more ordinary kinds of planning for significant change, citizens can contribute epistemically what they know and value. Moreover, their participation contributes to their education and to the emergence of new social habits in the culture, as Mead and Dewey argued. This is how real, twenty-first-century people move from abstract, formal citizenship, which may mean little to them, to substantial citizenship in which neighbors become real players in shaping their civic future. Democracy becomes grounded in real ways of living that shape cities in more sustainable ways through collaborative planning and shared citizen commitment to creating livable cities through interlinking the social/political, built, and environmental architectures.

Pragmatist reframing for transforming livable cities – an inclusive model

These last seven years of the Great Recession have seen times of human suffering and uncertainty on multiple levels of urban living that have led to a crisis in cities worldwide. This requires planning practitioners and scholars to develop a more nuanced and inclusive analysis of sustainable livability that reflects real inequalities in cities, and to bring forth a realistic and desirable, participatory democratic model of transformation that incorporates the social, built, and ecological architectures of sustainability.

It was not until the 1960s that federal, state, and local legislation required opportunities for affected stakeholders to participate in public decision-making, especially in areas of comprehensive planning that focus on visions for the future, land use, transportation, and environmental protection. My definition of 'affected stakeholders' is all those who are in the position to make or break a public decision and, more importantly, those who are directly affected by that decision. The 1960 election of John F. Kennedy as president of the United States, with his promise of youth, vigor, and the push for a "New Frontier," together with the beginning of the largest influx of youth to enter college at one time that the world has ever witnessed, created the basis for rethinking the role of city planners from passive reviewers of plans by developers who submitted them for review to a more activist role in developing the civic space in collaboration with affected stakeholders.

One of the most important paradigm shifts for the new role of urban planners was inspired by Jane Jacobs's *Death and Life of the Great American City* (1961). Jacobs was highly critical of 'business as usual,' whereby city planners only passively used their compulsion powers by reviewing plans based on the existing zoning code and passing these plans onto elected or appointed bodies to make decisions, instead of taking on the activist role suggested above (Woods 2013a, 2013b). Equally important was her criticism of the growing dominance of the automobile in the built environment; more specifically, she announced the imperative to plan for public spaces for people, not just the automobile, with safe streets, pedestrian activity, and public markets where citizens could meet and congregate. She called for citizens who were affected by decisions to stop being passive, and get out and organize for what they wanted, not what 'development czars,' such as Robert Moses, wanted.

The second key event that initiated a planning paradigm shift in the early 1960s was the Port Huron Statement in 1962, which brought the concept of a *contentious, countercultural, anti-authoritarian* participatory democracy to the American consciousness. During this historic era that shaped many young college students' generally shared world-view and broad social values, the inclusive principles of the Students for a Democratic Society's founding Port Huron Statement were also widely advocated by participants in the civil rights movement, the peace movement, the emerging women's movement, and the still-incubating environmental movement. The Port Huron Statement laid out several 'root principles' for participatory democracy:

> We would replace power rooted in possession, privilege, or circumstance by power and uniqueness rooted in love, reflectiveness, reason, and creativity. As a *social system* we seek the establishment of a democracy of individual participation, governed by two central aims; that the individual share in those social decisions determining the quality and direction of his [or her] life; that society be organized to encourage independence in men [and women] and provide the media for their common participation.
>
> (In Lemert 1999, 355)

These 'root principles' of "*contentious* participatory democracy of the 1960s" are still the basis for later "*collaborative* participatory democracy of the 1990s" (Woods 2012a, 3–4).

It is *collaborative* participatory democracy that emphasizes, among other factors, the 'educative function' of participatory events and planning processes, as these can affect both citizens and elected and appointed leaders. Participatory democratic city planners place relatively greater emphasis on how specific social issues develop through direct interaction among groups and individuals so as to produce shared community goals and values. Last but not least, a distinctive feature of participatory democracy in contrast to deliberative democracy is the presence of concerns about 'empowerment.' City planner proponents of participatory democracy are relatively more concerned about lessening inequalities between 'elites' and 'grass-roots' participants in decisions about the built, social, and environmental architectures. Participatory democracy seeks to help all citizens to influence representative bodies that have power to affect their lives.

For the last fifty years, participatory democracy has supplied such guiding ideals more than deliberative democracy, including questions about hierarchical inequalities between 'expert' leaders and grass-roots 'followers' that pose an ongoing (and perhaps never fully resolved) challenge. As planning theorist Charles Hoch articulated this shift,

> The pragmatists replace the model of the planner as an *expert* offering truthful *advice* to the public with that of the planner as a counselor, who fosters public deliberation about the *meaning* and *consequences* about relevant plans with those who will bear the burden and enjoy the benefits of *purposeful change.*
>
> (Hoch 1994, 294; emphasis mine)

The notion of 'empowered participatory democracy' was embraced by city planners as potentially offering a hopeful and preferable vision for future organizing and rebuilding cities starting with the 1964 Model Cities program as part of President Lyndon B. Johnson's 'War on Poverty.' The Model Cities program was designed to work with low- and moderate-income neighborhoods, planning with affected stakeholders, with the goals to eradicate poverty, create affordable housing, enhance local jobs, and strengthen schools, transportation options, and infrastructure (sewer, water, and parks). It was one of the first federal programs that required 'real' citizen participation by local stakeholders in developing these locally specific plans. While this program had lofty goals, it was only partially successful in transforming issues of low-income neighborhoods due mostly to the problem of finding local stakeholders who could pay the economic, educational, and opportunity costs of a robust citizen participation program of the kind required to be eligible for funding.

During these years, successful city planners started to take into account the importance of understanding who else needed to be at the planning table in order to make sure that city planners were planning 'with' instead of 'for' others, in Jane Addams's insightful phrase (Addams 1902; see also Follett 1918). City planners started to think about the kind of 'expert' dominance about which Dewey warned and to distinguish between fellow urban planners and to decide with the public at large what kinds of decisions call for direct and creative 'citizen voices,' what kinds call for aggregate expression of public opinion on others' public policy proposals (such as a hearing or referendum), what kinds are properly made by elected representatives, and what kinds are best left to expert bureaucrats (Forester 1999; Green 1999, 2008; Healey 2008; Woods 2012a).

Thomas Jefferson left us with insights on all these distinctions, arguing in letters and essays that, if ordinary people are given opportunities to develop the capabilities and experiences of democratic citizenship through appropriate kinds of active and direct participation in public planning and decision-making, they will contribute practical insights and creative suggestions that neither their representatives nor the always-necessary expert bureaucrats would be able to contribute without them. In this way, the people, the policies, and the implementation process all improve through the citizen participation process.

Important recent works in transformative social theory that combine ideas and methods from Jürgen Habermas on deliberative democracy and from Thomas Jefferson and his pragmatist inheritors on democratic citizen participation, have become effective and influential guides for scholars and activists (Green 1999, 2004; Forester 1999; Woods 2012a, 2012b; Fung 2004). As Richard Bernstein pointed out, Dewey argued that there is *"no dichotomy between theory and practice"* (Bernstein 2010, 197), or in Dewey's words:

> The depersonalization of the things of everyday practice becomes the chief agency of their repersonalizing in new and more fruitful modes of practice. The paradox of theory and practice is that theory is with respect to all other modes of practice the most practical of all things, and the more impractical and impersonal it is, the more truly practical it is. And this is the sole paradox.
>
> (Dewey 1916, 268)

However, we planners need to understand what participatory *and* deliberative democracy means in ways that highlight their specific differences as well as their similarities in order to identify and interrelate the strengths and weaknesses of each unique model and method as these impact civic, professional, and personal motivations and opportunities to organize and to participate in the public arena.

Rereading Mead's work has been decisive in shaping '*the pragmatist turn*' in the work of Jürgen Habermas and thus in the emergence of the influential, interdisciplinary school of deliberative democracy, which treats his work as a research platform. Habermas is one of the most important philosophers and sociologists of the late twentieth and early twenty-first century in rationalizing and guiding the legitimate incorporation of 'public' decision-making within democratic governance through his development of various ideal concepts, including the *ideal speech situation* leading to communicative action (Habermas 1984, 1998). Deliberative democracy focuses on creating the legitimate conditions for decision-makers to communicate respectfully and rationally with each other in order to make informed and inclusive democratic decisions based on shared procedural norms, values, and objectives. 'Public reason' is a limiting norm for what can be expressed and what reasons can be given for one's views in contexts of democratic public deliberation; what this means in practice is that feelings, personal commitments, and local 'habits of the heart' have no place in Habermasian deliberative democracy. This is a key point of difference between Habermas and Mead, Dewey, and William James, and recent works in social sciences and my urban-planning experience lead me to side with the latter.

Habermas highlighted constitution-guided communication among government representatives as paradigmatic of democratic deliberation, although other deliberative democratic theorists, such as James Fishkin (1991), have expanded his vision to include other citizens at carefully constructed, rule-governed communicative events. For Habermas, the public is to be involved in the decision process only as far as this is constitutionally mandated, e.g., to meet the letter of the law by holding 'official' public hearings on all land-use decisions. He does not see a general need to include the 'public' in developing the *vision* for which an urban plan was mandated in the first place. This is why Habermasian deliberative democrats believe it is legitimate to argue that a process that involves the 'public' might be inclusive, transparent, and deliberative but not necessarily *participatory* in giving citizens a 'real' voice in directly influencing final decisions of what livability means in their community, because their view can rightly be expressed by elected representatives and their expert appointees. Again, this is a key difference between Habermas and Mead, James, and Dewey on which I side with the classical American pragmatists, because an effective visioning process brings forth a shared vision that did not previously exist, and citizens could not be 'represented' until after the interactive exchanges that participating in collaborative planning makes possible.

Citizens' participation contributes to their education and to the emergence of new social habits in the culture, as Mead and Dewey argued and John Forester articulated:

> Because planning is the guidance of future action, planning with others calls for *astute deliberative practice*: learning about others as well as about issues, learning about what we should do as well as what we can do. So when city planners deliberate with city residents, they *shape public learning* as well as *public act*. Sharing or withholding information, encouraging or discouraging public participation, city planners can *nurture* public hope *or* deepen citizens' resignation.

> (Forester 1999, 1)

This is how real, twenty-first-century people develop substantial citizenship whereby neighbors become real players in shaping their civic future. Democracy becomes grounded in real ways of living that shape cities (and rural areas) in more desirable and sustainable ways through collaborative planning that can generate shared citizen commitment to key goals.

Resources from Dewey and Mead: values, process, habits, and institutions

While it is true that a radical democratic vision based on Dewey and Mead is not, in and of itself, a grand theory of economic equality and redistribution of wealth in the Marxist tradition, Dewey and Mead did argue that context-specific institutions and a more general vision of social and economic justice will emerge over time *if* participants are given opportunities for empowering education, collaborative democratic inquiry, and organized 'weight throwing.' It is through problem-focused processes of engaging and empowering citizens to provide direct input through collaborative, democratic participation that Deweyan radical democratic visions were instituted and now work to influence elected officials and economic leaders in many cities throughout America.

The role of planners in developing a pragmatist response to inequalities

Over the last twenty years, pragmatist philosopher and urban planner Judith M. Green and I have been working on a pragmatist model of livable cities. It is clear to us that *resilience* has emerged as a guiding concept in twenty-first century urban planning in response to experiences of terrorist attacks, earthquakes, tornados, hurricanes, and other climate-change-related disasters, as well as a key principle for dealing with inequalities to build more livable cities. Planners, architects, and landscape designers have worked with climate scientists, sociologists, community leaders, and diverse citizens in the aftermath of many such recent disasters, as well as in ongoing efforts to increase social equity, as a key element of livability. Their shared aim has been to

Table 11.1 Participatory and deliberative democracy matrix

		Deliberative *Yes (Habermas)*	*Deliberative* *No*
Participatory *(Dewey)*	*Yes*	Square no. 1: Town hall meetings Listening to the city 1 & 2	Square no. 2: Voting in elections Panel presentations
Participatory	*No*	Square no. 3: City council meetings 'Official' public hearings	Square no. 4: Implementation Bureaucracy

Source: Woods 2012a, 115.

restore hopes, lives, communities, and built environments in adaptive ways that prepare for related future contingencies while rebuilding livable cities after such disasters. In doing so, they have drawn on current knowledge and expert projections, as well as community values and individual inspirations, seeking to create *shared visions* that will make a necessarily changed place *beautiful, socially functional*, and *as safe as possible*. However, disputes and contrasting commitments have often emerged among experts and citizens during these processes, reflecting differences of opinion about how to think about democracy and the public good, as well as how to include citizens in *democratic decision processes* that include both science and architecture.

Planners and philosophers – especially those with a pragmatist orientation – can help to resolve these disputes and advance *the resilience factor* in such twenty-first-century civic rebuilding processes to create location-specific livable cities of equality by

1 adding a stimulus to reframe the political, scientific, social, and planning issues;
2 suggesting new ways to understand key concepts, such as 'democracy,' 'citizen standing,' 'property rights,' and the 'public interest,' in light of historical changes in their meaning and use;
3 highlighting unique aspects of a particular context, as well as similarities and 'family resemblances' to other events;
4 asking *the right questions* that clarify the current issues in terms that show knowledge of and respect for co-participating disciplines, as well as diverse communities; and
5 suggesting how to include citizens in *epistemically and politically effective democratic inquiry* that aims for broad agreement about how to adjust

   • individual memories, narratives, and aspirations,
   • changing community relationships,
   • the current array of public institutions, and
   • new relationships among the three intertwined elements of urban ecology: the natural, the social, and the built environment.

This pragmatist approach to civic engagement in theorizing and planning for transforming inequitable cities into livable cities would incorporate many of the following elements of livability:

• Walkability
• Efficient and affordable public transportation
• Affordable housing for all current and future residents
• Living wage jobs
• Parks and open space
• Cultural pluralism
• Educational institutions
• Religious institutions

- Financial institutions (lending institutions for local residents and businesses)
- Vibrant business sector
- Food, water, energy infrastructure
- Entertainment
- Public utilities
- Environmental sustainability
- Public safety
- Supportable streetscape
- Moderate density.

From PlaNYC 2030 to OneNYC 2030: economy, ecology, and equity

During the twelve-year period that Michael Bloomberg was mayor of New York City, his administration faced three major economic crises: a) rebuilding NYC after 9/11, b) the economic crash of 2008 that devastated one of the city's major industries (Wall Street investors and all of the support businesses), costing thousands of people their jobs, and c) rebuilding after Hurricane Sandy in October 2012. The Bloomberg administration learned from these three disasters to utilize the planning framework developed as part of rebuilding after 9/11 (Woods 2012a). Building upon this, the Bloomberg administration developed and unveiled on Earth Day in 2007 its PlaNYC 2030 as a blueprint for rebuilding New York City, including *economic development,* land use, transportation, and *environmental policies* especially focusing on waterfront development and sustainable parks. Building on and reframing these focuses of PlaNYC 2030, on Earth Day 2015, Mayor Bill de Blasio unveiled OneNYC 2030, which focuses on the key missing component of economic sustainability for a livable city: equity, especially in affordable housing, living wage jobs, and expanded affordable public transportation.

A framework for deep democratic engagement

What I have discussed above is aimed toward developing a framework for interweaving built architecture, environmental preservation, and a social architecture grounded in deep democratic engagement into a planning process that can create more naturally and socially sustainable, ideal, livable cities in the future. This last section will explore two main questions: How is planning with nature related to planning for human welfare in ideal cities of the future? What are some solutions to interweaving all three elements – social, built, and natural – that have arisen within collaborative planning for land use, transportation, economic development, and social-natural sustainability?

Bruce Knight, FAICP (Fellow of the American Institute of Certified Planners), the former president of the American Planning Association (APA) who represented the APA at the 2008 Earth Summit in Rio de Janeiro, has argued that planning must now focus on sustainability:

Planning for sustainability is the defining challenge of the 21st century. Overcoming deeply ingrained economic and cultural patterns that result in resource depletion, climate instability, and economic and social stress requires holistic problem solving that blends the best scientific understanding of existing conditions and available technologies with the public resolve to act.

(Godschalk and Anderson 2012, 1)

Even though the concept of sustainability has been used in the social sciences, the natural sciences, and the humanities at least since the 1992 UN Earth Summit, its use is generally undefined. What it means is the interlinking of three separate architectures – built, environmental, and social – deeply grounded in civic engagement in shaping the future of that context-specific area. Some pragmatist environmental philosophers, e.g., Andrew Light and Hugh McDonald, have argued that there really is no such thing as sustainable development, only sustainable preservation. However, I argue that the world really does not have a choice about sustainable development, given the natural population growth (births outnumber deaths, and life expectancy is longer). This means that we must find sustainable ways to house, feed, educate, and employ millions of people in the next fifty years in ways that do not totally deplete natural resources, while preserving environmental treasures, reusing already built areas more effectively, and providing opportunities for civic participation in the decision process. In doing so, we take an active role in the choice of where and, more importantly, *how* humans live in the future.

However, given the general principle of sustainability that links the three architectures, we need to learn from recent best practices that provide sustainable solutions for cities of the future, which include some changes in the patterns of land use, transportation, economic development, and social-natural sustainability. Land use is one of the most controversial areas to focus on in dealing with sustainable built environments, especially in Europe and the United States, perhaps less so in Latin America, Asia, and Africa. But, there still exist inequalities between extreme wealth and extreme poverty in some of the most rapidly developing cities in the world today, e.g., in Rio de Janeiro between the citizens who live near the world-famous Copacabana Beach and those who live in the shacks in the favelas only a few miles away. These are contexts in which real urban development projects need to put people to work and to provide healthy and safe living environments, while designing for clean air, water, and sanitation. This takes government action and will – it cannot be left to the 'free market,' which is not free but leads the wealthy to build for themselves and not for the less-well-off. Sustainability also means that new development must include more density in housing units, office buildings, and shopping areas located close to where there is employment, schools, and recreational opportunities. For sustainable development to work, affordable transportation systems must be built to lessen dependency on the automobile, including high-speed rail, light rail, dedicated bus lanes, bicycle lanes and lockers for bicycle storage, and more walkable designs for people to move around cities more easily. Such land-use changes and enhanced transportation systems can bring about living wage jobs, as well as enhance the ability of employers to locate businesses closer to employees. Whether these aspects of social sustainability are planned for and actualized depends on whether the everyday citizens they affect most intimately participate in the planning and the implementation processes. As Mead argued, such active citizen participation is the best, perhaps the only way to shape new social habits that reflect and actualize our ideals. In this century, deep democracy and sustainability go hand in hand. The only way to accomplish this sustainable agenda of inter-linking the built, environmental, and social architectures is through a deeply democratic engagement of citizens who know and care about specific locations, planning for Earth's survival at the same time as they work together to develop more ideal, livable communities.

References

Addams, Jane. 1902. *Democracy and Social Ethics.* Champaign, IL: University of Illinois Press, 2002.

Baiocchi, Gianpaolo. 2003. "Participation, Activism, and Politics: The Porto Alegre Experiment." In *Deepening Democracy: Institutional Innovations in Empowered Participatory Governance*, ed. Archon Fung and Erik Olin Wright. London: Verso Press.

Bernstein, Richard. 2010. *The Pragmatic Turn.* New York: Polity Press.

Dewey, John. 1915. *Democracy and Education.* Vol. 9 of *The Middle Works of John Dewey, 1899–1924*, ed. Jo Ann Boydston. Carbondale: Southern Illinois University Press, 1980.

Dewey, John. 1916. "The Logic of Judgments and Practice." In *The Essential Dewey*, vol. 2: *Ethics, Logic, Psychology*, ed. Larry A. Hickman and Thomas M. Alexander. Bloomington: Indiana University Press, 1998.

Dewey, John. 1927. *The Public and Its Problems.* In *The Later Works, 1925–1953*, vol 2: *1925–1927, Essays, The Public and Its Problems*, ed. Jo Ann Boydston. Carbondale: Southern Illinois University Press, 1984.

Dewey, John. 1939. "Creative Democracy – The Task Before Us." In *The Later Works of John Dewey, 1925–1953*, vol. 14: *1939–1941, Essays*, ed. Jo Ann Boydston, 224–230. Carbondale: Southern Illinois University Press, 1988.

Dewey, John. 1940. "Introducing Thomas Jefferson." In *The Later Works of John Dewey, 1925–1953*, vol. 14: *1939–1941, Essays*, ed. Jo Ann Boydston. Carbondale: Southern Illinois University Press, 1988.

Fishkin, James. 1991. *Democracy and Deliberations: New Directions for Democratic Reform.* New Haven: Yale University Press.

Follett, Mary Parker. 1918. *The New State: Group Organization the Solution of Popular Government.* University Park, PA: Pennsylvania State University Press, 1998.

Forester, John. 1999. *The Deliberative Practitioner: Encouraging Participatory Planning Processes.* Cambridge: MIT Press.

Fung, Archon. 2004. *Empowered Participation: Reinventing Urban Democracy.* Princeton: Princeton University Press.

Godschalk, David R., and William R. Anderson. 2012. *Sustaining Places: The Role of the Comprehensive Plan*. Planning Advisory Service Report Number 567. Chicago: American Planning Association.

Green, Judith. 1999. *Deep Democracy: Community, Diversity and Transformation*. Lanham, MD: Rowman & Littlefield Publishers.

Green, Judith. 2004. "Participatory Democracy: Movements, Campaigns, and Democratic Living." In *Pragmatism and Deliberative Democracy*, ed. Robert Talisse. Special issue, *Journal of Speculative Philosophy* 18: 60–71.

Green, Judith. 2005. "Pluralism and Deliberative Democracy." In *Blackwell Companion to Pragmatism*, ed. John Shook and Joseph Margolis. Oxford: Blackwell Publishing.

Green, Judith. 2008. *Pragmatism and Social Hope: Deepening Democracy in Global Contexts*. New York: Columbia University Press.

Green, Judith, ed. 2014. *Richard J. Bernstein and the Pragmatist Turn in Contemporary Philosophy: Rekindling Pragmatism's Fire*. New York: Palgrave Macmillan.

Habermas, Jürgen. 1984. *The Theory of Communicative Action*, vol. 1: *Reason and the Rationalization of Society*, trans. Thomas McCarthy. Boston: Beacon Press.

Habermas, Jürgen. 1998. *On the Pragmatics of Communication* ed. Maeve Cooke. Cambridge, MA: MIT Press.

Healey, Patsy. 2008. "The Pragmatic Tradition in Planning Thought." *Journal of Planning Education and Research* 28(3): 277–292.

Hoch, Charles. 1994. *What Planners Do: Power, Politics, and Persuasion*. Chicago: American Planning Association.

Lemert, Charles. 1999. *Social Theory: The Multicultural and Classical Readings*. Boulder, CO: Westview Press.

Mead, George Herbert. 1910. "Social Consciousness and the Consciousness of Meaning." *Psychological Bulletin* 7: 397–405. Repr. in *Pragmatism: The Classical Writings*, ed. H. S. Thayer. Indianapolis: Hackett Publishing Co., 1982.

Mead, George Herbert. 1915. "The Social Self." *Journal of Philosophy, Psychology, and Scientific Methods* 10: 374–380. Repr. in *Pragmatism: The Classical Writings*, ed. H. S. Thayer. Indianapolis: Hackett Publishing Co.

Mead, George Herbert. 1932. *The Philosophy of the Present*, ed. Arthur Murphy. Chicago: Open Court Press.

Mead, George Herbert. 1934. *Mind, Self, and Society from the Standpoint of a Social Behaviorist*, ed. Charles W. Morris. Chicago: University of Chicago Press, 1962.

Mead, George Herbert. 1938. *The Philosophy of the Act*, ed. Charles W. Morris. Chicago: University of Chicago Press.

Park, Robert E., Ernest Burgess, and Roderick McKenzie. 1925. *The City: Suggestions for Investigation of Human Behavior in the Urban Environment*. Chicago: University of Chicago Press.

Shalin, Dmitri. 1991. "G. H. Mead, Socialism and the Progressive Agenda." In *Philosophy, Social Theory, and the Thought of George Herbert Mead*, ed. Mitchell Aboulafia. Albany, NY: State University of New York Press.

Woods, David W. 2012a. *Democracy Deferred: Civic Leadership after 9/11*. New York: Palgrave Macmillan.

Woods, David W. 2012b. "A Pragmatist Philosophy of the City: Dewey, Mead and Contemporary Best Practices." *Cognitio-Estudos* 9(1): 73–74.

Woods, David W. 2013a. "George Herbert Mead on the Social Bases of Democracy." In *George Herbert Mead in the 21st Century*, ed. Tom Burke and Krzysztof Skowroński. Lanham, MD: Lexington Books.

Woods, David W. 2013b. "Persuasion and Compulsion in Democratic Urban Planning." In *Persuasion and Compulsion in Democracy*, ed. Jacqueline Kegley and Krzysztof Skowroński. Lanham, MD: Lexington Books.

Woods, David W. 2014. "Democratic Community Participation: Bernstein between Dewey and an Achieved Deeply Democratic Future." In *Richard J. Bernstein and the Pragmatist Turn in Contemporary Philosophy: Rekindling Pragmatism's Fire*, ed. Judith M. Green. New York: Palgrave Macmillan.

12 Deepening Piketty's pragmatism

Hopeful leadings for democratic political economy

Judith Green

> The present state of industrial life seems to give a fair index of the existing separation of means and ends. Isolation of economics from ideal ends, whether of morals or of organized social life, was proclaimed by Aristotle. Certain things, he said, are conditions of a worthy life, personal and social, but are not constituents of it. The economic life of man, concerned with satisfaction of wants, is of this nature ... Most philosophers have not been so frank nor perhaps so logical. But upon the whole, economics has been treated as on a lower level than either morals or politics. Yet the life which men, women and children actually lead, the opportunities open to them, the values they are capable of enjoying, their education, their share in all the things of art and science, are mainly determined by economic conditions. Hence we can hardly expect a moral system which ignores economic conditions to be other than remote and empty.
>
> Industrial life is correspondingly brutalized by failure to equate it as the means by which social and cultural values are realized. That the economic life, thus exiled from the pale of higher values, takes revenge by declaring that it is the only social reality, and by means of the doctrine of materialistic determination of institutions and conduct in all fields, denies to deliberate morals and politics any share of causal regulation, is not surprising.
>
> (John Dewey, *The Quest for Certainty*, 1929, in *Later Works* 4, 1988: 225)

Working with a global team of co-researchers, the French economist Thomas Piketty has launched a formidable challenge to the currently dominant, liberal-technocratic paradigm of economic theory in his internationally influential book, *Capital in the Twenty-First Century* (2014). Describing his intellectual standpoint as "pragmatist," Piketty calls for a methodological shift away from econometrics and an opening up of economics' disciplinary boundaries into wider inquiries in 'political economy' that include history, political science, psychology, sociology, and other disciplines for a threefold purpose: to better understand economic, social, and political trends over the last three centuries; to analyze adequately current global issues; and to guide public policy effectively in a desirable, democratic direction in the coming years. Although Piketty has not yet explicitly invited *philosophers* into this continuing inquiry, he has already demonstrated how to deploy new methods of inquiry that expand upon those economists typically use, including careful combing of historical tax records in order to plot data flows and trends in relation to world events, as well as reflecting on socially critical works of literature by masters like Jane Austen and Charles Dickens.

Moreover, Piketty's reflections on earlier and contemporary works of philosophy clearly play an important role in his thinking toward a new "pragmatist" paradigm of democratic political economy. His analysis of the most effective methods for understanding and transforming what he, like John Dewey, regards as the inseparable moral and practical problems in which political economy now must intervene "deliberately" reflects his inheritance of the contributions of those eighteenth- and nineteenth-century moral philosophers and social activists who initiated economics as a discipline, as well as the theories and practices of democratic politics. Piketty expresses definite views about the works of Adam Smith and Karl Marx, as well as a guiding commitment to the ideals of the French *Declaration of the Rights of Man and of the Citizen*, a general sense that advancing the common welfare matters more than achieving and maintaining economic equality, and moral disgust at extremely high incomes entirely from inherited capital and unproductively high corporate salaries.

In addition, Piketty mentions the work of six contemporary philosophers as either helpful or useless for guiding our reflections on the big issues of political economy in our times. He mentions the work of John Rawls, whose philosophical methods and liberal model of justice have permeated the social sciences, both in the main text and in three endnotes. He mentions and cites Amartya Sen's work several times, although he reads him as a leading economic theorist, rather than as a philosopher. In an endnote, Piketty assesses Jacques Ranciere's *The Hatred of Democracy* (2005) as "indispensable" reading. Finally, in a single footnote, Piketty alludes briefly to works on capital and class inequality by Jean-Paul Sartre, Louis Althusser, and Alain Badiou, dismissing them all as "a pretext for jousts of a different nature entirely" (Piketty 2014, 655n2). Taken together with his fuller discussions of political economy's classical thinkers and his ways of expressing his own moral sentiments, these brief contemporary references show that philosophy is a familiar discipline for Piketty that influences his ongoing efforts to frame a new "pragmatist" paradigm of democratic political economy. However, he has not yet imagined *an active role* for philosophers on his interdisciplinary 'dream team' of researchers, and *pragmatist philosophy* is not yet on his radar screen.

Piketty's philosophical literacy should not surprise the attentive reader – after all, Piketty is French, and the study of philosophy is part of a formative education for intellectuals and social leaders in all fields in France today, as it has been for more than a century. Regrettably, however, Piketty's formative philosophical education ended before the current worldwide revival of interest in pragmatist philosophy, and it probably did not include works by classical American pragmatists like Charles S. Peirce, William James, John Dewey, G. H. Mead, Jane Addams, and W. E. B. Du Bois, even though many of James's key concepts and phrases (such as the 'cash value' of an idea) appear without acknowledgment in works by countless contemporary philosophers, functioning as a kind of *lingua franca*. Thus, even though Piketty calls his methods of developing his already influential new paradigm of democratic political economy "pragmatist," and his ways of thinking clearly show the influence of his ongoing engagement with philosophy, *Capital in the Twenty-First Century* displays no specific awareness of *pragmatist philosophy*, classical and contemporary, which could offer valuable assistance to his project.

Therefore, my purpose here is to show how pragmatist philosophers can contribute actively in critical, interpretive, integrative, and creative ways to Piketty's hope-inspiring, interdisciplinary project of developing this new "pragmatist" paradigm of democratic political economy into an effective instrument for understanding the urgent problems of our times and for guiding specific local-and-global changes. I believe that Piketty will find the spirit, ideas, methods, and practical engagements of classical and contemporary philosophical pragmatism congenial with many aspects of his own way of thinking. At the same time, its critical and reconstructive approaches can help him to resolve *a moral and practical dilemma* within his current framework and also to give detail to some of its currently too-vague aspects. If we contemporary pragmatist philosophers do our interdisciplinary homework in order to be ready to join this highly demanding, already energized inquiry in mid-stream – and if we come prepared to explain our intellectual inheritance to our colleagues in economics and other social science disciplines and to demonstrate to them the kinds of social-intellectual tools, perspectives, and networks we bring – contemporary pragmatist philosophers can contribute valuable assistance in advancing the intellectually powerful and potentially transformative interdisciplinary inquiry that Piketty now leads in these times of economic, social, and ecological crisis.

Piketty's new "pragmatist" paradigm of democratic political economy

In *Capital in the Twenty-First Century*, Thomas Piketty offers historical data-driven answers to basic questions about the real, national and global processes of accumulating and distributing wealth during the past three centuries – answers that partially support Karl Marx's concern that "the dynamics of private capital accumulation inevitably lead to the concentration of wealth in ever fewer hands," while radically limiting the generality of the influential, mid-twentieth century American economist Simon Kuznets's claim that "the balancing forces of growth, competition, and technological progress [will lead] in later stages of [capitalism's] development to reduced inequality and greater harmony among the classes" (Piketty, 1). Kuznets's historical data set was inadequate to support this general claim, Piketty persuasively argues, as it largely reflects an unsustainable rate of economic growth to rebuild national infrastructures after two world wars, as well as policy-driven, post-war changes in taxation rates that allowed for the creation of much-needed public goods, including new housing, the expansion of education, and social insurance funds to provide for conditions of old age, disability, and unemployment, thereby renewing the basis and hope for democracy. Contrary to Kuznets's conclusion, the Piketty team's preliminary analysis of their much larger data set shows that *the rate of return on private capital generally tends to grow faster than do national economies,* leading to rapidly increasing, non-productive, and democracy-corrosive economic and social inequalities for which Piketty believes democratic countermeasures can and should be deployed.

> Let me say at once that the answers contained herein are imperfect and incomplete. But they are based on much more extensive historical and comparative data than were available to previous researchers, data covering three centuries and more than twenty countries, as well as on a new theoretical framework that affords a deeper understanding of the underlying mechanisms. Modern economic growth and the diffusion of knowledge have made it possible to avoid the Marxist apocalypse but have not modified the deep structures of capital and inequality – or in any case not as much as one might have imagined in the optimistic decades following World War II. *When the rate of return on capital exceeds the rate of growth of output and income,* as it did in the nineteenth century and seems quite likely to do again in the twenty-first, *capitalism automatically generates arbitrary and unsustainable inequalities that radically undermine the meritocratic values on which democratic societies are based.* There are nevertheless ways *democracy can regain control over capitalism* and ensure that the general interest takes precedence over private interests, while preserving economic openness and avoiding protectionist and nationalist reactions.
>
> (Piketty, 1–2; emphases added)

What kinds of democratic countermeasures may be feasible as well as desirable now is unclear: the much lower rates of growth in national economies since the Great Recession began in September 2008 are likely to be the new normal, Piketty suggests, but there is little public support now for expanding the kinds of redistributive programs that it was possible to institute in the wake of the shared suffering of World War II. Thus, given *the law of capital accumulation* that his team's historical data reveal, the gap in wealth between the top 1%, the top 10%, and everyone else is growing and will continue to grow, unless and until we adopt a reconstructed, democracy-focused model of international political economy or find ourselves in the midst of an even more devastating World War III. At the same time, already great social inequalities in power, influence on the future of nations, educational opportunities, practical choices in daily life, health and lifespan probabilities, exposure to violence, and variable senses of personal value that ensue in capitalist, market-led societies, will become even more exaggerated.

In analyzing these long-term trends toward increasing economic and social inequality, Piketty expresses the same kind of moral and practical concerns that drove both Marx's critique and Kuznets's defense of capitalism, as well as the French Revolution's rejection of vastly and permanently unequal inherited social positions: such institutional outcomes, even though rationalized by the philosophical claims and social habits of some, are *unjust and anti-democratic*, as well as *politically unstable and economically inefficient*. Writing as a French intellectual of the twenty-first century, Piketty reaffirms Article 1 of his revolutionary forbears' 1789 *Declaration of the Rights of Man and the Citizen*: "Social distinctions can be based only on common utility." Thus, his is not a leveling egalitarianism – "social inequalities are not in themselves a problem as long as they are justified, i.e., founded only upon common utility" (31) – but rather a practical one that draws both on historical data and on the culture-specific, yet inter-culturally influenced 'common sense' and moral sentiments of diverse contemporary peoples to conclude that this wide and growing wealth-gap within and between nations undermines instead of serving "common utility."[1] Although Piketty accepts limited inequalities in institutional outcomes on the basis of actually contributive "merit," incentives, and tolerable imperfections in the operations of social institutions, he rejects as "indecent" the heaps of inherited wealth that create unearned, lifelong social advantages for the few, and he rejects as unsound Kuznets's claim that minimally regulated capitalist markets in developed societies tend toward greater social equality in the long run.

Piketty does not regard this situation of growing, capital-based economic and social inequality as hopeless, but rather as requiring a new theoretical and practical paradigm of democratic political economy that can be deployed to adjust the current relationships between politics and the economy in various nations in ways that reinstate democratic norms, work toward common utility, and reflect an older, basic value of *social justice*, which he does not define, and for which his colleague Emmanuel Saez could give no more detailed defense than to say it is still important because "people care about it."[2] Developing and gaining acceptance for this new paradigm of democratic political economy and its public-policy implications will not be easy. It requires finding ways to overcome the theoretical and political "dialogue of the deaf" (Piketty, 3) of the post-Cold War years, which has prevented intellectuals and their fellow citizens from acknowledging, understanding, and transforming the growing threat of unproductive inequality in wealth, with all its "indecent" social implications. Thus, the method of developing the new paradigm matters: it must be widely inclusive of differing scholarly viewpoints as well as many kinds of data, and it must effectively engage the wider audience of thinkers, power-wielders, and social-change activists that it aims to influence.

In his own terms, the method of paradigm development that Piketty advocates and attempts to model in *Capital in the Twenty-First Century* is both 'pragmatic' and 'democratic.' Its *pragmatism* is expressed in its interdisciplinary, empirical, and historicist method, as well as its focus on "fundamental questions" that social sciences such as economics originally aimed to answer and must undertake again:

> If we are to *progress* in our understanding of the historical dynamics of ... wealth distribution and the structure of social classes, we must obviously *take a pragmatic approach* and avail ourselves of the methods of historians, sociologists, and political scientists as well as economists. We must start with fundamental questions and try to answer them. Disciplinary disputes and turf wars are of little or no importance. In my mind, this book is as much a work of history as of economics.
>
> (33; emphases added)

Such a new paradigm of political economy must also be *democratic*, Piketty more vaguely suggests, in that the test of the adequacy of its eventual answers to these "fundamental questions" about how to organize social institutions so that they will operate justly is to subject them eventually to "democratic debate."

> I am interested in contributing however modestly to the debate about *the best way to organize society* and *the most appropriate institutions and policies to achieve a just social order* ... effectively and efficiently under the *rule of law*, which should apply equally to all and derive from universally understood statutes subject to *democratic debate*.
>
> (31; emphases added)

Although it involves many other analyses supported by large, online data sets, Piketty's approach to developing this new "pragmatic" paradigm of democratic political economy has six key features that suggest the need for active contributions from participating philosophers:

1   It requires economics to shift its focus and methods from econometric analysis of the behavior of rational 'agents' in hypothetical situations within abstract ideal systems – "the profession's undue enthusiasm for simplistic mathematical models based on so-called representative agents" – to new methods of collaborative, empirical work with other social sciences, including history and sociology, in order to uncover the historical dynamics of wealth distribution, so as to "identify mechanisms at work and gain a clearer idea of the future" (16).
2   It involves "putting the distributional question back at the heart of economic analysis" (15); as Piketty emphasizes, "It is long since past the time when we should have put the question of inequality back at the center of economic analysis and begun asking questions first asked in the nineteenth century" (16).

3   It expresses doubt about the economic ideal of 'balanced growth' and anxiety about who will own the world in 2050 if the mechanisms of capital accumulation continue to operate unchanged as they have over the last several hundred years, as well as wariness of "any economic determinism in regard to inequalities of wealth and income," because the history of wealth is "deeply political" (20).

4   It acknowledges the ancient, widely shared, yet contextually plastic ideal of *justice*, as well as relative differences in *power*, as key factors in explaining historical changes in patterns and degrees of inequalities that social institutions produce through the interactive behavior of many, diverse human agents: "the history of inequality is shaped by the way economic, social, and political actors view what is *just* and what is *not*, as well as the *relative power* of those actors and the *collective choices* that result. It is the *joint product* of all relevant actors combined" (20; emphases added).

5   It focuses on understanding and influencing how "the dynamics of wealth distribution reveal *powerful* [*social*] *mechanisms* pushing alternatively toward convergence and divergence ... there is *no natural, spontaneous process* to prevent destabilizing, inegalitarian forces from prevailing permanently" (21; emphases added).

6   Its theoretical purpose is not only to *explain* but to *guide transformation* of local-and-global problem situations in political economy, using democratic institutional models and change methods to achieve *morally and practically preferable outcomes for real lives*.

Perhaps due to a 'philosophical hangover' from reflecting on earlier thinkers' unworkable methods of imagining the theory-practice relationship, Piketty runs out of words on the second part of this sixth point – how to develop the kind of empirically well-grounded, "pragmatic" and "democratic" new paradigm of political economy that, in turn, can guide twenty-first-century institutional transformations and public-policy developments in more "common utility"-serving directions. In Part IV of *Capital in the Twenty-First Century*, Piketty argues that the kind of "social state" that became the normal model of democracy after World War II is so deeply entrenched in modern societies now that there is no going back on its basic commitments to education, health care, unemployment insurance, and income replacement for senior citizens, but *none of these is adequately funded* because of budget-draining commitments to wars and the political impossibility now of the kind of general increase in taxes to pay for such programs that most voters supported in the late 1940s. In seeking a solution to this key problem, Piketty follows Rawls's philosophical approach of antecedently specifying a universal, ideal model of social relationships of political economy and then proposing a global strategy for achieving it by progressive approximations: to end the unequalizing and democracy-undermining trend toward a small number of people who have inherited capital-based wealth, increasingly owning almost everything, Piketty proposes *confiscatory taxation*, globally imposed, with no tax havens, that rapidly reduces the holdings of such individuals. Not only would such taxation curb the corruptive power of the wealthiest one thousandth per cent over elections and democratic policy-making processes, Piketty suggests, but it would also fund advances in education that could increase social equality and open up life choices for many who still bear the burden of colonial social structures and race-based oppression. What Piketty overlooks in developing and proposing this one-size-fits-all solution is this: unless the *current institutional guardians* and *other powerful actors* in local-and-global political economies are persuaded by the concerted efforts of *researchers* and *ordinary citizens* that such taxes must be adopted, they will effectively resist such changes until it is too late to make them. Moreover, unless such researchers and ordinary citizens are persuaded of the necessity of such a confiscatory tax policy and other changes by coordinated and effective initiatives in many social-institutional realms – education, political campaigns, community-building efforts, religion, and the arts – they are likely to affirm the widespread view that confiscatory taxation is neither feasible nor desirable and thus to do nothing. Concerning the crucial question of *how to solve this practical and moral dilemma* he so effectively frames and documents, Piketty has no ideas.

Thus, Piketty's interdisciplinary 'dream team' clearly needs thinkers who can offer assistance in resolving this practical and moral dilemma from both directions, thinkers who can not only propose persuasive strategies for overcoming the current resistance of the many and the powerful to providing needed funding and authorizing governmental and non-governmental organizations to take the necessary steps to reduce unjust and unproductive economic and social inequalities, but who can also suggest a preferable alternative to Piketty's and many others' current way of thinking about the relationship between theory and practice that has generated this dilemma. Many philosophers have written about each aspect of this dilemma; some of them have helped to create it. *Pragmatist philosophers* can offer helpful proposals of both kinds, in addition to being ready, willing, and able to play critical, interpretive, integrative, and imaginative roles in many other aspects of Piketty's wildly ambitious moral and practical project.

How pragmatist philosophers can helpfully reframe Piketty's "pragmatist" paradigm

In the critical phase of our contribution to resolving Piketty's dilemma – exposing theoretical missteps as well as widely shared conceptual errors that block otherwise feasible and desirable solutions to the moral and practical problems of economic and social inequality – pragmatist philosophers can show that economics, politics, and law, as scholarly disciplines, are rife with ill-considered and outdated philosophical assumptions and apparently harmless, simplifying devices that drive many of their mainstream research methods and public-policy proposals. So, too, is the slow-to-change 'common sense' of diverse modern peoples, which not only reflects the earlier influence of these disciplines and their public-policy proposals, but also guides the development of individuals' personal and culturally shared life plans, in which such theoretical assumptions and simplifying devices function as working generalizations about reality that many people take to be facts of experience. Such philosophical obstacles include a widely shared metaphysical assumption that human beings are ultimately *solitary individuals* driven by acquisitive, adversarial desires and guided in achieving their goals by instrumental rationality; that they are morally endowed by nature with equal, inalienable rights to life, liberty, and all the property they 'earn' through their own labors, and therefore are morally entitled to protect; and that they are politically best-served by a limited government that allows economic and intellectual markets to reward 'the best' for their individual hard work and ingenuity in a 'dog-eat-dog' struggle for survival, social leadership, and lasting cultural influence.[3] Many ideal theoretical visions of political economy – liberal, libertarian, and conservative – are grounded in this 'common sense' about the ultimate metaphysical, moral, and political solitariness of all individual persons, aiming to free such 'persons' from any historical encroachments on the liberty this implies and to establish this individualist ideal as the shared practical reality within and among nations by stage-wise approximations, *even if* the process of actualizing this ideal may lead to radical economic and social inequalities among real human persons and nations.[4] Such an unrealistic, foundational view of the 'solitary' individual underlies the methodology of contemporary econometrics, as well as libertarian and objectivist politics, many recent rulings of the United States Supreme Court, and the practical training that most Western business students receive in the classroom and on the job.

However, the theories of those philosophers, social scientists, and practitioners who focus on the ethical choices of solitary individuals *misfire*, both descriptively and normatively, while using up 'air time' we need to be devoting to studying, communicating, and making hard decisions – sometimes individually, sometimes collectively – about the important moral and practical issues that grow out of the ways in which our lives are inextricably entangled with those of others, creating unequal and unjust patterns of benefits and burdens that leave some in poverty and misery. As R. G. Lipsey and Kelvin Lancaster, the economists who developed "The General Theory of the Second Best," showed, in the 1950s, significant divergences in reality from theoretically ideal conditions do more than throw off prediction and guidance by a small, marginal factor; they make it *impossible to predict and control the outcomes of institutional and policy interventions*, which can have *the opposite effect from the intended, ideal-guided one*.[5] This is what happened with the European Bank's post-Great Recession 'austerity' requirements as a condition for bailing out floundering member political economies like Greece.[6] Such outcomes *discredit those nominally democratic social institutions* that cause or fail to mitigate them. They show that these institutions *defeat or evade their core purpose*: neither maximal reward for individual entrepreneurship and risk-taking, nor 'the wealth of nations' as an end-in-itself, but *advancing the 'common utility,' the 'general welfare,'* or what Jeffrey Sachs and others once again follow Aristotle in calling *"human happiness."*[7]

In contrast, students, scholars, and public-policy professionals in many of the younger social sciences, including psychology, sociology, anthropology, education, social work, and urban planning, generally reject such empirically unsupportable and trouble-making assumptions about 'solitary' individuals because the philosophical paradigms that inform their inquiries reflect the rival views of other eighteenth- and nineteenth-century thinkers, as well as the fresh, empirically oriented thinking of the classical American philosophical pragmatists – James, Dewey, Mead, Addams, Du Bois, and others – whom they count among their founders, along with European critical-social philosophers like Marx, Wundt, Herder, Weber, Durkheim, Simmel, and others. All of these thinkers treat human beings as fundamentally *social individuals,* inextricably entangled in their lives and destinies with others; as motivated by hopes for the future as well as saddled with unjust burdens of the past; as requiring both social and governmental institutions that intelligently foster education and collaboration in advancing mutual benefit; as dependent on others' social and intellectual contributions to live interesting, contributive, sustainable lives; and as entitled, therefore, to struggle to transform our various societies' outmoded institutions in order to achieve these fundamental purposes. Instead of reflecting a timeless, universal vision of the nature of human persons as a guide to institution-making and public policy, these classical pragmatists and most of these classical critical-social theorists treat their ideal-guided theoretical models as flexible, historically contextual, morally and practically pluralistic, and evolutionary, i.e., as developed through scholarly and popular analyses of diverse people's experiences of daily living, of broad economic and social trends, and of the effectiveness of 'deliberate' moral and practical efforts to influence social change by artists, orators, and social movements, as well as government policies and agencies.

Thus, these classical pragmatists and critical-social theorists and their contemporary inheritors argue that our reflections on purpose-driven and less intentional transformative practices must continuously inform theory development. In turn, social scientific theories should aim to offer better guidance to transformative efforts to help real people respond to real problems in particular contexts by drawing upon a broad, critically analyzed background of experience of how diverse human beings have tended to behave in broadly similar contexts, how their various cultures and languages frame the world, what kinds of generalizable successes and losses have come from earlier institutional formations and political strategies, what kinds of vague and variable but enduring values have come to matter to many of us human persons over time, *why* these values matter, and *what guidance* they can give to living and solving problems in specific current contexts. For these pragmatists and critical-social theorists, general theories and problem-specific transformative practice must develop simultaneously in mutually corrective ways; useful theories simply cannot be developed in advance of transformative practice.

Even if the existence of Plato's 'philosopher-kings' would not violate the democratic values that most modern people have come to regard as deeply important, there are no fully enlightened autocrats who can command the institutionalization of universal ideal theories while controlling all other human beings so as to prevent them from taking countermeasures or simply 'messing up.' Moreover, sources of insight as well as change are not and cannot be centralized in government, the academy, or power-guided markets – they are everywhere. Therefore, 'good-enough' theories,[8] as well as morally adequate and practically effective public policies, must reflect these metaphysical, epistemic, and political realities in their levels, tools, and focuses of analysis, as well as in their sources and methods of information-gathering and -sharing. At the same time, in both the theoretical and implementation phases of such an ongoing process, collaborating scholars, government and business leaders, artists, activists, and ordinary citizens must continuously develop and deploy their values, hopes, histories, shared visions, and emerging new formations of 'common sense' that retain some aspects of the old but revise other aspects in light of new experiences, more data, and better theories.

At present, Piketty's proposed method of collaboratively developing a new, interdisciplinary, "pragmatist" paradigm of democratic political economy calls for bringing together uncritically these two kinds of radically different philosophical frameworks and the social science disciplines they guide, without acknowledging the inevitable tensions and cross-purposes such intellectual and practical collaborations must overcome. Moreover, Piketty presently calls for including a wider process of "democratic debate" to validate changes in law and institutional structures, but he offers no suggestions about why and at what point in these change processes a wider public should be included. These two gaps in his intellectual framework are important factors in generating his current practical dilemma.

Contemporary philosophers of both kinds of metaphysical, moral, and political-theoretical orientation have written on these issues, but those of the first kind – including Rawls, Jürgen Habermas, Ronald Dworkin, Robert Nozick, and other liberals and libertarians whose work is easiest for mainstream economists, political scientists, and legal theorists to import into their theoretical frameworks because of their more quantifiable 'solitary individualist' orientation and their ideal-theory-leads-transformative-practice methodology – cannot so easily guide collaboration with sociologists and other social scientists. Nor can they help Piketty to solve his moral and practical dilemma of how to engage the hearts and minds of power-wielders and ordinary citizens in authorizing and funding new, justice-focused initiatives of 'the social state.' This is why Piketty's ongoing, interdisciplinary project needs contributing *pragmatist philosophers and congenial critical-social theorists.* These philosophers, who bring the second kind of meta-theoretical perspective, can intelligently interpret, critically reframe, and persuasively integrate the views of rival disciplinary experts, as well as those of ordinary citizens in diverse modern cultures who also must be brought into a shared, operative framework of inquiry about how to resolve our real-world crises, in order to assure public contribution to and uptake of reliable information that can support the emergence of an effective, governing consensus about what is to be done.[9]

John Dewey's suggestion is that those philosophers and philosophical thinkers in other disciplines who deploy a pragmatist perspective and a broad, well-informed intellectual background can serve as "liaison officers" within interdisciplinary scholarly inquiry and that public-inclusive inquiries can help to reframe Piketty's ambitious project in ways that overcome his moral and practical dilemma.[10] Playing this "liaison officer" role among brilliant and confident scholars in rival fields and among deeply conflicted citizens of contemporary societies will be no easy task, and few philosophers today – including pragmatist philosophers – are adequately prepared to undertake it. In addition to knowing what various pragmatists have said and now say about the background assumptions that underlie current critical issues, one must know the wider history of philosophy in its adverse and constructive impacts on the social sciences and on modern cultures, as well as key contemporary bodies of social science literature, various perspectives on contemporary social issues, and 'how life lives' for diverse contemporary peoples in diverse cultural contexts. 'Liaisons' also must have excellent intellectual tools to listen, to analyze, to generate alternative practical hypotheses and strategies, to communicate orally, visually, and in writing with differing kinds of audiences, and to assess the import of others' suggestions and empirical findings for the ongoing development of general 'ground maps' that can guide effective, democratic transformation processes. Therefore, those who propose to offer their services as pragmatist philosophical "liaison officers" have their homework cut out for them, as those from the diverse disciplines and 'publics' to whom they offer their services will rightly expect them to show their worth or get out of the way.

Nonetheless, the intellectual function of pragmatist liaison officers is necessary for the effective further development of the new interdisciplinary paradigm of *democratic political economy,* for which Piketty and his global team of researchers have already offered such hopeful leadings. Without such a pragmatist philosophical contribution, the tensions between law and sociology, for example, become irreconcilable in thinking about what kinds of 'persons' can be bearers of rights, what forms rights should take in the twenty-first century, and how they can be deployed justly and effectively to advance human welfare. Moreover, with help from well-qualified pragmatist philosophical liaisons, Piketty's interdisciplinary team of collaborating scholars can overcome the practical dilemma that seems to have stumped him by also including, educating, and learning from diverse 'publics,' who know and can transform their diverse cultures from within and can initiate and stabilize the kinds of democratic transformation processes within their local, national, and international institutional frameworks, economic strategies, tax policies, and social welfare programs for which Piketty rightly calls.[11]

Lessons from Dewey's reflective, democratic method of moral and practical inquiry

In preparing for and playing this liaison role among diverse scholars and publics, pragmatist philosophers can at the same time make a second kind of theoretical contribution that Piketty's paradigm also needs: using and stimulating others' moral imagination concerning the meaning of the democratic ideal as a guide to interpreting the meaning of the important ethical concepts he aims to deploy, including their implications for public policy and in the lives of each of us as citizens. Some of the key ethical concepts that Piketty's educated intuitions and cultural loyalties tell him *must matter*, though neither he nor his Emmanuel Saez can explain how or why, include *justice, merit, human dignity, common utility, the general welfare, liberty, equality, property, poverty*, and *humanly worthy personal goals in living*. An accessible starting point for illuminating the meaning of the democratic ideal and how each of these various ethical concepts relates to it and to each other is Dewey's 1932 *Ethics*, which frames these concepts in pragmatist ways that are both compatible with the best aspects of Amartya Sen and Martha Nussbaum's "capabilities theory" and preferable to Rawls's powerful, but easily misused ideal liberal account of individual civil liberties and fair opportunities to share in "primary social goods."[12]

What we need to develop in order to understand and desirably transform the kinds of moral and practical problem-situations that increasingly plague modern life, Dewey argues in the first of the chapters he contributed to the 1932 *Ethics*, is *a reflective social morality* that draws on many interdisciplinary sources in an ongoing process of critically reconstructing our social institutions, as well as our diverse moral traditions, our rival ethical theories, and our particular individual characters, goals in living, and felt responsibilities to others. Dewey writes,

> When social life is stable, when custom rules, the problems of morals have to do with the adjustments which individuals make to the institutions in which they live, rather than with the moral quality of the institutions themselves … When social life is in a state of flux, moral issues cease to gather exclusively about personal conformity and deviation. They centre in the value of social arrangements, of laws, of inherited traditions that have crystallized into institutions, in changes that are desirable. Institutions lose their quasi-sacredness and are the objects of moral questioning. We now live in such a period.
>
> (Dewey, in Dewey and Tuft 1932: 314–15)

Dewey quotes Jane Addams's *Democracy and Social Ethics* (Addams 1902) as rightly expressing the *social* nature, scope, and complexity of the theoretical and practical moral challenges modern people face, as well as the social focus and developmental process of adequate ethical theories, of ethically justifiable institutions, and of the kinds of ethically responsive public policies we must pursue in these troubled times.

> To attain *personal* morality in an age demanding *social* morality, to pride one's self on the results of personal effort when the time demands social adjustment is utterly to fail to apprehend the situation ... All about us are men and women who have become unhappy in regard to their attitude toward the social order itself. The test which they would apply to their conduct is a social test ... They desire both a clearer definition of the code of morality applied to present day demands and a part in its fulfillment, both a creed and a practice of *social* morality.
>
> (Dewey, in Dewey and Tufts 1932, 315; Addams 1902, 1–4; emphases added)

This real, human demand that we as individuals and as social group members must have opportunities to participate in interpreting and creatively reshaping the values as well as the institutions that shape our lives is both reasonable and capable of fulfillment, Dewey argues. It requires raising our own and others' awareness of the values, forces, and institutions within our social world that influence the development of our desires and characters by shaping our shared "fast" habits of "intuitively" feeling, thinking, and acting.[13] When we are aware of these values, habits, and institutions, we can take responsibility for the roles we play in sustaining or changing them, and we can respond in intelligent, active ways to affirm or oppose them. Dewey has awareness of the guiding-values and institutions of political economy explicitly in mind here:

> To many persons at present the economic system, in all probability, seems to exist in the same way that the order of nature exists. It is something to which we must accommodate ourselves as to sunshine and storms, taking advantage of it when possible, protecting ourselves against its inclemencies when necessary, and so on. But in the degree in which there develops in the mind of any one a consciousness of its operation and effects, it is no longer the bare institution which acts, but that institution as it is reflected in the imagination; in desire, hope, fear, intention to support or to change. In short, the contention is not in the least that our will, the body of our desires and purposes, is subservient to social conditions, but that the latter are incorporated into our attitudes, and our attitudes into social conditions, to such an extent that to maintain one is to maintain the other, to change one is to change the other.
>
> (Dewey, in Dewey and Tufts 1932: 342–42)

When we become aware of how our shared social values, habits, and institutions affect who we are and how we live as particular individuals – what our opportunities are in comparison to those of others, what kinds of powers we and they can develop and deploy, what obligations we recognize and to whom, and what plans of betterment make sense to us – we can reflect on these morally and practically, affirming them or seeking ways to make changes in them, individually and collaboratively.

In discussing the kinds of individual and collaborative habits as well as the intellectual tools that support a reflective social morality that can guide the resolution of real conflicts within our modern problem situations and among our personally felt values and obligations, Dewey suggests that we must reconstruct at least some of the norms and practices of the customary morality with which we were raised, understanding this moral inheritance as a complex, creative construction of generations of our forebears and those in other cultural streams who lived through both ordinary and extraordinary times. Like James, Dewey argues that effective ethical reconstruction always has a conservative aspect, combining what we might call 'historic preservation' – i.e., valuing and continuing to use elements of our own and others' inherited morality that are still functional and beautiful as part of honoring and connecting with the ethical resources of our collective past – as well as a transformative aspect, i.e., demolition of dysfunctional elements of our ethical inheritance and replacement of these with new habits, social institutions, and practices that will serve both our continuing ethical ideals and our emergent needs and aims better in this new era.

Dewey suggests that some of the best resources for developing a pragmatist moral theory that can guide reflective social morality's reconstructive work within modern conflict zones are inherited tools from the past, which we can study and then refine or repurpose as needed: earlier moral codes, legal theory and practice, human institutions, biographies, and histories of world civilizations (Dewey, in Dewey and Tufts 1932, 179–80). The other resources we will need to employ in order to create appropriate new ethical tools for both the demolition phase and the creative reconstruction phase of transforming social-and-personal problem situations must be mined or harvested from the biological and social sciences, with Dewey's caveat that *these will need continuing moral transformation* to fit them for the job of shaping new theoretical guides for reflective morality (179–80). The goal of this pragmatist tool-creation process is not to create a one-size-fits-all-situations ethical "cookie cutter" – some kind of pragmatist version of Kant's categorical imperative – but rather a set of value prompts, duty reminders, fact-checkers, moral gravity monitors, inspiration devices, and communicative frequencies that will allow individual ethical artists to focus reflective intelligence critically and reconstructively on rival demands emerging within their own psyches, while similarly coordinating the differing moral perspectives of a community's diverse members whose active aim is to solve moral problems that emerge within their shared social life.

Both the historical preservation and the demolition-and-reconstruction aspects of reflectively transforming personal-and-social problems come together in Dewey's way of choosing and refining intellectual tools from three earlier traditions in moral theory: Aristotle's orientation toward the good, Kant's evaluation of personal motives in light of duties, and Mill's emphasis on promoting the general welfare while positively influencing the development of individual characters. Drawing from the Aristotelian tradition, Dewey critically sharpens and repurposes the development of *reflection-endorsed, inclusive, and enduring personal aims* linked to *wider, shared ideal ends* or overarching values as *guiding interests for conduct*, the correlative development of character, and the framework within which *practical wisdom* chooses ends-in-view and particular courses of action to achieve these. From the Kantian tradition, Dewey adopts the insight that duty is a different, equally important moral factor that must be considered in choosing a course of conduct, but he broadens this into *a general sense of duty* that leads to *sensitivity* to other persons and situations in determining what is *the right thing to do in a particular situation*. From Mill's way of developing the utilitarian tradition, Dewey adopts a *two-sided standard of conduct at both personal and social levels*: act collaboratively with others in ways that promote *the general welfare*, being open to learning with others what this may mean in particular contexts while making sure that *the growth of one's own and others' characters* is advanced at the same time, with special attention to *interest-linked virtues* of personal commitment, persistence, and thinking inclusively and in terms of the big picture in which particular interests play a role. In brief discussions at the ends of these three chapters, Dewey deploys each of these three kinds of reconstructed tools from earlier ethical theories in his critiques and calls for reconstruction of social institutions and practices in order to solve some of the same local, national, and global problems of modern life on which the more recent Piketty's analysis focuses.[14] Dewey argues that a *mature moral self* deploys all of these intellectual tools habitually, creatively, and in relation to insights from the biological and social sciences in reflectively analyzing particular situations and judging wisely about what course of conduct is best in that situation as part of a larger picture that has both personal and social dimensions.

Deploying all of these ethical tools effectively in diverse contexts in order to advance the process of resolving the real moral and practical problems that blight people's lives is not a process of discovering and applying a universal 'best solution' like Piketty's "confiscatory" international tax policy, but rather an *experimental method* guided by *the democratic ideal*. Key aspects of Dewey's pragmatist experimental method (344), include: analysis of the kinds of conflict involved in the particular problem situation (328); inclusive inquiry to identify the facts and values involved (329–31); imagination of the alternative courses of conduct and their consequences (336–38); implementation of experimental solutions; assessing their results; and revising strategies accordingly.[15] Finally, Dewey argues, solving real modern problems for political economy through such an experimental method of devising, deploying, and revising moral and practical tools that can achieve contextually feasible, socially desirable, and individually affirmable personal, social, and institutional transformation requires the directional guidance and process-focused prompts of *a shared, pluralistic, historically grounded, but valuably vague and open-ended ideal* that gains more specific content through reflection on experience in change processes, both at social institutional levels and in daily life.

This is the imagination-guiding, experience-reflecting role of *the democratic ideal*, which conjoins the French revolutionary ideal concepts of *liberty, equality*, and *fraternity* in mutually conditioning, context-specific ways (348).

> For democracy signifies, on one side, that every individual is to share in the duties and rights belonging to control of social affairs, and, on the other side, that social arrangements are to eliminate those external arrangements of status, birth, wealth, sex, etc., which restrict the opportunity of each individual for full development of himself [or herself]. On the individual side, it takes as the criterion of social organization and of law and government release of the potentialities of individuals. On the social side, it demands cooperation in place of coercion, voluntary sharing in a process of mutual give and take, instead of authority imposed from above. As an ideal of social life in its political phase it is much wider than any form of government, although it includes government in its scope. As an ideal, it expresses the need for progress beyond anything yet attained; for nowhere in the world are there institutions which in fact operate equally to secure the full development of each individual, and assure to all individuals a share in both the values they contribute and those they receive. Yet it is not "ideal" in the sense of being visionary and utopian; for it simply projects to their logical and practical limit forces inherent in human nature and already embodied to some extent in human nature. It serves accordingly as a basis for criticism of institutions as they exist and of plans of betterment ... Most criticisms of it are in fact criticisms of the imperfect realization it has so far achieved.
>
> (Dewey, in Dewey and Tufts 1932, 348–49)

It is crucial to the effectiveness of the experimental method that we understand such a guiding ideal as an experience-based generalization, "*a hypothesis*, not a dogma; something to be tried and tested, confirmed and revised in future practice; having a constant point of growth instead of being closed" (343). Theorists and practitioners in the various allied fields of political economy who have misunderstood the nature and function of guiding ideals have done enormous harm in the past, Dewey writes; in fact, "it would be hard to say whether the world has suffered more from the attempt to regulate social affairs by a rule of thumb empiricism, by sticking to precedent and such rules as have evolved in the past, by refusing to admit constructive imagination and rational insight, or from doctrinaire creeds framed without reference to actual conditions, from dogmas supposed to proceed from some source beyond all experience and immutable" (343–44). Therefore, we must remember that "the democratic ideal poses, rather than solves, the great problem: How to harmonize the development of each individual with the maintenance of a social state in which the activities of one will contribute to the good of all the others. There is no shortcut to it, no single predestined road which can be found once for all and which, if human beings continue to walk in it without deviation, will surely conduct them to the goal" (350).

The kinds of transformative strategies Dewey thinks the democratic ideal would guide us to pursue experimentally are not only interdisciplinary, but also public-inclusive and motivating to the efforts of diverse individual persons and social groups to develop their own characters and capabilities, to develop networks and movements of people working to change their cultures and social institutions, and working to influence power-wielders in government and in business to curb the abuses of those whose enormous and growing heaps of capital currently allow them to anti-democratically 'rig the system.' Dewey's emphasis on the importance of focusing on what human individuals and social groups can become and achieve if they are given opportunities to participate actively in shaping their social world finds echoes in Sen and Nussbaum's capabilities theory: "The [democratic ideal as a] moral criterion attaches more weight to what men and women are capable of becoming than to their actual attainments, to possibilities than to possessions, even though the possessions be intellectual or even moral ... estimating what they can grow into instead of judging them on the basis of what conditions have so far made of them" (348). From a theoretical perspective, the ongoing democratic inclusion of ordinary people and "publics" is morally, epistemically, politically, and economically necessary to the ongoing development of a "good-enough" new paradigm of democratic political economy, as well as to the achievement of feasible and desirable personal, cultural, and institutional changes. From a transformative perspective, it is both inspiring to and inclusive of a large scholarly-and-public team of participants. Like Mohandas Gandhi, Dag Hammarskjöld, and Martin Luther King, Jr., after him, Dewey advised us to become the changes we want to see in our families, our communities, our nation, our world, and our own lives, working intelligently and democratically with others or resolve current conflicts and transform the problem situations we now face.

Thus, as even this brief sketch suggests, Dewey's pragmatist and democratic method of transformative social inquiry offers useful guidance for reframing Piketty's new paradigm of democratic political economy as an interdisciplinary, public-inclusive, twenty-first-century experimental process of discovering and deploying effective solutions to moral and practical problems like poverty, hunger, homelessness, joblessness, and hopelessness that Sen describes as "capabilities deprivation," as well as to related problems of fast-growing social and economic inequalities, local-and-global environmental degradation, and increasing interpersonal violence, war, and terrorism. Instead of attempting to spur approximations of a universal, antecedently specified, ideal tax policy that would apply across all countries and contexts, Piketty would be wise to adopt Dewey's pragmatist experimental approach in seeking interim national and regional tax policies that bend the steep curve in capital-based wealth accumulation in particular, diverse geopolitical contexts while simultaneously working to change cultural norms that glorify wealth accumulation in favor of those that emphasize economic justice and educational opportunity for all, providing incremental opportunities to build and deploy democratic capabilities in ways that continuously increase the pool of researchers and ordinary citizens who can envision and effectively advocate for the further democratic changes we will need in the future.

Notes

1 At no point in *Capital in the Twenty-First Century* does Piketty explain what he means by "common utility," and he gives no reason to interpret his use of this concept in utilitarian terms such as Jeremy Bentham, John Stuart Mill, Henry Sidgwick, or Peter Singer variously use. Instead, he seems to mean something more like 'the general welfare,' another vague term variously defined by economists, political scientists, and philosophers.
2 In his keynote address to the 2014 Annual Meetings of the American Sociological Association, this was Emmanuel Saez's only explanation of why economic and social justice still matters, in spite of entrenched and growing inequalities. When I engaged him on this point during the question-and-answer part of the session and at the reception that followed, Saez expressed his joy in entering and crunching large sets of historical data, as well as his interest in but lack of training to address the moral questions, as a way of showing why this new paradigm-framing project in which he works closely with Thomas Piketty requires interdisciplinary collaborators with differing focal interests and skill sets, including philosophers.
3 I encounter this 'common sense' in my students on the first day of my required classes in ethics at Fordham University, the Jesuit university of New York City, not only among the many business students, but among many others studying the social sciences and the humanities – a peculiar mixture of the seventeenth- and eighteenth-century analyses of Hobbes, Locke, Jefferson, and *The Godfather* that their parents, teachers, and fellow students seem to share. I should add that most of my students also take Kantian ideas about human dignity and Catholic ideas about social justice seriously, and that most of them would help others and seek help from them in times of emergency such as a great storm or civic disaster like the terrorist attacks on New York's World Trade Center on 9/11. They have more trouble seeing and responding to race- and poverty-linked daily emergencies in many other people's lives, even though these are epidemic in many parts of our city.
4 This way of relating ideal theory to practice includes the liberal theories of a wide range of contemporary thinkers, from Rawls and Habermas to Robert Nozick. Its underlying model of the relationship between universal ideal theory and feasible transformative practice dates back to Plato.
5 See Lipsey and Lancaster 1956, 11–32.
6 On the disastrous effects for Greece's political economy, as well as for the Euro-zone and the larger European Community, of the national sovereignty-damaging, misery-deepening "austerity" measures as a condition for humanitarian aid as well

as for new loans to bail out failing banks that German leaders of the European Bank and the European Union have demanded – over the opposition of French leaders of the International Monetary Fund – on the basis of such an abstract, individualist ideal-guided economic model, as well as an ahistorical moral rhetoric that confuses personal irresponsibility with crises in national economies whose troubles arise in part out of their relationships with other nations, see a series of critical analyses and opinion pieces in *The New York Times* by Joseph Stiglitz, Paul Krugman, and others, as well as a series of generally concurring columns in *The Economist*.

7 See Jeffrey Sachs, *The End of Poverty* (Sachs 2006) and subsequent works, but more importantly for this purpose, see his collaborative work with global-and-national teams of scholars, local informants, and the United Nations to understand and advance human happiness pluralistically in culturally, politically, economically, and ecologically diverse national-and-global contexts.

8 This category of "good-enough theories" reflects Herbert A. Simon's thinking about non-ideal, "satisficing" economic rationality: decisions must be made in real time on the basis of the best information we can get, guided by the values we think matter most concerning the matter at hand, while reflecting what classical pragmatists like James, Dewey, and Mead call effective habits of thinking, which factor in many other implications for ourselves and others, not just the "interests" of the individual, the firm, or the agency for which one may be acting as a fiduciary. See Simon's (1976) essay, "From Substantive to Procedural Rationality," as well as Amartya Sen's (1976) essay, "Rational Fools," in *Philosophy and Economic Theory* (ed. Hahn and Hollis 1979).

9 Critical social theory in the interdisciplinary tradition of the Frankfurt School has taken a pragmatist turn in recent years under the influence of Karl-Otto Apel, Hans Joas, Axel Honneth, and other scholars. An international workshop there (April 2015) focusing on "Freedom in View: The Critical Theory of John Dewey," in which I had an opportunity to participate, highlighted both pragmatist aspects of their recent work and a valuable theoretical remainder of their earlier tradition that is not so easily absorbed, but requires continuing critical conversation between representatives of these two schools of thought across their differing cultures of origin, current geopolitical locations, and intuitive 'hunches' about what must be done.

10 In fact, thinking about what Piketty's project needs from pragmatist philosophers helps to clarify what Dewey meant by the role of "liaison officer" in interdisciplinary inquiry, which he suggested in many of his later works. For some complementary suggestions on the need for this liaison role and how to fulfill it, see Dewey's *Experience and Nature* (Dewey 1925), as well as "The Need for a Recovery of Philosophy" (Dewey 1917), "Philosophy and Democracy" (Dewey 1919), *The Public and Its Problems* (Dewey 1927), "Creative Democracy – The Task before Us" (Dewey 1939b), "Time and Individuality" (Dewey 1940).

11 Dewey uses 'public' and 'publics' as technical terms, meaning neither the general data pool of sociologists nor the constitutionally specified ranks of the citizenry, but rather an emergent social group(s) of individuals who are adversely affected by spillover effects from others' private contracts and differently focused government decisions, which motivate them to begin to communicate with one another and to strategize who to influence the kinds of changes that will give them relief, and perhaps help them to live more fully according to a shared, emerging ideal-guided vision of their lives together. See Dewey's *The Public and Its Problems* (Dewey 1927).

12 See Dewey and Tufts' *Ethics*, revised edition (Dewey and Tufts 1932), as well as Sen's *Development as Freedom* (Sen 1999) and *The Idea of Justice* (Sen 2009), Nussbaum's *Sex and Social Justice* (Nussbaum 1999) and *Creating Capabilities: The Human Development Approach* (Nussbaum 2011), and Rawls' *A Theory of Justice* (Rawls 1971) and *Political Liberalism*, paperback edition (Rawls 1996).

13 I am thinking here of the relevance of Dewey's analysis of socially shared habits of feeling, thinking, and acting for Nobel Prize-winning behavioral economist Daniel Kahneman's as yet unexplained intuitive, "fast" thinking in his best-selling book, *Thinking, Fast and Slow* (Kahneman 2011).

14 For Dewey's brief, chapter-end discussions of how to deploy reconstructed ethical 'tools' from Aristotle, Kant, and Mill, see Dewey, in Dewey and Tufts 1932, 211–12, 233–34, 259–60.

15 For more details about this social ethics-inclusive experimental method of problem-solving inquiry, as well as historical contextualization and theoretical justification, see Dewey's *Logic: The Theory of Inquiry* (Dewey 1938). For more details about imagining alternative courses of conduct and their consequences as a phase of good judgment guided by practical wisdom, see his *Human Nature and Conduct* (Dewey 1922). For more details about how and why to alternate hypothesis-guided action toward ends-in-view, evaluation of consequences at social and individual levels, and corrective revision of strategies and even the ends-in-view themselves to better track with the developmental direction and methodical guidance of the democratic ideal, see his *Theory of Valuation* (Dewey 1939a). For my earlier discussion of how all of these elements of Dewey's transformative method fit together, see *Deep Democracy: Community, Diversity, and Transformation* (Green 1999).

References

Addams, Jane. 1902. *Democracy and Social Ethics*. Champaign: University of Illinois Press, 2001.

Dewey, John. 1917. "The Need for a Recovery of Philosophy." In *The Essential Dewey*, vol. 1: *Pragmatism, Education, Democracy*, ed. Larry A. Hickman and Thomas M. Alexander. Bloomington: Indiana University Press, 1998.

Dewey, John. 1919. "Philosophy and Democracy." In *The Essential Dewey*, vol. 1: *Pragmatism, Education, Democracy*, ed. Larry A. Hickman and Thomas M. Alexander. Bloomington: Indiana University Press, 1998.

Dewey, John. 1922. *Human Nature and Conduct*. Vol. 14 of *The Middle Works of John Dewey*, ed. Jo Ann Boydston. Carbondale: Southern Illinois University Press, 1983.

Dewey, John. 1925. *Experience and Nature*. Vol. 1 of *The Later Works of John Dewey*, ed. Jo Ann Boydston. Carbondale: Southern Illinois University Press, 1981.

Dewey, John. 1927. *The Public and Its Problems*. In *The Later Works of John Dewey*, vol. 2: *1925–1927, Essays, The Public and Its Problems*, ed. Jo Ann Boydston. Carbondale: Southern Illinois University Press, 1984.

Dewey, John. 1929. *The Quest for Certainty*. Vol. 4 of *The Later Works of John Dewey*, ed. Jo Ann Boydston. Carbondale: Southern Illinois University Press, 1988.

Dewey, John. 1938. *Logic: The Theory of Inquiry*. Vol. 12 of *The Later Works of John Dewey*, ed. Jo Ann Boydston. Carbondale: Southern Illinois University Press, 1986.

Dewey, John. 1939. *Theory of Valuation*. In *The Later Works of John Dewey*, vol. 13: *1938–1939, Essays, Experience and Education, Freedom and Culture, and Theory of Valuation*, ed. Jo Ann Boydston. Carbondale: Southern Illinois University Press, 1988.

Dewey, John. 1939. "Creative Democracy – The Task before Us." In *The Essential Dewey*, vol. 1: *Pragmatism, Education, Democracy*, ed. Larry A. Hickman and Thomas M. Alexander. Bloomington: Indiana University Press, 1998.

Dewey, John. 1940. "Time and Individuality." In *The Essential Dewey*, vol. 1: *Pragmatism, Education, Democracy*, ed. Larry A. Hickman and Thomas M. Alexander. Bloomington: Indiana University Press, 1998.

Dewey, John, and James Hayden Tufts. 1932. *Ethics, Revised Edition*. Vol. 7 of *The Later Works of John Dewey*, ed. Jo Ann Boydston. Carbondale: Southern Illinois University Press, 1985.

Green, Judith M. 1999. *Deep Democracy: Community, Diversity, and Transformation*. Lanham, MD: Rowman & Littlefield.

Green, Judith M. 2008. *Pragmatism and Social Hope: Deepening Democracy in Global Contexts*. New York: Columbia University Press.

Hahn, Frank and Martin Hollis, ed. 1979. *Philosophy and Economic Theory*. Oxford: Oxford University Press.

Kahneman, Daniel. 2011. *Thinking, Fast and Slow*. New York: Farrar, Strauss & Giroux.

Lipsey, R. G., and Kelvin Lancaster. 1956. "The General Theory of the Second Best." *Review of Economic Studies* 24(63): 11–32.

Nussbaum, Martha C. 1999. *Sex and Social Justice*. New York: Oxford University Press.

Nussbaum, Martha C. 2011. *Creating Capabilities: The Human Development Approach*. Cambridge, MA: Harvard University Press.

Piketty, Thomas. 2014. *Capital in the Twenty-First Century*, trans. Arthur Goldhammer. Cambridge, MA: The Belknap Press of Harvard University Press.

Rawls, John. 1971. *A Theory of Justice*. Cambridge, MA: The Belknap Press of Harvard University Press.

Rawls, John. 1996. *Political Liberalism*, paperback ed. New York: Columbia University Press.

Sachs, Jeffrey D. 2006. *The End of Poverty: Economic Possibilities for Our Time*. New York: Penguin Books.

Sen, Amartya. 1976. "Rational Fools: A Critique of the Behavioural Foundations of Economic Theory." In *Philosophy and Economic Theory*, ed. Frank Hahn and Martin Hollis, 87–109. Oxford: Oxford University Press, 1979.

Sen, Amartya. 1999. *Development as Freedom*. New York: Alfred A. Knopf.

Sen, Amartya. 2009. *The Idea of Justice*. Cambridge, MA: The Belknap Press of Harvard University Press.

Simon, Herbert A. 1976. "From Substantive to Procedural Rationality." In *Philosophy and Economic Theory*, ed. Frank Hahn and Martin Hollis, 65–86. Oxford: Oxford University Press, 1979.

Index

For Product Safety Concerns and Information please contact our EU
representative GPSR@taylorandfrancis.com
Taylor & Francis Verlag GmbH, Kaufingerstraße 24, 80331 München, Germany

www.ingramcontent.com/pod-product-compliance
Ingram Content Group UK Ltd.
Pitfield, Milton Keynes, MK11 3LW, UK
UKHW020953180425
457613UK00019B/663